Upper Intermediate

Just Right

American Edition

Jeremy Harmer
& Carol Lethaby

Teacher's Book

Marshall Cavendish
Education

© 2007 Marshall Cavendish Ltd

First published 2007 by Marshall Cavendish Education

Marshall Cavendish is a member of the Times Publishing Group

All rights reserved; no part of this publication may be reproduced, stored
in a retrieval system, transmitted in any form, or by any means, electronic,
mechanical, photocopying, recording, or otherwise, without the prior written
permission of the publishers.

Marshall Cavendish ELT
119 Wardour Street
London W1F 0UW

ISBN: 978-0-462-00026-8

Designed by Hart McLeod, Cambridge
Editorial development by Ocelot Publishing, Oxford, with Geneviève Talon

Printed and bound by Times Offset (M) Sdn. Bhd. Malaysia

Contents

Introduction

Welcome to JUST RIGHT Upper Intermediate, a course for students of English as a foreign language.

JUST RIGHT Upper Intermediate comprises a Student's Book with a separate Mini-grammar and Audioscript, a Workbook, audio material on CDs for both the Student's Book and the Workbook, and a Teacher's Book.

JUST RIGHT Upper Intermediate provides material for between 90 and 120 classroom hours.

What *upper intermediate* means

Although people use terms like *beginner, pre-intermediate, intermediate, upper-intermediate* and *advanced* in different ways, students who use this course are assumed to:

- have studied successfully for between 330–400 classroom hours, and/or
- have a grasp of more than basic vocabulary areas and grammar patterns, and/or
- be able to read and listen to a wide range of texts which use a variety of non-technical language
- have some experience of recognizing varieties of language style and of drawing inferences from texts ("reading between the lines").

What's in this Teacher's Book?

The Teacher's Book contains:

- a statement of principles (pages 4–6)
- methodological guidelines (pages 6–11) (how to make things work)
- a description of the Student's Book (page 12) and the Workbook (pages 12–13)
- an introduction to the lesson-handling notes (page 13)
- lesson-handling notes, including answers to the activities where appropriate (pages 14–112)
- an answer key to the Workbook (pages 113–128).

A statement of principles

The design of JUST RIGHT is based on a number of pedagogical and linguistic principles. The summary below explains what these principles are and how they have influenced the final design of the course.

Design principles	Design principles in action
Topic principles: different topics interest different people. Some topics are of universal, general interest; they should be included within a varied topic syllabus designed to reach the widest student audience. But given the topic in question, everything depends on how it is exploited by the Student's Book, teacher and students.	JUST RIGHT offers a selection of unit topics, in order to cater for the widest range of student interests. These include: • *experiences with money* (Winning, hoping, giving—Unit 1) • *human attitudes to wild animals* (Wolf—Unit 3) • *anger management* (Getting angry—Unit 5) • *thinking about the future* (Looking forward—Unit 6) • *judging by appearances* (First impressions—Unit 9) • *climate change* (Heavy weather—Unit 10) • *fame and celebrity* (Famous for 15 minutes?—Unit 11) • *books and movies* (Writing and writers—Unit 12) • *justice systems* (Crime and punishment—Unit 13) • *storytelling* (Stories from the heart—Unit 14) These topics are expanded and enlarged upon in reading and listening texts in the JUST RIGHT Workbook.
Grammar principles: people learn in different ways. For some, the most effective learning techniques involve controlled practice exercises. For others, the most important thing is to draw their attention to language in use so that they "notice" it in action—and therefore acquire their knowledge of it. Grammar materials need to cater for both types of learner. At the upper intermediate level we want to draw on students' existing knowledge as well as offer them new information.	In JUST RIGHT, grammar is dealt with in four distinct ways. • **Revision stages:** students' previous knowledge is activated with straightforward explanations, examples and exercises. • **Extension stages:** having reactivated their knowledge in the revision stages, students now learn and practice new and more detailed facts about the language point(s) using JUST RIGHT's unique "Mini-grammar". • **Noticing:** at various stages in each unit students are asked to notice language features in, for example, a reading text. This is designed to keep language features current in their minds. • **Review:** each unit has a review section where grammar is recycled and practiced. There are also grammar exercises in the JUST RIGHT Workbook.

Vocabulary principles: vocabulary is more than words. Our students should also be able to use language in chunks (that is words grouped to make phrases or multi-word units); they should learn how certain words collocate with other words and, crucially, they should see how words are used. They should also be encouraged to "get personal" with words, identifying which ones they like best, which they find most useful and difficult, etc.

In JUST RIGHT, vocabulary is dealt with in five main ways.
- **Teaching stages:** students are introduced to word meaning, word formation, collocation, etc. and are given a chance to practice with their new knowledge.
- **Words in context:** students study the use of words and phrases in reading and listening texts.
- **Language in chunks:** students look at words which group together in lexical phrases and other multi-word units. This is a special feature of reading and listening activities and also forms the basis for much of the functional items which they study.
- **Word choice:** students are shown how to discriminate between words with related meanings.
- **Speaking and writing:** students look at the way language is used differently in speech and writing in terms of grammar and vocabulary choice.
- **Review:** as well as more standard practice, students are also encouraged to "get personal" with words from the unit that they have just worked through.

There are also vocabulary revision exercises in the JUST RIGHT Workbook.

Functional language principles: students benefit greatly from seeing/hearing how language is used in social situations, particularly since such language is frequently made up of language chunks and various lexical phrases. It is particularly important for students to be able to act empathetically in English.

In JUST RIGHT, students study functional areas such as asking for help and giving warnings, but they also study interpersonal / social language, including:
- *expressing sympathy* (Unit 1)
- *buying "thinking time"* (Unit 4)
- *taking something to be fixed* (Unit 7)
- *checking understanding* (Unit 11)
- *expressing likes and dislikes* (Unit 14).

Each unit in the JUST RIGHT Workbook has a section which revises functional language.

Pronunciation principles: good pronunciation depends on the students' ability to hear differences and variations as well as on their own pronunciation skills. You can't have one without the other. That's why students need to have their attention drawn to a variety of pronunciation features, such as word stress and sentence intonation. They also get practice in recognizing and producing unusual ("marked") stress to express strong feelings.

In JUST RIGHT, pronunciation issues are dealt with in two main ways.
- **In the main units:** students study topics such as stress patterns in sentences, interpreting intonation clues to meaning, different sounds (and their spellings) and weak forms in informal speech.
- **In the review sections:** students do a variety of pronunciation exercises focusing on different phonemes, word stress, etc.

There is extra pronunciation material in the JUST RIGHT Workbook, and exercises to familiarize students with phonemic script.

Reading principles: the more students read, the more language they acquire and the better they become at reading. But they need to see language in a variety of formats, used to discuss a variety of attractive topics. A student's book should provide exploitation which will help students to cope with reading texts, and train them in skills they need for reading both specific and general texts.

Among the different reading text types in JUST RIGHT are the following:
- *magazine articles* (e.g. Units 1, 6)
- *extracts from stories, novels and memoirs* (e.g. Unit 10)
- *website articles* (e.g. Unit 5)
- *movie scripts* (e.g. Unit 12)
- *book advertisements* (e.g. Unit 12)
- *poems* (e.g. Unit 14).

The JUST RIGHT Workbook includes a variety of further reading texts including web pages, newspaper articles, extracts from novels and chat forums.

Listening principles: even though students find listening difficult they need to be exposed to a wide range of speaking styles. This will help them to acquire the skills necessary to extract information from what they hear in a variety of situations. At all times the listening extracts should be comprehensible (even if challenging) for students at this level.

JUST RIGHT offers a range of listening examples and activities, including:
- *authentic interviews* (e.g. Units 11, 14)
- *autobiographical memories* (e.g. Unit 2)
- *extracts from novels read aloud* (e.g. Units 3, 12)
- *personal conversations* (e.g. Units 6, 7)
- *songs* (e.g. Unit 10)
- *newscasts* (e.g. Unit 13)
- *poems* (e.g. Unit 14).

There are more listening exercises in the JUST RIGHT Workbook, including a song, recorded messages and interviews.

Speaking principles: speaking is one of the key skills in learning a language. When students use language for communication (in the safety of the classroom), they have the chance to rehearse what they have learnt and test their own ability. Not only that, but the processing skills needed are thought by many to actually aid the language acquisition process itself.

In JUST RIGHT students are encouraged to speak through a variety of tasks, including:
- *expressing views and making decisions* (e.g. Units 2, 7)
- *discussion and debate* (e.g. Units 1, 13)
- *making presentations* (e.g. Unit 4)
- *role-play* (e.g. Units 5, 9)
- *telling jokes or stories* (e.g. Units 8, 12)
- *consensus reaching* (e.g. Unit 10)
- *information gap tasks* (e.g. Unit 13)
- *reading aloud* (e.g. Unit 14).

Writing principles: many people have given writing less prominence than it deserves. Writing practice trains students in this most important of skills and gives them time to reflect on what they have learnt, encourages them to process their knowledge and, crucially, gives them a chance to produce work that they can take pride in.

JUST RIGHT offers a variety of writing tasks, including:
- *making mind maps* (Unit 1)
- *newspaper headlines* (Unit 2)
- *answering interview questions* (Unit 4)
- *leaflets and brochures* (Unit 5)
- *planning compositions* (Unit 6)
- *instructions* (Unit 7)
- *describing graphs and charts* (Unit 8)
- *resumés* (Unit 9)
- *diaries* (Unit 10)
- *book reviews* (Unit 12)
- *screenplays* (Unit 14).

More writing practice is provided in the JUST RIGHT Workbook.

How to make things work

The following methodology topics are dealt with in this section:
- correcting students when they speak
- correcting written work outside the classroom
- learner training
- putting students in groups
- reading and listening
- speaking and writing
- the teacher's role
- using the Student's Book
- using the Workbook.

In the lesson-handling notes, which start on page 14, guidance is given on how to approach particular exercises and activities in the various units and sections of the Student's Book. Here, however, some general methodological issues are discussed.

- **Correcting students when they speak**: most students want teachers to tell them when they are getting their English right and when they are getting it wrong, but they are also deeply affected by the way we do this. One student interviewed a few years ago spoke for many when she said that a teacher "should be able to correct students without offending them."

  A lot depends upon how and when correction takes place. If you and your students are concentrating on a piece of grammar or vocabulary, or if you are working on an aspect of pronunciation and focusing on it in detail, then it seems sensible to show students how they are doing and offer them help to correct mistakes.

  Correction in such "accuracy-focused" sequences has two basic stages. In the first you show students

that a mistake has been made, and in the second (if necessary) you guide the student to the right answer or way of doing something.

There are a number of ways of showing incorrectness. You could repeat what the student just said with a questioning intonation, e.g. "Do that again and I *get* angry?" (see the Functional language section in Unit 4), hoping that he or she will be able to correct themselves. You could ask "Do we say *I get* or *I'll get*?," or you could just say, "That's not quite right. Can you try again?" In all these cases we hope / expect that the mistake the student made was just a "slip," and that since the student really knows the answer—even though it came out wrong—he or she can correct it easily.

The second stage happens if and when students can't correct themselves. One possible response to this is to ask "Can anyone help Sara here?" hoping that another student can give the correct answer, and in so doing, support his or her colleague. Such student-student correction can be very valuable and help to bind classes together. But there may be serious disadvantages too: it may be humiliating for a student to realise that everyone else in the class knows the answer except them!

Sometimes you will want / have to explain the correct version yourself, e.g. "We don't say *I get*, we say *I'll get* because we are talking about what will happen in the future so instead of saying "Do that again and I *get* angry," we say "Do that again and I *will*—*I'll*—get angry." (See "The teacher's role" on page 10.) This way, you can get students to form the sentence, or word/pronunciation aspect, correctly.

A technique that many teachers find appropriate is sometimes called *reformulation*. Here the teacher simply repeats what the student has just said, reformulating it so that it is now correct, e.g.

STUDENT: Do that again and I get angry.
TEACHER: ... and *I'll* get angry.
STUDENT: Oh ... Do that again and I'll get angry.
TEACHER: Good.

During fluency work—in speaking activities, or when students are writing creatively—we may not want to correct quite so directly as we do in more formal accuracy-focused sessions, for to do so might inhibit the students' fluency practice and / or creative abilities. Instead we can listen and watch and make a note of both good and bad language use and tell students about it when the activity is over. However, in such circumstances we will probably not want to identify the individual student(s) who made the mistakes. Instead we can write up the mistakes on the board without saying who made them and ask the class to correct them. Another technique is to write on individual cards examples of both "good" and "bad" language use that we have heard. The students then have to stick them up in either one of the two columns ("Wonderful" and "Could be better") that you have put on the board.

If we think we can do it helpfully—and without compromising the activity—we may want to prompt the students using techniques such as reformulation or showing incorrectness so that students can, if they wish, correct themselves as they speak.

The point about correction is that it is difficult to make hard-and-fast rules. What is appropriate for one class or, more importantly, for one student, may be quite wrong to use with another. In some speaking activities it may be possible to use techniques such as reformulation in a helpful and non-intrusive manner, whereas to do so in others would completely disrupt the proceedings.

The only way to be sure of getting it right most of the time is to be constantly alert, watching and listening to students to judge whether our correction techniques are appropriate and successful, and being prepared to change our approach when our observation shows this to be necessary.

• **Correcting written work:** the way we respond to students' written work is just as crucial as the way we give feedback when they are speaking. Once again a lot will depend on what the writing is for. If students have done a grammar exercise, then we may want to correct every error we come across. If, on the other hand, we have asked them to do a creative writing exercise, they may well get very dispirited if we cover their work in red ink.

There are a number of considerations to bear in mind when giving feedback on written work; in the first place we may want to respond to the content of what is being written rather than only correcting mistakes. This might involve including positive comments in the margin or writing comments at the end of the piece of work.

Rather than cover a text with marks and comments, some teachers prefer to use correction symbols, so that they make a small mark in the text, and then, in the margin, write a series of symbols such as these:

Symbol	Meaning	Example error
S	A spelling error	*The answer is obvius.*
WO	A mistake in word order	*I like very much it.*
G	A grammar mistake	*I am going to buy some furnitures.*
T	Wrong verb tense	*I have seen him yesterday.*
C	Concord mistake (e.g. subject & verb agreement)	*People is angry.*
⅄	Something has been left out.	*He told that he was sorry.*
WW	Wrong word	*I am better in jazz music.*
{ }	Something is not necessary.	*He was not {too} strong enough.*
?M	The meaning is unclear.	*That is a very excited photograph.*
P	A punctuation mistake	*Do you like london.*
F/I	Too formal or informal	*Hi Mr Franlin, Thank you for your letter ...*

From *How to Teach Writing* by Jeremy Harmer (Pearson Education Ltd).

When the teacher hands written work back to the class, students should be given time to look at the comments that have been made, and then make any necessary corrections and amendments.

One way of avoiding over-correction is to tell students that you will only comment on specific aspects of writing for a particular written task (e.g. punctuation, tense usage, spelling). This has the advantage of focusing their minds on that particular aspect whilst, at the same time, ensuring that the student does not feel completely discouraged by a piece of writing which appears to be full of mistakes.

• **Outside the classroom:** however hard teachers try, they cannot expect to teach students a language all on their own! Students need to learn too, and part of this learning involves working on English outside the classroom.

For some students this presents no problem. Such motivated pupils study by themselves, reading extra English, listening to English-language songs, watching English-language movies, and visiting English-language sites on the Internet. Teachers generally find these people to be self-motivated and easy to have in their classes. They also tend to be in the minority.

The rest of the class will have varying levels of commitment and enthusiasm depending not only on their motivation, but also upon other aspects of their lives, and how much time they have to give to the study of English. They may have other homework and self-study demands placed upon them. They might have pressing work and family involvements. They might have motivational problems. Left on their own they might find it difficult to dedicate time to self-study.

In the face of such student variety, we need to be positive about the value of studying outside the class. We need to explain to students how important it is and what the benefits are. We can tell our students that research has shown unequivocally that the more self-study people do the better they learn in the end. We can remind them that it takes time to learn languages, so the more time they give it the better!

One of the ways we can encourage students to study on their own is by our own behavior. This means that where we give homework, and ask for it to be in on a certain date, we should check that it is handed in. Crucially, we should then give it back, corrected appropriately, in a reasonable time. If teachers take for ever to hand back homework, or lose it, or don't seem to mind whether or not it is handed in on time, students pretty soon get the message that it's not that important.

Another way of helping students to study outside the classroom is to give them study programs. Tell them what to do, which Internet websites to visit, which books to use for grammar revision, which bits of JUST RIGHT to look at before they come to class, and what they can do to improve, say, a particular skill. One way of doing this is through "learner training."

- **Learner training:** many teachers believe that it is helpful for students to think about how they learn, and to reflect upon their progress, difficulties and strategies. This is because a student who is involved in the process of learning as well as just the learning itself is likely to have a greater understanding of how to be successful.

Teachers can encourage students to think about learning in a number of ways. We can, for example, make it a point of most lessons to ask them how they got on, what they liked / didn't like, and how they are going to use what they have learned in the future. We can lead discussions (at various stages) on the best way to tackle reading texts or on why pronunciation is difficult. We can talk to them about correction (see above) and what kind they find the most effective and appropriate. We can, in other words, let students into the mysteries of teaching and learning! Each teacher, however, will have to decide how far he or she wishes to take such approaches, depending, of course, on who the students are.

In JUST RIGHT Upper Intermediate students are given time to reflect on things they have learnt and to prioritise their language-learning needs through a form of self-evaluation. These sections are in the Workbook, at the end of each unit.

- **Putting students in groups:** many of the activities in JUST RIGHT are designed for students to work in pairs or groups. This is thought to be a good idea for four main reasons: in the first place, students in pairs or groups each have much more chance of talking and interacting generally than they would have if the class were working all together. Students who work together are students who are cooperating, and this sharing of information and effort is important for creating good relationships in the class. Many good activities are more suitable for pairs and groups, especially when there is an information gap (see Student's Book page 36, Activity 38 for an example of this). Finally, asking students to work in pairs and groups demonstrates to them our belief that learning is just as important as teaching.

Care needs to be taken when selecting which students should work with which. We could, for example, always put the same students together, perhaps depending on where they normally sit. There may be nothing wrong with this, especially where students get used to working well together, but there is the danger that students get stuck in groupings which are not very effective, or which they get tired of.

In order to counter these dangers we may wish to choose who works with who; we can decide whether to try and group people according to ability, or personality (depending on our observation of who gets on with who). Alternatively, we can use different devices to pair and group people more randomly. For example, to make pairs we could have the class standing in concentric circles facing each other. The circles rotate in different directions. When they stop, students work with the person opposite them. We could also have students line up according to height, age or birthdays and then choose pairs or groups based on where they are standing in the line. We can give each student a letter from A to E and then have all the As sit together, all the Bs sit together and so on.

Once we have decided which pairs or groups students should be in, we will want to observe what is going on quite carefully. This is not just so that we can see how well they are completing their tasks, but also so that we can observe how well they are getting on with each other—in order to be able to group them better in the future.

Pairwork and groupwork allow us to monitor individuals or groups of individuals. It is important to be sensitive to how much this help is needed or wanted. We will also need to make sure that the rest of the class does not get impatient while we are working with just one pair or group. There is more about monitoring in "The teacher's role" (on page 10).

Finally, it is worth remembering that pairwork and groupwork are not the only ways to organize students. Having the whole class working together can be very motivating for the identity of the class, and is often the most appropriate grouping for certain activities. It is worth being aware, too, that not all students are as enthusiastic about working with their colleagues as teachers tend to imagine—and sometimes they show this by refusing to maintain an appropriate level of discipline. There is no reason why the pair and groupwork activities in JUST RIGHT should not be done, in such circumstances, by the whole class. One half can work as one side of the "pair," the other half can represent the other side. Or the class can be divided three or four ways for groupwork.

- **Reading and listening:** students often have difficulty understanding written and spoken English in class. The act of processing language is complex, involving as it does not only understanding separate sounds (in listening) and words, but also the way in which words group together, the relationship between them, and the way texts are organized into a coherent whole.

One of our aims in getting students to read and listen in class is to get them reading and listening for gist (general understanding) before getting into the detail of specific information and the understanding of every last word they see or hear. One of our main tasks, in other words, is to help students become proficient in the ability to deal with spoken and written text out there in the real world even if they do not understand every single word. That is why it is so important to give them chances to predict the content of what they are going to see and hear, and to activate what *schematic knowledge* (knowledge about the topic or about a particular reading genre) they have to help them in the task ahead.

In the lesson-handling notes you will find detailed suggestions for dealing with the various reading and listening sections in the units. But, however teachers approach each text, it is always useful to get students to look at questions, pictures or even the appearance of the text itself, so that they get an idea in their minds about what they are going to be faced with. Even if their predictions are completely wrong, their curiosity, hopefully, will have been aroused.

It is important to differentiate between the testing and the teaching of reading and listening. In the case of the former, students answer questions so that we (and they) can gauge their comprehension abilities. When teaching reading and listening, however, we are involved in a different process—namely helping students to be better readers and listeners. Even where questions look the same in both cases, the way we treat them will be completely different. In testing, for example, students work individually. In teaching, on the other hand, we may allow them to work together to see if they have understood the same things. When we then ask them if they think a statement about the text is true or false (for example), we allow them to tell us about joint conclusions, rather than shining the spotlight on an individual who, if they get it wrong, may feel uncomfortable or demotivated.

In testing, students see or hear the text for a given period or a pre-set number of times. In teaching, a basic principle is to let students read and listen for as long (within reason) as they need to. That is why we should always ask students if they want to hear the recording again, so that they get maximum benefit from it.

In testing, it is the answer that counts. In teaching, it is the discussion of the answers that matters.

Although when teaching reading and listening we want students to read and listen for general understanding, at least at first, we will also want them to go back to texts for details of vocabulary, grammar and pronunciation. Seeing the details of language in use like this is one of the best ways we have of helping students acquire language.

Many students want to analyze the meaning and use of every single word in a text. This can present a problem, however, since if you answer every single one of their questions, you might pass the whole lesson explaining individual words. This would leave you with no time for any follow-up or discussion. In such circumstances, it is wise to restrict the time you will give to such questions, or set a limit on the number of words you will answer questions about.

Finally, it is worth remembering that unless students are engaged with what they are reading or listening to they are unlikely to derive too much benefit from it. One of the most important responses they make to a reading text, for example, is whether or not they like what they have read: were they amused, moved, or horrified by it? What is their opinion of what they have just listened to? Do they agree with it or not? These are questions we should always encourage them to discuss even where they are not overtly present in the material. By doing so we are helping students to experience the language in a way that is more personal than some of the drier comprehension tasks that are included (important as they are).

- **Speaking and writing:** when we ask students to take part in speaking and writing activities, they have the opportunity to try out all and any language they know in the safety of the classroom. Unlike the vocabulary, grammar and functional sections in each unit of JUST RIGHT, the speaking and writing sections ask them to "have a go," using the English they know to discuss, take part in a role-play, write newspaper articles, or create the opening scene of their first great film!

Many teachers remember instances where discussions, for example, have failed because their students had nothing to say, or didn't appear to want to talk. Sometimes students seem to find writing creatively an almost insurmountable challenge. Yet, with the appropriate support, such depressing outcomes can be made far less likely.

One of the reasons that speaking activities sometime fail is because students really don't have anything to say—at least not immediately. When they are asked to give opinions, instantly and coherently, they just clam up, causing both themselves and the teacher to feel extremely uncomfortable. On the other hand, if they are given time in small groups before the activity takes place to prepare what they are going to say—or at least, with the guidance of the Student's Book or the teacher, to think of ideas which they can use when the discussion or the role-play starts—then although they may have trouble getting the words out, they won't also be fighting to come up with ideas at the same time.

Another way of ensuring that students have the best chance of success in speaking activities is to be certain that they understand instructions quite clearly. This is especially important when they are involved in an oral presentation (as in Student's Book Unit 4, for example), or a story reconstruction activity based on different pictures in a sequence (like the one in Unit 12).

While speaking activities are taking place, you may well want to go around the class prompting and participating to help the activity along. (See "The teacher's role," below).

Creative writing, too, is greatly enhanced if students are given time and help to come up with ideas, and if the teacher then goes around helping those with student-writer's block. When we ask them to write a scene from their first great movie (!), for example, it is immediately apparent that while some find such tasks (whether treated seriously or facetiously) easy to do, others just go blank. Yet if the activity is preceded by a discussion of dramatic openings and the kind of language a movie writer would use, as a result of which students (and the teacher) make suggestions, if we allow students to work in pairs or groups, especially where they don't seem to be able to come up with very much, if we are prepared to go and help the ones who are having trouble, then there is every chance that we will end up with some amusing lines which can then form the basis of an enjoyable writing text.

Speaking and writing activities offer students the chance of doing something they can be proud of. In the case of the latter, we can get people to read each other's efforts. We can put writing samples up on a class noticeboard, collect them in a folder, or even post them on the Internet or on an e-group site. If we have a chance to video speaking activities, we can show students how well they are doing.

Having followed the kind of approaches suggested here, students should get a very positive feeling when doing speaking and writing activities, which will affect their motivation and hence their learning.

An extra feature of this Student's Book is provided by a number of "Speaking and writing" sections where students investigate some of the stylistic and linguistic differences between these two alternative language manifestations.

- **The teacher's role:** in any lesson, teachers will play a number of different parts. When explaining a grammar point, for example, you may well find yourself standing at the front of the class with everyone listening to you. This traditional teacher behavior has always been important and useful, and continues to be so in a number of different situations. On the other hand, when students are working in pairs or groups (see above), teachers will behave in a completely different way: *monitoring* student performance by walking around and watching or listening to what is going on. This allows us to work with individuals, pairs or small groups, *explaining* things they don't understand, *correcting* obvious mistakes they are making and, crucially, *prompting* them by giving them ideas and suggestions in situations where they are stuck for ideas. In discussions and role-plays, too, we may want to be more like *prompters* (nudging students with ideas and perhaps language), *participants* (taking part in the activity ourselves as a way of inspiring students), *resources* (being available to answer questions or clarify things when needed) or *tutors* (giving advice in pre-arranged consultations).

The important thing, however, is not so much which role we are "playing," but how we play the role(s) we have chosen. Acting as a controller, for example, means being clear, calm and audible. We would be unsuccessful if we were confusing or so quietly spoken that no one could hear us. A good tutor listens and counsels rather than talks, talks, talks. A prompter pushes students gently and sparingly most of the time and only occasionally feels the need to re-ignite student participation with more forceful behavior.

Perhaps the most important role a teacher plays is that of *observer*, not just of students, but also of lessons, activities, exercises and the effect of different teacher behaviors on the class. It is absolutely vital that we do this so that we can come to a view about the best way to do things. Such a reflective approach involves looking at what we do, and have done, so that next time we can do it better. Apart from helping to make teaching more interesting, and more open to change and development, such an approach will have huge benefits for our students. Our own performance will keep improving, we will get more out of it, and we will be more effective because of it.

- **Using the Student's Book:** although care has been taken in JUST RIGHT to provide the best possible material, both in terms of topics and activities, most teachers will want to use the book in their own way—though there is nothing to stop them using the material in the book exactly as it is written, of course.

Using a coursebook is a skill. It involves looking at the material on the page and deciding if, when and how to use that material. It may be, for example, that a particular exercise, activity or even, in some situations, a whole section is not quite appropriate for your class. In such circumstances you may decide to either omit that material or, if you have something better up your sleeve, replace it with your own activities. There is nothing wrong with this, unless of course you do it all the time, in which case both you and your students may wonder why you are using the coursebook at all!

You may decide that you want to use part of a unit, and teach it very much in the way it is written; this represents a "no change" option. On the other hand, you may think that, for various reasons, you wish to adapt the extract in the Student's Book. You might want to add an extra stage to make it "richer;" you might decide to "rewrite" a particular activity whilst keeping to the main design of the section; you might get students to read the text in a unit, for example, but use your own activities to go with it in preference to the ones provided, or you might have reasons for doing things in a different sequence from that in the material. Finally, you might decide not to use absolutely every activity.

These various options can be summarized as follows:

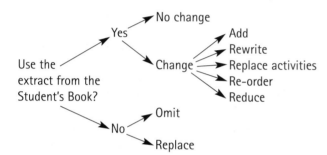

It is not being suggested that teachers will want to change the material in JUST RIGHT all the time. On the contrary, the book has been designed to be reliable. But a coursebook is only a coursebook! It is only when teachers and students get hold of it, change and mould it to their own purposes that it comes to life. That is why you need to feel free to adapt it to suit your own tastes and your students' own needs.

- **Using the Workbook:** the JUST RIGHT Workbook has sections on vocabulary, grammar, functional language, pronunciation and writing. Each unit ends with a "reflective" section, including "Culture and language," in which learners are encouraged to consider similarities and differences between how things are said or done in their language or culture and how they have been presented in JUST RIGHT (this material can be used as an introduction to cross-cultural studies). This final section also has a self-evaluation exercise, as well as "Test your knowledge," which either asks students to translate language from the unit or identify which items are correct or wrong. There is also a small exercise to practice recognizing phonemic symbols (a skill that will help students when using dictionaries, or when receiving instruction from classroom teachers).

It is up to teachers and students to decide when to use individual activities. In general, we assume that the activities will be done for practice after the topics

have been dealt with in class (and we have indicated this in the lesson-handling notes). Thus, the activities on functional language, for example, would follow the section on functional language in the Student's Book. However, some teachers and students may well want to use the Workbook activities to form a preview of a section they are about to work through.

In the case of reading, listening, pronunciation, "reflective" and phonemic script activities, there is no reason why these should not be done at any stage of the learning cycle—from before the beginning of a Student's Book unit, to post-unit study. Because the listening and reading sections are linked closely to the Student's Book unit topic, however, we suggest that teachers should not leave too long a time after working through a Student's Book topic before dealing with them.

The "Test your knowledge" section is designed to be worked through when the Student's Book unit has been completed.

Teachers can get students to use the Workbook in a number of ways: for example, students can do individual exercises for homework and you can then go through them in class. Parts of the Workbook can be used during lessons to break up the routine and, perhaps, provide some quiet "concentration time" for individuals. Students can do the reading or listening sections on their own at home and then compare their answers with those of other students when they next come to class. These reading and listening sections provide useful in-class material too.

Further reading

Teachers may wish to consult some or all of the following books.

Methodology

Harmer, J. (2001) *The Practice of English Language Teaching* (3rd edition). Pearson Education.

Harmer, J. (2004) *How to Teach Writing*. Pearson Education. (Other books in the same 'How to' series include *How to Teach Grammar, How to Teach Vocabulary*, and *How to Teach Speaking* by Scott Thornbury, *How to Teach Pronunciation* by Gerald Kelly and *How to Teach English* by Jeremy Harmer.)

Grammar and vocabulary

McCarthy, M. & F. O'Dell (1994) *English Vocabulary in Use*. Cambridge University Press.

Lott, H. (2005) *Real English Grammar*. Marshall Cavendish.

Parrott, M. (2000) *Grammar for English Language Teachers*. Cambridge University Press.

Swan, M. (1995) *Practical English Usage* (2nd edition). Oxford University Press.

Dictionaries

There are many excellent dictionaries available for students at this level. Our current favorites are:

- *Longman Dictionary of Contemporary English* (4th edition).
- *Macmillan English Dictionary*.

Both these dictionaries are comprehensive and will, once students have discovered their riches, be invaluable resources for many years.

A description of the Student's Book

- **Units and sections:** the JUST RIGHT Student's Book has 14 units, each with enough material for between six and eight hours of classroom time. How long each unit takes will obviously depend on how much time teachers decide to spend on individual exercises and activities (see "Using the Student's Book" above) Each unit is divided into a number of sections. These are:
  - Vocabulary
  - Grammar
  - Functional language
  - Speaking
  - Reading
  - Listening
  - Writing.

  The order of these sections varies from unit to unit.

  There are also shorter sections on "Word Choice" (looking at easily confusable groups of words) and "Speaking and Writing" (which looks at differences between these two varieties). A "Language in chunks" section (where word phrases are highlighted) occurs with each reading text.

  Each section is designed to be free-standing, though they are all connected, both by language and also by the thematic material which ties each unit together.

  Each unit ends with a review section which recycles grammar, functional language and vocabulary, as well as providing further pronunciation practice.

- **Mini-grammar:** grammar explanations for JUST RIGHT are given in the Mini-grammar. This is part of a separate booklet which you can find in the inside back cover of the Student's Book. Teachers and students can refer to the explanations and examples in the Mini-grammar whenever they want. In the grammar sections in the Student's Book, they are frequently asked to refer to material in the Mini-grammar, like this:

  Look at **3A–3F in the Mini-grammar** to check your answers.

- **Pronunciation:** the pronunciation activities are designed to be used at any convenient stage. Teachers should not feel obliged to tackle them the moment they appear on the page (see "Using the Student's Book" above). That is why they appear in separate boxes.

- **Activity Bank:** at the back of the Student's Book students will find the reference materials they will need when working with information-gap material in pairs or small groups.

- **Audioscript:** a complete script of all recorded material is found on pages 1–30 in the booklet at the back of the Student's Book. This is to help both students and teacher follow and / or study scripts in order to enhance the listening sections. Though it is taken as axiomatic that students should listen, at least at first, without having recourse to the printed text (since we wish to cultivate their listening skills), the Audioscript is designed for subsequent study and / or for those students who are having particular trouble and who depend upon the printed word to assist comprehension and / or revision.

- **Word Choice:** the booklet inside the cover of the Student's Book also contains explanatory material for the words in the Word Choice section.

A description of the Workbook

The JUST RIGHT Workbook has the same number of units as the Student's Book.

The content of each unit follows the sequence in the Student's Book. The following elements will always appear, but not necessarily in the same order.

- **Vocabulary exercises:** designed to practice and extend the vocabulary in the Student's Book unit.

- **A reading text:** related to the same topic area as the Student's Book unit, the reading texts are accompanied by comprehension and vocabulary exercises.

- **Grammar exercises:** these exercises give further practice using the grammar from the Student's Book unit.

- **Functional language:** these exercises practice the functional language from the Student's Book unit.

- **Listening:** a variety of different listening genres are offered, together with comprehension exercises.

- **Pronunciation:** these audio-based exercises are designed to increase students' ability to hear differences in sound, stress and intonation.

- **Writing:** further practice of the writing task, focus or theme from the Student's Book.

The following activities occur at the end of each Workbook unit:

- **Culture and language / Self-evaluation:** students are invited to compare how their own culture handles the topics and issues presented in the unit, but they are also asked to reflect upon their own learning or look at ways of learning better. This material is designed for them *either* to think about language and learning on their own, *or* (and this is preferable where possible) to discuss with other students and their teacher.

- **Test your knowledge:** students are asked either to translate sentences and questions which contain language from the unit or to sort out correct from incorrect utterances.

- **The phonemic alphabet:** because it is useful for students to recognize the phonemic symbols (both for classwork and dictionary work), each unit contains some words and phrases written in phonemic script. The students have to write these in normal orthography and then listen to the recording to check their answers.

An introduction to the lesson-handling notes

Lesson-handling notes give the following information.

- **What a section is all about:** in this Teacher's Book, there is a brief statement of what each section is about and what its purpose is.

Example (from Unit 3):

Reading: wolves

In this section, students read about different perceptions of wolves, distinguishing fact from opinion and comparing different points of view.

- **Suggested procedures:** these explain how you may want to proceed for the different stages of each activity.

Example:

- Ask students to read through these questions. Start with the second question. Ask students to find the paragraph where Hedley expresses his view (answer: the last paragraph). Then get students to summarize this view, along these lines:
  According to Hedley, we hate wolves because they have something we have lost—the ability to be natural.

- **Answers:** these are supplied for the different activities.

Example:

Answers:
a because they killed their livestock
b a character in a fairy story
c a musical fable (by Prokofiev)
d the devil
e bones and twigs
f lions
g Romulus

- **Sample dialogues:** these give examples of the kind of dialogue that might be engendered by a class discussion (in pairs or groups) of a particular point.

Example:
Ask student to say why they'd like to be a particular animal. The rest of the class can quiz them about their choice, e.g.:
S1: I'd like to be a fox.
S2: A fox? Why?
S1: Because foxes are beautiful.
S3: But they smell bad.
S1: Also they're very clever.
S4: But people hunt them and kill them.
These samples are meant to be an indication of how such dialogues might go—they are not intended as a model to be followed.

- **Workbook activities:** the earliest point at which these activities could normally be introduced is flagged throughout.

Example:

 Workbook Activities 1–3 *can be used at any stage from now on.*

Abbreviations

The following abbreviations are used in the lesson-handling notes.

[I] We suggest that the activity is done by individuals, e.g. students working on their own.

[P] We suggest that the activity is done by students working in pairs.

[SG] We suggest that the activity is done by students working in small groups (of up to five).

[I/P] We suggest that the activity can be done by students working individually or in pairs.

[P/SG] We suggest that the activity can be done by students working in pairs or in small groups.

For more on uses of pairwork and groupwork see page 8.

UNIT 1 Winning, hoping, giving

Vocabulary: money words and sayings

Students study a variety of sayings and expressions about money and use them to talk about people and money.

Activity 1a
- Introduce the activity by asking students what they think about money. Is money always a positive thing in people's lives? Can it sometimes be a bad thing?
- Students look at the sayings. Check that they understand them. Get them to explain the meaning of each phrase in other words (e.g. *Money doesn't grow on trees.* = "You shouldn't waste money.").

Activity 1b
- [SG] Students discuss these sayings in groups, saying which they agree with and which they don't. After a few minutes, ask for feedback. See if groups generally agree with each other.
- Ask students to suggest examples for each saying that they agree with (e.g. a friend who gambled money on a horse race and lost it for *A fool and his money …*).
- [I/SG] Ask students to quote sayings about money in their own language and then try to explain / translate them. This can be done in groups or individually.

Activity 2
- [P] Ask students to match the statements to the pictures. Elicit the first answer from the class.
  Answers:
  a 5   b 3   c 1   d 2   e 4
- [P] Students can use their dictionaries to find the meanings of the words and phrases in blue. You might need to explain the colloquial *broke* (= "without any money") and the idiomatic *make ends meet* (= "have enough to pay for what you need").

Activity 3
- Choose one of the pictures and ask students to say something about the person shown. For example, for picture 4, you can ask "Why is the woman sad? Why can't she make ends meet?"
- Then choose a student to ask similar questions about one of the other pictures, for the class to answer.
- [P] Students act out the role-play as shown in the Student's Book. Remember they can't ask directly about money. Some questions they could ask are:
  Picture 1: "Do you have your own boat?"
  Picture 2: "Wouldn't you like to have a job?"
  Picture 3: "Do you think that gambling should be illegal?"
  Picture 5: "Do you have somewhere to live?"

Activity 4
- Get students to give an example word from the box for each of the three headings, e.g.
  wise: *save*   foolish: *gamble*   kind: *lend*
- [P] Ask students to copy the table and complete it with the appropriate verbs. Tell them that they may decide that some words do not go in the table—that is something you will discuss with them.
  Possible answers:
  What a wise person does
  earn, invest, make, get money (by working), put money (in a bank account), save, spend money (on important things), pay money (that you owe)
  What a foolish person does
  blow, gamble, lose, borrow, take money (from a bank), spend money (on useless things), pay money (that you don't need to pay)
  What a kind person does
  donate, give, lend
- [P] Students compare their tables. Are there any differences? Is spending money wise or foolish? Is winning the result of wisdom or foolishness? Is lending money (e.g. to a friend) wise or foolish? The point of the exercise is to provoke discussion between students.

Activity 5
- Do the first example with the class, then ask students to complete the phrases with appropriate verbs.
  Answers:
  a save / spend / invest   b borrow   c give
  d spend   e give   f donate   g put   h spend
  i take   j pay   k invest   l lend   m earn
  n win / lose
- Accept alternative answers, as in the Student's Book example, but try to get students to justify them.

Activity 6
- Here's another example you can use:
  A friend of mine worked for a stockbroker. She invested their money. She made millions for the company but they didn't pay her very much. So she started her own company. She borrowed money from a bank and gambled on oil stocks. She blew all the money she'd borrowed. Then the oil market crashed and she lost all her money. Now she's working in a fast-food restaurant. She asked me to lend her $1,000. What do you think I should do?
- [SG] Groups of students make up their own story. Each student contributes a sentence. Groups appoint an editor to produce the final story. Go round groups and see how they're getting on. Invite group leaders to read out their stories. The class votes on the best story.

Activity 7

- [I] Students work on their own and try to find the meanings of the phrases.
- [P] Give students the example in the book and then ask them to make similar phrases of their own as suggested in the book. Select individual pairs to repeat their definitions and matching phrases, for the whole class to hear; correct if necessary.

Answers:
- a a way of saying "not for any reason"
- b a way of saying "something is not worth the money that was spent on it"
- c a (spoken) way of saying "I want to know that you can pay for this!"
- d a way of saying "to not have enough money"
- e a way of saying "to have loads of money"
- f a way of saying "to make someone work hard for something"
- g a way of saying "to have too much money"
- h a way of saying "to marry a rich person"
- i a way of saying "to prove that you will do as you say by spending money on it or betting on it"
- j a way of saying "to spend a lot of money on something (usually a business venture), that is eating up the money quickly and is not worth the investment"

 Workbook Activities 1 & 2 *can be used at any stage from now on.*

Reading: lottery dreams

In this section students read about people who have won a lot of money and how this has affected them.

Activity 8

- If there is an important sporting event coming up (e.g., a soccer match, a race, a championship) ask students who they think will win. Ask if they would bet money on the outcome of the event. Why? / Why not? If appropriate, get students to exchange views on betting.
- [P] Students compare answers to questions *a* and *b*. See if anyone has answered "Yes" to either / both questions. Now give students more time to respond to question *c*. Take a vote and see which option most students take. Ask them to say why.
- For the final question, see who can come up with the most outrageous suggestion. If nothing very exciting comes up, offer your own crazy ideas, e.g. have your body frozen for 100 years, travel round the world until the money runs out.

Activity 9

- Tell students that they are going to read about people who have won a lot of money in a lottery. Check that students know what a lottery is. Do they have one in their country? How often is it drawn? How big is the first prize?
- [I] Students first read the text through fairly quickly to get the general idea. Then they put the sentences in the correct place in the text. (Note: busboy = "the

person in a restaurant who clears away dirty plates from the tables")
Answers: a 2   b 4   c 1   d 6   e 5   f 3

Activity 10

- [I/P] When the missing sentences are in place, students read the full text and complete the table as follows:

Answers:
- a busboy   b sales clerk   c $2 million
- d he lent or spent all his money
- e huge credit card debts   f bookkeeper
- g $17 million
- h she and her husband fought over money
- i she divorced her husband   j accountants
- k $12 million   l their kids lost their friends
- m they worried about safety
- n they lost their jobs

Activity 11

- [I/P] Elicit the first match with the whole class. Then students match the remaining pairs.
  Answers: a 3   b 4   c 2   d 1
- Ask students if they agree with the first statement. If they do, ask them to find evidence in the text for this. They could choose the example of Lynette Nichols. Or they could quote paragraph 4 which suggests general problems of poor people suddenly becoming rich. Try to get students to be as specific as possible. Quoting evidence to back up an opinion is an advanced skill for most people—even in their own language!—but one that's well worth acquiring.

Activity 12

- Depending on your students' experience, you could ask if they know any US English words that are different from British English words. Give a few easy examples yourself of the US English word followed by the British English equivalent, e.g. *sidewalk / pavement*, *sick / ill*, *pants / trousers*.
- Students complete the box with the correct matches.
  Answers:
  - a an expensive neighborhood
  - b neighbors
  - c blue-collar backgrounds
  - d pay-check to pay-check
  - e putting their kids through college

Activity 13

- Students can do this orally. The object here is to find an approximate equivalent of these words rather than a precise dictionary definition.
  Answers:
  - a complained about   b unexpected gift of money
  - c separates them from   d sensibly   e very bad
  - f devour, consume   g suddenly

Language in chunks

In this section, we look at aspects of language more closely. In particular, students learn to use idioms they have met in the reading text.

Activity 14

- In this activity students look more closely at the language used in the text, specifically at some of the idioms the writer uses. An accurate use of idioms is a good indication of an advanced level of English fluency.
- [I/P] Get students to identify which phrase goes in which sentence, then ask them to make the appropriate alterations (if any) to make the phrases fit grammatically.
  Answers:
  a time on her hands   b to make matters worse
  c Money is no object.   d ended up
  e way too much   f a dream come true

Activity 15

- Take the first phrase and show students how they can use it in a question, e.g. "Have you ever had a dream come true?" "Do you have a dream? What would you do if it came true?"
- [I] Tell students that you want them make questions from the other phrases. Explain that they should write questions that they can use to interview a fellow student about his / her attitude to money. Go round and check students' questions and make suggestions where necessary. There is a wide range of possible questions. Here are some suggestions:
  "What would you end up doing if your car broke down?"
  "What do you do when you have time on your hands?"
  "Have you ever said 'Money is no object?'"
  "Do you think it's possible to have way too much money?"
- [P] All students should write their questions. Then in pairs they should take turns in asking and answering them. Go round the pairs and listen to the exchanges. Choose a few pairs and ask them to report to the rest of the class on the questions asked and answers given.

Activity 16

- The questions in the text can be divided into two types—questions that can be answered *Yes* or *No*, and "open-ended" questions that begin with a question word, e.g. *Why?* Get students to identify these questions in the text. Ask them to suggest answers, e.g.:
  "Did it bring her happiness?"—"No."
  "Who lives in wealthy neighborhoods?"—"Rich people."

Activity 17

- [SG] Give students time to discuss these questions. Ask additional questions if students get stuck, e.g. "How would it change your life?" "How would your partner / wife / boyfriend etc. feel about it?" "Would he / she feel the same as you?"

 **Workbook Activities 3–6** can be used at any stage from now on.

Grammar: question forms

Students look at different types of questions and learn how to use them.

Activity 18

- [P] This activity follows on from the question-identifying task of Activity 16. Go over the examples of each question-type given in the table then ask students to fit the remaining questions into the table.
  Answers:
  Question type 1   a, b, c, g
  Question type 2   f, h, i, j, p
  Question type 3   e, l, o
  Question type 4   d, k, m, n
- For further information on these different question forms, students can refer to Section **1A in the Mini-grammar.**

Activity 19

- Do an example conversation with a student for the class to hear. Write on the board the names of a friend and a relative, the place you were born and the place you visited on holiday last year. Now the student asks you questions about these people and places. All four question types should be used. You can help the student with ideas for questions, e.g.:
  "Is that your best friend?"
  "She's your daughter, isn't she?"
  "When did you live there?"
  "Who went there with you?"
- Answer the student's questions.
- [P] Students interview each other in the same way. Remind them that they should try and use each of the four question types.

Activity 20

- [I] Students read extracts *a–i* from Track 1 and should look out for them when they then listen to Track 1.
- [P] Students read the functions (*1–6*) and try to match the functions to the questions. Do an example with a student.
  Answers: a 6 b 4 c 3 d 1 e 4 f 2 g 5 h 4 i 4
- Students should refer to Section **1B in the Mini-grammar** for further information on the use of these different question types.
- [P] Ask students to match question forms to the functions (*1–6*), e.g.: "When we want to make sure that we heard a statement correctly, we often use an echo question."

Workbook Activities 7 & 8 can be used at any stage from now on.

Activity 21

- Check that students know which functions they are to use, namely *4* (asking to make sure we heard a statement correctly) and *5* (asking to make sure that we heard a question correctly). Go over example *a* with the class, perhaps acting it out with a student.

Then choose a pair to do the same with *b*, e.g.:

A: I'm late for work!

B: You're late for work? Why? What happened?

A: I didn't wake up until eight o'clock.

- [P] Now ask students in pairs to act out the remaining situations. Here are some suggested opening questions to set the conversation going:

c It's going to be a busy day? Why?

d "She gave all her winnings to a what?"

e "She invested how much in the stockmarket?"

f "You won $500? That's great. What are you going to do with it?"

g "They finished dinner at 2, did they? Why did they finish so late?"

h "They invited how many for dinner? Fourteen! Where did they all sit?"

i "You waited for six hours? Why did you have to wait for so long?"

j "Why am I investing all my money? I don't know why. It just seems a good idea. Don't you think it is?"

k "Why don't I like buying lottery tickets? Because it just seems a waste of money. Have you won anything on the lottery?"

Activity 22

- [SG] Divide the class into groups of four; each person in the group chooses, or is assigned, one of the topics (*a–d*). Basically, the questions offer a skeleton, which each student uses to write the notes of a story. Explain that the story can be real or imaginary. Go around the groups and help with suggestions, as and when necessary.

- Each person in the group tells their story to the rest of the group. The listening students interrupt with questions designed to elicit more detailed information.

Functional language: expressing sympathy

Here students practice using language to express sympathy over a range of situations. They take part in conversations and are encouraged to describe disappointments in their own lives.

Activity 23

- Go over the expressions of sympathy in the box with the class. Which is the strongest? (answer: *I'm really sorry about that.*) Which is the weakest? (answer: *What a pity.*)

- Go over the example (*a*) with the class. Note that all the expressions can be used here, except for the following:

What a pity. (This sounds too uncaring.)

It's a real shame things didn't work out for you. (This is not appropriate, as it's a response to a series of events in someone's life.)

It's a pity you're not feeling up to it. (This is not appropriate, as it's a response to how someone feels and not to something that has happened to them.)

- [P] Students do the activity. When they have finished, ask individual pairs to say which expressions they

could use for each situation. Correct where necessary.

Possible answers:

I'm so sorry to hear that. a, b, c, f, g

I'm really sorry about that. a, b, c, d, f

That's such a shame. a, b, c, d, e, f, g

That's so sad. a, b, c, e, g

What a pity. c, d, e, f, g

It's a real shame that things didn't work out for you. b, c, f

It's a pity that you're not feeling up to it. h

That's a shame. a, b, c, d, e, f, g, h

Activity 24

- [I] Play Track 2 more than once, if necessary. Students work in pairs to complete the table.

Answers:

Conversation	Statement	Situation
1	I'm so sorry to hear that.	c
2	That's a shame.	e
3	I'm really sorry about that.	d
4	What a pity.	g
5	It's a real shame that things didn't work out for you.	f
6	That's so sad.	a
7	It's a pity that you're not feeling up to it.	h
8	That's such a shame.	b

Activity 25

- [P] Students work in pairs to complete the table.

Answers:

a sorry   b shame / pity   c shame / pity
d sad   e pity   f shame   g shame / pity
h shame   i pity   j sad   k sorry

- Point out that some of the words in *a–k* are in parentheses, and explain that this means that we can leave them out. Still in pairs, students consider the effect of using the words in parentheses.

Answers:

The effect of using words like *so*, *really*, etc. is to strengthen the expression of feeling.

▶ **Workbook Activity 10** *can be used at any stage from now on.*

Pronunciation: stress

Students are introduced to aspects of word and sentence stress.

Activity 26

- Syllable, word and sentence stress are all very important in understanding and being understood in English. In this activity, students listen to Track 3 and learn to hear which words or syllables are stressed in sentences.

Answers:

a I'm ⟨so⟩ sorry that you lost your job!

b It's ⟨so⟩ sad that he lost all the money.

c It's ⟨such⟩ a shame that they had to leave that beautiful house.

d It's such a pity that you didn't save the money.
e That's such bad luck.

Activity 27

- [I] Students practice saying these sentences themselves, putting the stresses on the appropriate syllables. Don't correct for any other factor, such as word pronunciation; concentrate here on getting the stress right. It may help to play Track 3 again either before or after the students have done the activity.

Activity 28

- [P] Students work in pairs to react to these situations. One student reports the situation to the other person and the other student expresses sympathy. Students should stress the appropriate words to show how much sympathy they feel, for example:
  S1: Guess what? My sister lost her bill-fold and all her money on the first day of her holidays.
  S2: That's such a shame! She must have been so miserable about it.

Activity 29

- Get two students to act out the example (*a*). Check that they use natural-sounding patterns of stress.
- [P] Students work in pairs to act out the remaining situations. Go around the class listening to the pairs and making any suggestions (particularly about which syllables to stress) that are appropriate.

Activity 30

- Ask students to tell you about a disappointment they have had. Write examples on the board, e.g. failing an exam, not getting into a team, having a new camera stolen. You could start the ball rolling with an example of your own.
- [P] Students work in pairs and have conversations for these situations.

Workbook Activity 9 *can be used at any stage from now on.*

Speaking: making a decision

Students are introduced to the topic of charity. They read about a number of different charities and decide which ones are most deserving of help. They also look at ellipsis in speaking.

Activity 31

- [SG] This is a warm-up activity to prepare students for reading about charitable organisations. A brief discussion in groups is all that is necessary. Get individual groups to give feedback on their rewrite of the sentence about charities.

Activity 32

- [SG] Put students in five groups. Each group reads about one of the five charities. They then discuss and make notes about what they have read and why they think the charity is a good idea.

- When the five groups have read about their charity and made notes, form new groups of five, comprised of one person who has read about each one of the texts. Each person in the group gives feedback to the rest of the group about their charity. There are two points to be covered here: the nature of the work the charity does, and the reasons why the charity is worth supporting.

Activity 33

- [SG] The groups of five now decide on which charity they would choose to donate money to and why. Let the different groups compare their decisions stating clearly why they chose that particular charity to donate the money to.

Speaking and writing: ellipsis

Activity 34

- Go through the examples of how we leave out words when we speak. Ask students to comment on which kinds of words we often leave out.
- [P] Discuss what words are left out in *a*, with the whole class. Then ask students to write down the full forms of the utterances. Point out that some (not all) of B's utterances could be expanded too. As they go through the exchanges, the pairs can discuss where they think each exchange took place, e.g. in *a*, it may be two people talking about how one of them has just got a promotion in their work which they did not expect.
  Answers:
  a A: Are you surprised?
     (B: Yes, I am just a bit surprised.)
  b A: Was it a difficult exam?
     (B: No, it wasn't too bad.)
  c A: Would you like a cookie?
     (B: No thanks. I have just eaten.)
  d A: That's a nice car.
     (B: Thanks. I'm glad you like it.)
  e A: It's going to rain.
     (B: Yes, I think you're right.)
  f A: Shall we have a drink / something to drink?
     (B: Yes, let's have a drink / something to drink.)
  g A: I'm starting a new job tomorrow.
     (B: You're doing what?) ?
  h A: It's hot!
     (B: Yes, it is hot.)

Listening: money advice

In this section students listen to a financial adviser and a student talking about how to handle money.

Activity 35

- Brainstorm with the whole class possible answers to the first question. You can create different categories, e.g. people in their twenties, people in their thirties.
- Then ask individual students if they would consult a financial adviser. Ask them to suggest reasons why they might consult an adviser. Write a few of these on the board, e.g.:

Why?   *Because I can't handle money. / Because I'm always in debt. / Because I'd like to invest for the future.*

Activity 36

- Ask students to read the options (*a–d*) for what Don wants to do, and then to listen to Track 4 and choose the correct option.
  Answer: d

Activity 37

- Students read through Suzanne Moore's notes about Don. Some of the words and numbers are missing. They can put in their guesses now and correct these when they listen to Track 5. Explain that Track 5 is the continuation of Suzanne and Don's conversation. (Note: college [in US English] = university [in British English])
  Answers: a 100   b supermarkets   c the local store
  d once   e $500   f a couple of CDs
  g once every two weeks   h college cafeteria

Activity 38

- Play Tracks 4 and 5 again. Ask the students to complete the gaps in the sentences as they hear them on the tracks.
- [P] After they have completed the sentences, they should work out and write down the meaning of the words they have put in the gaps. They should try and do this without a dictionary, at least at first. Go round the class checking their answers.
  Answers: a spendthrift (= "someone who spends money carelessly")
  b major [in American English] (= "undergraduate" [in British English], e.g. "English literature major"—someone who has English literature as their main subject of study)
  c dilemma (= "difficult choice")
  d budget (= "plan of what you earn and what you save")
  e expenditure (= "the money that you spend")
  f cut down (= "reduce")
  g groceries (= "food")
  h varies (= "changes")
  i specials (= "reduced offers")
  j roommates (= "friends who share a room or apartment")

Activity 39

- The first thing students need to be clear about is what advice Suzanne gave Don. Ask questions to check that with the whole class, e.g. 'What did she suggest cutting back on?'
- [SG] Students work in groups to come up with opinions and ideas on these questions. Spokespersons feed back to the whole class. (Make sure groups don't appoint the same spokespersons all the time; if necessary, choose a spokesperson yourself).
- Listening students should ask spokespersons the reasons for their opinions.

 **Workbook Activities 11–14** *can be used at any stage from now on.*

Writing: mind maps

Students learn to use mind maps to organize their thoughts when they are doing a piece of writing.

Activity 40

- [P] Students work in pairs to study the mind map and decide what the theme is. If students are having problems deciding what the theme of the map is, suggest that they look back at the article on page 8.
  Answer: a

Activity 41

- [I] Students draw up their own mind maps individually on the topic of money and their attitudes and approaches to it.
- Students compare their maps with their partners, explaining why they chose the topic headings they did. Their partner then does the same with their mind map.

Activity 42

- Have students look back at page 8 and at the way the article finishes.
- Give students time to think about what they might want to say. You can discuss this with the whole class, or they can talk in groups.
- Tell students to look at the structure for the three paragraphs, and then start to write a letter which follows that structure.

Activity 43

- [P] Students exchange letters and compare them. Go around the class. Ask students if their letters are broadly similar. If there are major differences, what are they?
- Collect in the students' letters and take them home to mark them. When you hand them back, make sure students rewrite the parts which you had identified as having problems.

Workbook Activities 15 & 16 *can be used at any stage from now on.*

Review: grammar and functional language

Students review the key language introduced in this unit.

Activity 44

- Ask students to look at the picture of the woman. How does she feel? How old is she? Is she married?
- Now brainstorm questions from the class they would ask her and write these on the board. Some likely questions might be the following: "How do you feel?" "What are you going to do?" "Is this going to change your life? How?" It doesn't matter if the students' questions don't match the questions the interviewer actually asks: this isn't a right / wrong exercise. The point here is to get the students to think about what lines of questioning are possible.

Activity 45

- [I /P] Now students read the interview and supply the interviewer's questions. Do the first example orally with the class.
  Answers:
  a how do you feel?
  b Have you played the lottery before?
  c Why did you buy a ticket?
  d Then what happened?
  e How did you pay for it?
  f Did anyone help you?
  g don't you?
  h Where did you buy the ticket?
  i how did you find out that you had won?
  j What did you do?
  k What did she do?
  l Who called?
  m what are you going to do (first)?
  n are you?

Activity 46

- First of all, ask students to tell you from the pictures what the situation is, e.g.:
Top The boy has failed his math test. His mother is sympathetic but wants to know what happened.
Middle The woman is sick and probably tired after a hard day's work. Her partner is comfortable and at home. Is he going to be sympathetic? How is she going to react if he isn't?
Bottom The family's home is burning down. They feel terrible. What kind of questions is the reporter going to ask? If he isn't sympathetic, how are they going to react?
- [P] Now get students to choose one of these situations and act it out. They will need to write down the dialogue they have made up. Encourage dialogues which involve argument and misunderstanding. For example, in b, we could have something like this:
WOMAN: I feel terrible.
MAN: That's too bad. What's the matter?
WOMAN: Can't you see? I've got a cold.
MAN: What a shame. Why don't you make yourself a cup of coffee and take an aspirin?
WOMAN: I'm really tired. I've been working all day.
MAN: You shouldn't work so hard.
WOMAN: What have you being doing all day?
MAN: Me?
WOMAN: Why don't you make me a cup of coffee?

Activity 47

- [P] The kind of person students could think of are sports or music stars, politicians, artists, TV personalities, etc. Tell students they can use the kind of questions the interviewer asked in Activity 45.

Review: vocabulary

Students check the vocabulary used in this unit.

Activity 48

- [P/SG] Students can exchange opinions on questions *a* and *b*.
- For *c*, you could suggest other topics, e.g. saving money, borrowing money, difficulties with money.

Pronunciation

Activity 49

- Ask students to find as many words as they can for each column in the table. Explain that they have to be words that contain the same sound.
  Answers:
  /ʌ/ money
  bankrupt, up, one's, come, color, love, run
  /æ/ gamble
  bankrupt, hands, matters, marry
  /e/ get
  credit, invest, lend, objected, spend, let's, end
- Students can check their answers by listening to Track 6. Other words from the lists include *much* (under *money*), *at* (under *gamble*), *object* and *ends* (under *get*). Students then can add more words of their own to the table.

Activity 50

- Students listen to Track 7. In the first sentence, *object* (here a noun) has the stress on the first syllable; in the second sentence, *object* (here a verb) has the stress on the second syllable.
- [P] Students practice saying these sentences to each other with the stress on *object* in the right place each time.
  Answers: a ˈobject b obˈject c obˈjected
  d ˈobjects
- Students can look through dictionaries to find words which are stressed differently as nouns and verbs. If they find it difficult, you can suggest they look at *export, permit, record, subject, suspect, transport.* Have them write sentences with these words as nouns and verbs. Students read out their sentences. Make sure they use the correct stress in each case.

Activity 51

- Ask students to think of a friend who is either successful at managing money or completely hopeless at it. Then ask them to read the example. Which of these expressions could they use in telling the story of their friend?
- [P] Students work in pairs and tell their stories to their partners. Pairs decide which story is the more interesting or uses more of the key expressions from this unit. Then they tell that story to the whole class.

Workbook Activities 17–20 *can be used at any stage from now on.*

UNIT 2 Photographs

Speaking: choosing a photograph

Students talk about their attitudes to photography and choose the best picture from a set.

Activity 1

- [P] This activity is a warm-up for the topic of this unit. Allow a few minutes for pairs to discuss these questions. Ask one or two pairs to report to the class on what they found out from their partner.

Activity 2

- Two criteria are given here. Brainstorm other criteria with the class and write these on the board. Possible further criteria are:
  (the picture is) *historical   well-composed beautiful   dramatic   emotional exciting   amusing   frightening*
- [SG] Students discuss these criteria (and any others of their own) and decide on their top five. Check all groups' criteria, but don't comment at this stage or try to influence their decision.

Activity 3

- [SG] Now groups study these pictures and choose the best in terms of their five criteria.

Activity 4

- Find out which picture each group has chosen. Ask them to justify their choice.
- Work with the whole class to answer as many of these questions as possible about each picture. The answers are going to be approximations rather than "correct." For example, for photo *a*, the answers might be as follows:
  Answers:
  a Forty or fifty years ago.
  b In South Africa or the USA.
  c The white people are angry with the black woman.
  d The white people are angry; the black woman is hurt and upset.
  e The black girl walked through the crowd of white people.
  f The white girl shouted at the black girl. / The black girl kept on walking.
  g Photos like this are important as they show us differences in the way people behave now from how they used to behave.

Reading: more than a moment

Students read about an incident in the battle for racial equality in the USA.

Activity 5

- Students skim-read the text and decide which of the four pictures in Activity 3 fits with it. Don't allow more than a few minutes for this activity.
  Answer: photo a

Activity 6

- [P] This activity requires students to read the text more carefully. They can work in pairs to decide where the sentences *a–g* should go.
  Answers: b 1   c 6   d 5   e 4   f 2   g 3
  Sentence *a* is not needed.

Activity 7

- Elicit from students what Hazel Bryan's actions were at these two ages:
  15—she shouted abuse at the black student (Elizabeth Eckford)
  55—she met Elizabeth Eckford and they were reconciled
- Take the first action. Ask students to give you words to describe what she did. Possibilities include: "What she did at 15 was ugly / aggressive / racist / stupid."
- Do the same for Hazel's later action. Here students might choose words like brave, courageous, mature, sincere, honest.

Activity 8

- [I/P] The next three activities go together. Students can work in pairs or individually. To begin with, they read the text again—even more carefully—and fill out the information table.

Answers:

Hazel Bryan	white student at Little Rock's Central High School	—shouted at a black student	1957
		—apologized	1962
		—reconciled with the black student	1997
William Counts	photographer	—took photo of black student entering white school	1957
		—took photo of Hazel and Elizabeth	1997
Bill Clinton	President, USA	—awarded medal to black students	1997
Dwight Eisenhower	President, USA	—ordered federal troops to escort students	1957
Orval Faubus	Governor, Arkansas	—sent soldiers to stop black students	1957
Elizabeth Eckford	black student at Little Rock	—first of nine black students at Little Rock school	1957
		—met Hazel	1997

Activity 9

- Tell students that they need to choose words from the text to justify each of these statements.

  Answers:

  a segregated education
  b unconstitutional
  c shouting abuse at
  d they were yelling
  e she just remained so dignified
  f They caused outrage
  g the objections of the Arkansas governor
  h their innocence
  i her face screwed up in anger and hatred
  j immature

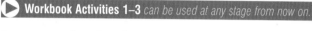 **Workbook Activities 1–3** *can be used at any stage from now on.*

Language in chunks

Activity 10

- [P] Ask the students to do this exercise without referring back to the text on page 18. If they are having problems then suggest that they look back at the text and find the phrases there to see if this helps them.

  Answers: a 3   b 4   c 7   d 1   e 6   f 5   g 2

Activity 11

- Make sure that the students realize that they will be using the same phrases that appear in Activity 10.

  Answers:

  a She never lost her composure when the police arrested her.
  b It's a fact of life that everyone gets colds and flu from time to time.
  c The Industrial Revolution changed the course of history.
  d I can never fully repay my debt to you.
  e I am bitterly opposed to your plan.
  f They built new flood defences in the wake of the terrible storm . / In the wake of the terrible storm, they built new flood defenses.
  g When he saw the people in the stadium, he knew there would be trouble.

Activity 12

[P] See how many examples of these tenses each pair can find in the text on page 18. Point out to students that they can also use the sentences that they inserted in the text, namely *b–g*. These are shown below in square brackets.

Possible answers:

past simple of *be*:
segregated education was unconstitutional
racism was a fact of life
Americans were bitterly opposed to
he was a local man
he was able to take
the crowd were right in her ear
[And so there was.]

past simple of other verbs:
he arrived at the scene
he said
she called up Elizabeth Eckford

passive sentence:
he was not attacked
many photographers from out of town were (attacked) that day
nine black students were awarded the Medal of Honor five years after the photo was taken
[the photographs ... were soon published]

past continuous:
determined in what she was doing

past perfect:
Counts had recognized
Desegregated education had begun
[William Counts had been a student]

Activity 13

[SG] Students discuss their choices in groups. You could guide their discussion by suggesting various categories of people we should be grateful to, e.g. inventors (Bell / the inventor of the telephone), scientists (Fleming / the discoverer of penicillin), reformers (Wilberforce / the campaigner against slavery), national heroes (Napoleon).

Functional language: asking for help

Students learn to make requests and to agree to requests or refuse them politely.

Activity 14

Students listen to the photographer on Track 8 telling the Fowlers where to sit in the photo. His instructions are quite complicated, so students may need to listen to the track more than once.

Answer: The mistake in the picture is that Sam is standing up instead of sitting on the ground in front of the others.

Activity 15

- [I] Ask the students to listen to Track 8 again. All these different kinds of requests occur on the track. Students complete the sentences with the infinitive (*stand*) or the *-ing* form (*standing*), as they listen.

  Answers:

  a stand over there   b stand over there
  c stand over there   d stand over there
  e standing over there   f standing over there
  g stand over there

- Ask the students to think about which are the more polite requests and which are less polite or less formal.

  Answer: These requests are in ascending order of politeness. Thus, *Can you ... ?* is the most direct and informal, and *You couldn't ... , could you?* is the most indirect and therefore the most polite. In Britain, people tend to prefer more indirect ways of asking people to do something, while in the USA people tend to ask in a more direct way.

Activity 16

- [SG] This activity gives students an opportunity to practice different types of request. Try to get as many different forms used as possible. Groups can monitor each other here; thus, while one group is getting itself into position for the photo, another group can be checking how many of the request forms listed in Activity 15 they use.

Activity 17

- [P] Students work in pairs to produce requests. Explain that they should use some of the expressions in Activity 15, such as *Can you* and *Could you*, as well as the words in the boxes. Point out that only some combinations are possible—we can't say ~~Could you do me a hand~~ or ~~Could you do me out~~, for example.

Answers:

Can you / Could you / etc.	do me a favor?
	give me a hand?
	help me out?
	lend me a hand?

Activity 18a

- [P] This activity follows on from the one before. Explain that in this activity students are looking at ways to respond to requests in English: we can agree to a request (1), we can neither refuse nor agree (2), and we can refuse a request (3).

Answers:

1 Agreeing to a request	Certainly.
	No problem.
	Of course I could / would.
	OK.
	Sure.
	Yes, of course.
2 Could be either "yes" or "no"	That depends on what it is …
	Well …
	Why should I?
3 Saying "no" to a request	I can't really.
	I'd rather not.
	I'm afraid I …
	Sorry, but …

Activity 18b

- This can be done as a whole-class activity. Students should suggest all the positive replies given in the table they've just completed, e.g. *Certainly, Of course.*
- You may like to add other common ways of agreeing to a request for a favour, e.g. *That's no problem, Fine.*
- In real life, most people would ask what the problem was and what the requester wanted them to do. So you could teach students expressions like the following:
  Sure. What's the problem?
  Fine. What's the matter?
  OK. What would you like me to do?
  Certainly. What can I do for you?

▶ **Workbook Activities 4 & 5** *can be used at any stage from now on.*

Pronounciation: intonation clues

Activity 19

- Students listen to Track 9. Speaker A is making a request and Speaker B is responding to it. The question students have to decide is whether Speaker A should repeat the request or not. You wouldn't normally repeat a request if it has been refused: you would only do so if there was some room for doubt in the reply you received. So which of these requests would you repeat?

Answers:

a Yes. B's intonation suggests he is not giving a definite "no."

b No. B's intonation indicates a definite "no."

c Yes. B may be protesting, but his tone of voice and intonation suggest he might be persuaded.

d Yes, for the same reasons as in *c*.

e No. B's intonation suggests a definite "no."

Activity 20

- [P] Students practice the exchanges in Activity 19, in pairs. Explain that Student B should use a fall-rise intonation at the end of the sentence if he / she is not absolutely refusing, and a falling intonation at the end of the sentence if he / she is saying "absolutely not." Student A has to decide whether to continue the conversation or not. Choose a pair to demonstrate.
- When students have practiced different ways of saying the exchanges, you can ask students to continue the conversation in two of the exchanges where Student A hasn't received a straight refusal. Here's an example:

A: Can you help me tidy this room?

B: Sorry, but I've got a lot to do.

A: Come on. It won't take long.

B: No, really. I've got to write this report.

A: Can't you do that later?

B: How long will it take?

A: Ten minutes. That's all.

B: OK then. Let's get started.

Activity 21

- [P] Ask one pair to act out exchange *a*. Get the students to notice that when we refuse a request with *could*, we often use *can't* in the answer, and not *couldn't*. Point out that after requests with *would* we also use *can't* in refusals.
- Students can now act out the exchanges in pairs.

Possible answers:

a I can't really. (I have to wash my hair!)

b I'd rather not. (There's something wrong with my car.)

c I'm afraid I can't. (I must go home now.)

d Sorry, but I can't. (It belongs to my mother.)

e Why should I? (Paint it yourself!)

f I can't really. (I've got a bad back.)

g I'm afraid I can't. (I'm in a hurry.)

h Sorry, that's not possible. (I'm meeting my friends in five minutes.)

i I'd rather not. (I'm going out tonight.)

- Ask students to act out some of their exchanges for the whole class to hear. The other students can decide if the replies are polite, neutral, or quite definite / strong.

Activity 22

- [P] Students choose one of these situations. Make sure that each situation has been chosen by at least one pair. Remind students that they can use the expressions that they learnt in Activity 17 to ask for help.
- Act one situation out with a student as a demonstration. For example, for situation *b*, you might have a conversation as follows:
  A: Could you do me a favor?
  B: Sorry, but I'm busy at the moment.
  A: Oh, please help me out. I need to make some food for everyone and need some help in the kitchen. Could you give me a hand?
  B: OK. What are you going to make for everyone?
- Students can act out more than one situation before deciding which one they want to write out. Choose pairs to act out the scripts they have written. Pay close attention to the intonation of refusals.

Vocabulary: photography

Here students learn words and phrases that are used in talking about photography. There is particular emphasis on compound nouns.

Activity 23

- [P] Students work in pairs to do the next three activities. Here they match the phrases to the pictures of the two cameras (the picture at the top shows the front and back of a throwaway camera, the picture at the bottom shows a digital camera).
  Answers: a both   b both
  c second camera (at the bottom)
  d second camera (at the bottom)
  e first camera (at the top)

Activity 24

- Students can do this quick activity individually. Check the right answers with the whole class.
  Answers: photo c   photograph b   snap a

Workbook Activities 6 & 7 *can be used at any stage from now on.*

Activity 25

- [P] Students match the activity phrases with the pictures.
  Answers:
  put the memory card in the camera   b
  send the CD to a friend   f
  upload the pictures to a computer   d
  burn a CD with the pictures   e
  take pictures   c
  view pictures on the screen   g
  buy a memory card   a

Activity 26

- [SG] Students can start off in small groups for this. One student talks about his / her favorite photo and the other students can ask questions about the photo. Each student talks in turn about their favorite photo.
- If students mostly choose photos of family members, mention the possibility of talking about other kinds of photos, e.g. photos of famous landmarks or historical buildings, of landscapes, of animals, of activities (cycling, swimming, playing basketball).
- When the groups have finished talking about their favourite photos, then each student can write down a description of their photo, etc.
- Individual students can read what they have written to the rest of the class.

Activity 27

- Discuss the example (*a*) with the class. Elicit what a *compound noun* is (i.e. a noun made up of two words, for instance two nouns).
- [P] Students attempt to come up with words for the definitions.
  Answers: a photo booth   b cameraman
  c wedding photo   d passport photo
  e photo opportunity   f darkroom
  g photo frame   h video recorder
- [P] Students should try and guess the meaning of *photogenic* and *photo finish*. Ask individual pairs for their ideas. If no one knows, they can look in a dictionary or you can tell them the answer.
  Answers:
  photogenic = a description of someone whose appearance looks attractive in photographs
  photo finish = a very close race where the first two competitors can only be separated by looking at a high-speed photo

Activity 28a

- [I] Explain that this activity is also on compound nouns. Students should do this activity individually after you have done one example with them (e.g. *alarm clock*).
  Answers:
alarm clock	birthday card	contact lens
credit card	greenhouse effect	heart attack
human rights	mother tongue	
newspaper article	race relations	
shopping bag	steering wheel	
washing machine	windshield wiper	

Activity 28b

- [P] Students work in pairs to test each other on these compound nouns. You may need to help individual pairs with how to form the questions, e.g. "What do you call a card that people send at birthdays?" "What do you call a lens that people put in their eye?"

Activity 28c

- [I] Students work individually to complete this description of compound nouns.

Possible answer:
Some compound nouns are one-word only (example: *darkroom*). Some are two separate words (example: *heart attack*).

Activity 29
• Start this activity off by talking about one of these topics yourself and encouraging students to ask you questions about what you tell them.
  T: I bought a photo album last year.
  S1: Why?
  T: Well, I wanted to put all the photos I had taken in one place.
  S2: What kind of photos did you put in your album?
  T: They were mostly photos of me and my family.
  S3: Were there any photos of places?
  T: Yes, I put in photos of our holiday last year.
• [P] Students work in pairs and discuss another of the topics. Go around the class listening to the pairs and making any suggestions that may be appropriate.

Grammar: the past (tenses and habits)
Students learn to describe habitual actions in the past using a variety of past tense forms.

Activity 30
• [P] Students have to put the sentences in the correct order to make a story.
  Answers: a 1 b 12 c 2 d 3 e 4 f 9 g 7
  h 5 i 11 j 6 k 10 l 8 m 13

Activity 31
• [P/SG] Students can re-tell the story to their partners or group members. Encourage them to focus on the main events: the party / not drinking / police / breathalyser / brake light / relief. Don't worry too much about absolutely correct grammar—the point of this activity is for students to identify the important things that happened.

Activity 32
• [P] Students read through the examples and questions *a* and *b*.
• Go through the questions with the students, drawing their attention to the crossed-out sentence.
  Answers:
  a We can use both *used to* and *would* to describe habits in the past.
  b When we talk about past states, we cannot use *would*. We have to use *used to*.

Activity 33
  Answers:
  used to live
  used to / would get sick
  used to / would walk
  used to work
  used to / would complain
  used to / would listen

used to complain
used to / would look after
used to / would use
wouldn't have enough money
used to / would take in
used to be a real struggle

Activity 34
• Begin by asking students if their grandparents are alive. Do they live with the family? If not, how often do students see them? Do their grandparents ever talk about their lives when they were young? Do students ever ask them?
• Brainstorm the kind of things students could ask about, e.g. school, work, housing, travel, conveniences (TV, washing machines, etc.).
• If students have access to one or more grandparents, you could get them to ask questions on these topics and report back to the class on the answers they received.

Word choice: *remember, remind* and *forget*
Activity 35
• [I/P] Students should study the Word Choice notes on page 56 of the booklet at the back of the Student's Book. Then they can work in pairs and complete the sentences, checking back to the Word Choice notes if they need to.
  Answers: a remember   b forget   c forgot
  d remember ... forgotten   e Remind   f forget
  g remember ... remember   h forget
  i remind ... forget

Activity 36
[I] Students work on the exercise and then refer to **2E–2F in the Mini-grammar**. They can change their answers after they have studied the Mini-grammar.
  Answers: a use   b use   c wouldn't   d didn't
  e used
• We use the auxiliary *do* in the past tense.
• With *used to*, we form the tag question with the auxiliary *do* in the past tense.
  With *would*, we form the tag question with *would*, as it is an auxiliary verb.
• Sentence *e*, *I am not used to living in an apartment*, is about present habits.

▶ **Workbook Activities 8 & 9** *can be used at any stage from now on.*

Activity 37
• First, brainstorm the precise questions students will need to ask. Try to elicit these from the class.
  "How did you get to school?"
  "What did you do there?"
  "What happened in the mornings / afternoons?"
  "Did you have any special friends?" "What did you do together?"
  "Did you have any teachers with special habits?"
  "Is there anything else you can remember about school?"

- Write these on the board as a reminder to the interviewers.
- [P] Students work in pairs to ask and answer these questions. Monitor these pairs sessions. If you hear any particularly interesting or unusual responses, ask pairs to share these with the whole class.

Listening: what our photographs remind us of

In this section, students listen to people talking about photographs.

Activity 38
- [I] Students listen to Track 10 and match the photographs with the names of the speakers.
  Answers: Peter d   Jane b   Kate a   Betty c

Activity 39
- [I] Give the students time to read through the questions and then see if they can answer the questions from memory. The students need to say who did each thing.
  Answers: a Peter   b Peter   c Kate   d Kate
  e Jane   f Jane   g Kate   h Betty   i Peter
  j Jane   k Kate (and her family)

Activity 40
- [P] Students listen to the track again and then discuss the answers to the questions.
  Answers:
  a Peru: The old Inca trail is there, so is Machu Picchu. They went there after they went to Chile and Bolivia.
  The Spaniards: They got to Peru in the 16th century.
  Cuzco: It's the old capital of the Inca empire.
  Machu Picchu: It's fantastic, better than any photograph of it and as good as everyone says.
  b It's fantastic. It dates back to the 18th century, when King Rama I had it built. It has temples and pagodas and wall paintings. She went there quite a few times.

Activity 41
- Students may find it easier to work from the Audioscript in the booklet for this activity.
  Answers: a 10   b 8   c 5   d 6   e 7   f 2   g 12
  h 11   i 9   j 4   k 3   l 1

Activity 42
- Provide an example by first talking to the class about a particular photo of yourself. Describe how you look and where you are, in the photo. If you look totally different from how you look now (especially if it's somewhat ridiculous!), so much the better. For example, you may have very long / short hair, a beard, big glasses, or absurd-looking clothes. Get students to ask you questions about the photo, e.g. "When was it taken?" "How old were you?" "What

were you doing then?" etc. It's best if you then show the class the photo that you were talking about.
- [P] Now ask students to talk in pairs about a photo of themselves, or about a photo that they took, that they particularly love. It could have been taken in a particular place (a favourite vacation destination, for example) or could show them at a particular point in their life (leaving school, their first day in their first job). The rest of the class ask questions to find out why this photo is important.
- In these question and answer sessions, encourage conversation. Be careful not to interrupt the exchange of information by over-correcting minor faults of grammar, lexis or pronunciation.
- Students report back to the class on what they've learned from their partners.
- Again, it's good if they can bring their photos in to the next lesson so that they can look at each other's actual photos.

 Workbook Activities 10–13 *can be used at any stage from now on.*

Writing: headlines (précis)

The focus here is on newspaper headlines and the complete story.

Activity 43a
- [P] Students work together to decide the main point of these stories as revealed in the headlines. There is a certain amount of guesswork involved here, as you need to read the full story to find out exactly what happened. But such guesswork is a vital part of successful reading and should be encouraged.
  Possible answers:
  There's going to be a big change in charges for parking cars.
  A family was caught in a fire and escaped because a smoke alarm warned them about the fire.
  A photographer who took a famous photo at Little Rock has died.
  Someone suspected of killing someone in a photo booth has been arrested.
  A horse belonging to the Queen won a race, but it was a very close race.

Activity 43b
- [P] Students work together and see which words in their complete sentences are missing from the headlines. You can also point out that headlines often use present tense verbs to talk about past events, in order to make them more dramatic.
  Answers:
  Words frequently omitted from headlines include the following:
  definite and indefinite articles (*the* Queen's horse, *a* family)
  the verb *be* (there *is to be* a shake-up, a suspect *has been* arrested)

Activity 44

- Do the first example with the class, eliciting as much as possible. The result should be something like this: *mother of three escapes injury as car plunges into river*
- [SG] Students work in groups to compose further headlines relating to the rest of the story.
  Answers:
  mother rescued by passing bike rider
  bike rider dives to pull woman from car
  mystery hero

Activity 45

- [P] Students work in pairs to identify the key words in these stories.
  Answers:
  a student   photographs   shock
    robbers   bank   police
  b singer   airport   attack
    photographer   sue
- [P] Get pairs to compete against each other to produce the most exciting / interesting headlines.
  Possible answers:
  student's photo in robbery shock
  lucky shot for police
  bank robbers caught by student's photo

  singer attacks photographer in airport row
  photographer sues angry Carla after airport attack

 Workbook Activities 14 & 15 *can be used at any stage from now on.*

Review: grammar and functional language

Students review the key language introduced in this unit.

Activity 46

- Elicit possible activities for each of these three areas, e.g.:
  a watching TV / reading / playing with toys / having a story read to you
  b playing with friends / riding your bike / exploring / going to visit places / swimming
  c going to the movies / visiting relations / playing football
  Remind students that they should use *used to* and *would*.
- [SG] Each student in the group tells the others about his / her own experiences. The other students can ask questions; they should try and use expressions like *Did you use to ... ?*

Activity 47

- Before students start this activity, ask them to look back at Activities 14–22 to remind themselves of the language used in requests.
  Answers: a 3   b 5   c 4   d 6   e 2   f 1

Review: vocabulary

Students check the vocabulary used in this unit.

Activity 48

- [SG] Students should discuss which words are most useful and agree on the answers. A spokesperson can convey the group's answers to the rest of the class. It's a matter of opinion which are the most useful words. Students should be prepared to defend their choice, e.g.:
  S1: Why did you choose an alarm clock for a backpacker?
  S2: Because he has to get up in time to catch his bus / train.
- In this activity the aim is to encourage fluency in conversation. There are no absolutely right answers.

Pronunciation

Students learn to distinguish between similar consonants used in words from this unit.

Activity 49

- [I] Students can work on their own for this activity.
  Answers:
  /θ/—birthday, booth
  /ð/—mother
  /f/—fabulous, film, flash, effect, finish, fit, frame, photo, photograph, viewfinder
  /v/—develop, VCR, viewfinder

Activity 50

- [SG] Treat this as a game, with groups working in teams. This should be a fun activity, which will work well at the end of a lesson.

 **Workbook Activity 16** *can be used at any stage from now on.*

Activity 51

- Bring in some examples of newspaper headlines. Many of these may be funny, and some may be difficult to understand at first glance. See if students can work out what they mean. This will give them a stimulus to write their own headlines.

Activity 52

- Get the class to help you generate another situation using one of these phrases. For example, to use the expression *not a patch on*, you might say the following: "I don't think modern DVDs are a patch on proper movies. You can't beat sitting in a movie theater with your friends."

Workbook Activities 17–20 *can be used at any stage from now on.*

UNIT 3 Wolf

Reading: wolves

In this section, students read about different perceptions of wolves, distinguishing fact from opinion and comparing different points of view.

Activity 1

- This activity draws attention to figurative language associated with wolves. It introduces students to some of our common ideas about the animal.
  Answers:
  a wolf
  b wolf in sheep's clothing
  c keep the wolf from the door
  d crying wolf
  e lone wolf
  f wolf whistle
  g wolf (down) your food
- This is the first of three pre-reading activities. In other words, students should not read the text before doing them.

Activity 2a

- All of these figurative uses of the word *wolf* are negative. You may need to lead students to this conclusion by asking questions about each example, e.g.:
  T: Is a man who chases women a nice person?
  S: No, he isn't.
  T: What about eating too quickly? Do you like to see people doing that?
  S: No.

Activity 2b

- Ask the whole class this question. Write (or have students write) examples on the board and get the class to translate the sayings into English.

Activity 2c

- Ask students to compare attitudes and expressions in their own language with those in Activity 1.

Activity 3

- [P] Pairs can discuss this, giving reasons for their choice. Since they haven't read the text, they will have to guess what Peter Hedley's view is. Students then read the text quickly (scanning it) to see if their guess was correct.
  Answer: b

Activity 4

- Ask students to read through these questions. Start with the second question. Ask students to find the paragraph where Hedley expresses his view (answer: the last paragraph). Then get students to summarize this view, along these lines:

According to Hedley, we hate wolves because they have something we have lost—the ability to be natural.

- Students can express their opinions about this. You could take a vote: make three columns on the board—*Agree, Disagree, Don't know*—and record students' votes under each heading.
- Come back to the first question and ask students if they were surprised by Hedley's opinion. Was there anything else that they found surprising, e.g. that the devil was portrayed as a wolf?

Activity 5

The next three activities demand that students read the text more carefully. Allow sufficient time for this.
Answers:
a because they killed their livestock
b a character in a fairy story
c a musical fable (by Prokofiev)
d the devil
e bones and twigs
f lions
g Romulus

Activity 6

- [P] This activity requires students to read the text more carefully. They can work in pairs to find the best explanations of these words and expressions. Elicit explanations from several pairs. Try to get a consensus from the whole class as to the best explanation for each word / expression.
  Answers:
  a traveled, moved around
  b person or animal who is attacked
  c fable, traditional story told to children
  d cruelly
  e pictured, illustrated, shown as
  f very old story which is passed down through the generations
  g friendly
  h regard as evil
  i deserts of Siberia

Language in chunks

In this section (Activities 7–10), we look at aspects of language more closely. In particular, students learn to use idioms they have met in the reading text.

Activity 7

Answers:
a keep out of my way
b in the end
c do my best
d get my hands on
e just for the fun of it

f for a start
g ashamed of yourself

Activity 8

- Do an example for the class, e.g. with *to get (your) hands on*: "I'm a great fan of (noted pop band or singer). I'd love to get my hands on a copy of his / their first CD."
- Get students to give you further examples of this idiom, using a different context. Remember that this idiom can be used to mean that you'd love to catch someone who has done something bad, e.g. "Someone broke the window of my car last night. If I get my hands on the person who did it, I'll … "

Activity 9

Answers:
a When?
b Where?
c Where?
d How?
e When?
f How?
g How often?
h How?
The words / phrases are adverbial (they describe verbs).

Activity 10

- [P] While students are completing this table, complete it for yourself.
- Make sure they can give you an example of a wild animal (bear, lion) and a domestic animal (dog, horse).
- There should be plenty of variety in the answers you get, especially to question *c*. Ask students to say why they'd like to be a particular animal. The rest of the class can quiz them about their choice, e.g.:
  S1: I'd like to be a fox.
  S2: A fox? Why?
  S1: Because foxes are beautiful.
  S3: But they smell bad.
  S1: Also they're very clever.
  S4: But people hunt them and kill them.
- You could also give your own answer first and allow students to question you about your choice.
- For the last question, encourage students to be as imaginative as possible. Check on the questions pairs are producing. If there is a particularly interesting question, ask the pair to share it with the rest of the class.

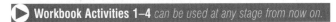 **Workbook Activities 1–4** *can be used at any stage from now on.*

Vocabulary: animal metaphors

In this section, students find out about how the characteristics of other animals are reflected in metaphor and idiom.

Activity 11

- [SG] Students take it in turn to describe one of these animals. They should give one piece of information at

a time. The other students in the group ask *Yes / No* questions to find out what animal the student is describing, e.g.:
S1: It's quite big.
S2: Has it got a tail?
S1: Yes, it has.
S3: Is it a pet?
S1: No, but you can ride it.
S4: Is it a horse?
S1: Yes, it is.

- Then other students in the group pick another one of these animals and describe it in the same way.

Activity 12

- [P] Students work in pairs for this activity and the next one.
  Answers:
  dogs bark
  sheep bleat
  chickens cluck
  cocks crow
  dogs growl
  pigs grunt
  snakes hiss
  dogs howl
  horses neigh
  cats purr
  lions roar
  rats squeal
  There are a few other possibilities that you could mention: *cats hiss, pigs squeal,* etc.

Activity 13

Answers:
a barked
b roared
c bleated
d grunted
e hissed
f purred
g crowed

Activity 14

- This task can be set to be done over a period of time (from a couple of days to a week). Elicit as many of these as possible from students' own language knowledge. For expressions students don't immediately know, ask them to use dictionaries, grammar books and other reference books as appropriate.

Answers:
a they looked guilty
b they criticized people unfairly
c they had long hair tied into one bunch at the back
d they were overconfident
e it was battered / worn
f it felt wrong / seemed suspicious
g they were shy or timid
h it was very untidy

i they were bad-tempered
j it was a failure

Activity 15
Answers:
a hold your horses
b the lion's share
c from the horse's mouth
d kill two birds with one stone
e smell a rat
f in the doghouse
g going to the dogs
h let the cat out of the bag
i fishing for compliments
j making a real pig of

Activity 16
- [P] Get the class to complete the sample sentence, i.e. *pig*. Ask the class to supply another sentence with a blank space to be filled with a phrase from Activities 12–15, e.g.:
  I'm really … . I came in late last night and woke my wife up! (answer: *in the doghouse*)
- Now ask students to write similar sentences and give them to their partners to complete. Partners should swap roles for this activity, so that both get practice in writing and completing sentences.

> **Workbook Activities 5 & 6** *can be used at any stage from now on.*

Grammar: adverbs

In this section, students learn to use adverbs to describe how and when actions are carried out.

Activity 17
- Do the first couple of examples with the class. *Sharp* here means *precisely*, *exactly*, so it's an adverb; whereas *late* describes *meeting*, a noun, so it's an adjective.
- [I] Students work on their own to decide on the functions of the remaining words.

  Answers:

a adverb	b adjective	c adverb
d adverb	e adjective	f adverb
g adverb	h adjective	i adjective
j adverb	k adjective	l adverb
m adjective	n adverb	o adjective
p adverb	q adverb	r adjective
s adverb	t adverb	

- [P] Students work in pairs to complete the three observations about adverbs and adjectives. Point out that those adverbs that have more than one form (*late*, *lately*; *hard*, *hardly*) also have distinct meanings.
  Answers:
  1 deadly, cowardly
    sharp, late, rough, wrong, flat, short, fast, hard
  2 sharp, late, rough, wrong, fast, hard
  3 late, lately; hard, hardly

Activity 18
Answers:

basically	calmly	chronically
clearly	definitely	extremely
fantastically	funnily	futuristically
happily	possibly	sadistically
terribly	tidily	vertically

Activity 19
- [P] Get students to act out the model exchange.
- [SG] Then get them to look at the adverb box. Do any of these words have to be changed to make adverbs (*rudely*, *softly*)? Are there any that don't need to add *–ly* (*fast*, *loud*)?
- When you've got that agreed, ask students which of these adverbs can be paired as opposites (*intelligently / stupidly*). Some words have more than one opposite (*tidily*: *untidily / messily*).
- See if you can generate the first two-line exchange from the students. Ask the class to choose a verb, e.g. *drive*, and a pair of adverbs to go with them, e.g. *fast / slowly*. What might the first line of the dialogue be?
  A: Don't drive so fast!
    And what might the reply be?
  B: I'm not driving fast, I'm driving slowly.
- More interesting exchanges are possible, e.g.:
  A: Why are you driving so fast?
  B: Because I'm on a freeway. You don't drive slowly on a freeway!
- [P] Students work out similar exchanges. Get pairs to perform the most interesting exchanges for the rest of the class.

Activity 20
Answers:

Manner	angrily, clearly, in a friendly way, noisily, very well, with great patience
Place	in my room, in the park, out of the window, upstairs
Time	at 6 o'clock, before, eventually, finally, next week, on April 30th
Indefinite frequency	a lot, from time to time, hardly ever, now and then, often, soon
Definite frequency	daily, every evening, never, twice a year
Certainty	certainly, probably

> **Workbook Activities 7 & 8** *can be used at any stage from now on.*

Activity 21
- [P] Tell students to look through the sentences. They should think about whether the words—especially the adverbs—are in the right order.
- Go through the answers with the students. Point out that with borderline sentences, the adverb isn't exactly in the right place, but that it can be used like this and not be totally wrong either.

Answers: a wrong   b borderline   c wrong
d correct   e borderline   f borderline   g correct
h borderline   i wrong   j correct   k wrong
l correct

Suggestions for improvements:
a I always try to watch …
b I only go to the movies a few times a year.
c I haven't often seen …
e On January 23rd I saw my first wolf …
f I will almost certainly have finished reading this
   wildlife book before I see you.
h She talked enthusiastically this evening when we
   were in the living room.
i This evening she went enthusiastically to the party.
k They didn't go home quietly.

Activity 22

* Brainstorm a selection of hobbies (genuine) from the
  class. You could include sports, if students don't have
  many hobbies. Ask students to think of adverbs and
  adverbial phrases that could go with these activities,
  e.g.:
  *I go to a chess club once a week. I play chess
  enthusiastically.*
* [P] Do the same for the other activities here
  (studying, working, next week's plans). Then get pairs
  to tell each other about these activities, following the
  models they have heard.

Activity 23

* Brainstorm this with the whole class. Build up the
  sentences by asking students to add adverbials to each
  sentence, e.g.:
  She got home late.
  Last night she got home late.
  Last night she eventually got home late.
* Make a game of this by seeing how many adverbials
  you can add to these basic statements, e.g.:
  Suddenly she heard a noise.
  Suddenly she heard a noise in the bathroom.
  Suddenly she clearly heard a noise in the bathroom.
* The story could either have an amusing ending (a
  dripping tap) or a dramatic ending (a strange woman
  standing in the bathroom looking in the mirror). The
  more imaginative ending you can elicit from students,
  the better.

Functional language: warnings and threats

Here students learn how words, phrases and
grammatical constructions can be used for issuing
warnings and making threats.

Activity 24

* Tell students to look at the sentences and questions.
  They should come up with as many possibilities as
  they can about the settings in which the words might
  be spoken.
* Go through the answers with the class, and accept
  any suggestions which make sense—or which make
  people laugh!

Possible answers:
a a man being threatened by a burglar in his house,
   or a cowboy in a western film, or a man pointing
   a gun at an elephant who talks English
b on a bottle / plastic bottle with chemicals in it
c a colleague suggesting you don't go into the
   boss's office because he or she is in a bad mood,
   or a student advising another student not to go
   into the principal's office because he or she has
   found out something about that student, or
   someone telling someone else not to go into a
   room because there's something terrible (an alien
   space monster) behind the door
d a friend who's upset with a friend, or an angry
   father talking to his son, or a couple arguing
e on a cigarette packet

Activity 25

* Students can discuss these different sentences and
  you can point out that some threats are not as
  'obvious' as others.
  Answers: a threat   b threat   c warning
  d threat   e warning   f threat / warning
  g threat   h threat   i threat   j warning

Activity 26

* [I/P] Students can either work in pairs or individually
  for this.
  In the case of description 5 ("Threats / Warnings
  with *If + would* sentences"), point out that *if* (*I was
  you*) can be omitted.
  Answers:
  a 2
  b 3
  c 1
  d 5
  e 5
  f 6
  g 4
  h 3
  i 2
  j 1

> **Workbook Activity 9** *can be used at any stage from now on.*

Pronunciation: main stress

Students identify stressed words in sentences then
practice using stress in this way themselves.

Activity 27

* Ask a number of students to read aloud the first
  sentence, putting a strong stress on '*ever*.
* [P] Students work in pairs to guess where the strong
  stress will fall in sentences *a–g*. Warn them that more
  than one word in each sentence may be strongly
  stressed for effect.
* Then play Track 14 and let students hear if they are
  right or not.

Answers:
a 'ever
b 'out
c 'very
d 'don't
e 'never ... 'that
f 'stop ... 'right 'now
g 'out ... be'hind

Activity 28

- [I/P/SG] Play Track 14 again and after each sentence get students to repeat it, copying the stress. You can start this exercise with large groups (even the whole class), then with small groups, pairs, and then individuals.

Activity 29

- This activity gives students great scope for imaginative improvisation and creative use of language. Try to get them to use a wide range of the threats and warnings outlined in Activity 26. Choose two or three students to read aloud the model sentence.
- [P] Students work in pairs to think up appropriate warnings / threats. Here are some suggestions.
  Possible answers:
  a I wouldn't go in there if I was you.
  b If you do that again, I'll have to kill you.
  c If you do that, I'll never speak to you again.
  d Never say that to me again.
  e Watch out!
  f I'm warning you not to park here again.
  g Do that again, and I won't let you use it.
  h Please don't do that again.
  i I wouldn't pick that plate up if I was you!
  j Can't you be more careful?

Activity 30a

- Having studied the pictures with the class, work out a sample scene together. Build up the dialogue by getting suggestions from some students with other students giving ideas for improving / changing the dialogue. Take picture 3 (two gangsters squaring up for a fight) as a start. You could end up with something like the following:

  A: If you tell the Boss, I'll kill you.
  B: Don't threaten me like that. The Boss will find out anyway.
  A: I'm keeping an eye on you. So watch out!
  B: You watch out yourself. You're not leading this gang, you know.

Activity 30b

- [I/P] Students choose one of the four scenes in Activity 30a and write out the conversation, complete with "stage directions." They can use the adverbial phrases they find in Activity 20, or others modelled on those phrases.

Listening: a story about wolves

Students listen closely to a story and answer detailed questions on it.

Activity 31

- Students should be able to answer this after a quick listen to the introduction on Track 15. The clues include the wooden hut, the presence of her father, the fact that it's not written in the first person (so not an autobiography).
  Answer: *Little House on the Prairie*

Activity 32

- Tell students to look at these questions. Can they answer any of them? Some students might be able to. Don't ask for their answers yet, but play Track 16. Having now heard both Tracks 15 and 16, more students should be able to answer.
  Answers:
  a the moonlight
  b her father holding a gun
  c a wolf's howl
  d her father and Jack, the dog
  e the fact that the wolves couldn't get in

Activity 33

- [SG] This activity is best done in a group. Not many students will have seen a wolf, but they will have some childhood experience that was frightening. Or, better, an experience where they should have been frightened but weren't. Encourage students to tell their stories, but don't press unwilling students to talk: not all childhood memories are pleasant to recall.

Activity 34

Answers:
a a bed covering; two
b a dog
c because there's no glass in them
d Laura's older sister

Activity 35

- [I/P] Go over the Word Choice notes on page 56 of the booklet with the class then let students work either alone or in pairs to decide which of these words best fit the gaps in these sentences.
  Answers:
  a hear
  b listening
  c to listen to
  d listening
  e hear
  f hear
  g listen to
  h listen to
  i listening

Activity 36

- Depending on how well the class has understood the story, you may wish to play Track 16 once or twice more before students answer these questions. As before, allow students to read the questions before listening to the track again.

  Answers:
  a growled and showed
  b she knew better than to
  c lifted her up
  d folded her arms ... looked at that wolf
  e moved back a little
  f take care of you all
  g on the other side of

Activity 37

- Introduce this by telling the class your favorite childhood story, preferably one students might be familiar with.
- [P] Students work in pairs to tell each other stories. Encourage the listeners to ask questions to clarify or explain points they don't understand.

Speaking: comparing pictures

Students look at different pictures and ask questions to find similarities and differences between the pictures.

Activity 38

- [P] Divide the class into pairs. In each pair, one student is A and one student is B. Tell all the A students to look at the picture on page 36. All the B students should look at the picture on page 156. The students should not look at each other's pictures.
- While students are involved in the activity, go round the class offering help where appropriate.
- When the activity is over, go through the similarities and differences with the class.

  Possible answers:
  similarities: both pictures have a tree; both have hills; the weather is fine; both have an animal; both have grass; both are probably taken in Africa, etc.
  differences: one picture has a lion, one a giraffe; the giraffe picture has clouds, the other one doesn't; the giraffe is closer to the camera than the lioness; the giraffe is standing up, the lioness is lying down, etc.

Activity 39

- [P] Here students are asked to express their opinion on various issues arising from the relationship between elephants and human beings. Pairs should be encouraged to debate these questions (make it clear that there are no "right" answers here). Monitor the discussions and ask the pairs for feedback, some of it in front of the whole class. It's helpful if there is a wide range of views on these issues. The important thing in such discussions is to learn to express an opinion and defend it against questioning.

Possible feedback:
a Ayesha and I discussed the correct punishment for ivory poachers. She thinks they should just get a fine, as they are only trying to make money for their families, but I think they should go to prison.

 Workbook Activities 10–14 *can be used at any stage from now on.*

Writing: linking words and phrases

Students plan a short composition on issues related to animals, focussing on the use of linking words and phrases.

Activity 40a

Answer: not in favor

- As an extension of this, you could ask students to look back at the opinions they expressed in the previous exercise. Which of these would the writer agree with?

Activity 40b

- [I/P] Students can work on their own or in pairs for this activity. Do the first example with the class. Students can check their answers in Activity Bank 2 on page 156.

  Answers:
  but—however
  and—and furthermore
  and—moreover
  but—on the other hand
  and—not only that, but
  so—therefore
  but—in contrast
  so—as a result
  so—in conclusion
  but—nevertheless

Activity 41

- Let students make notes, then brainstorm ideas for and against. Write them up in note form on the board, e.g.:

FOR	AGAINST
—animals safe in zoos	—animals best protected in natural habitat
—can breed	—zoos unnatural habitat
—enables research	—conservation best left to experts in field

Activity 42

- Work with students to draw up an outline plan for their compositions. A series of boxes works well. Draw these on the board and gradually fill them in. Elicit as much material as possible from the class. Much of this material will be drawn from the discussion in the previous activity.

Example plan:

1 Intro: introduce topic—discuss zoos, need for protection of species, rapid rate of extinction of species. How can animals best be protected? Language: *I'd like to start by outlining the problem.*

2 For: arguments for zoos as best protection Language: *Many people believe … It is true that …*

3 Against: arguments for other forms of protection / conservation Language: *On the other hand … However …*

4 Conclusion: decide for one argument or the other Language: *In conclusion therefore … Finally … To sum up …*

Activity 43

This is best set as an out-of-classroom task. Set aside a period for this and let students read their compositions to the class. Invite comments and questions. There is much time and effort involved in writing a composition of this kind, so it is a good idea to get the most out of it.

 Workbook Activity 15 *can be used at any stage from now on.*

Review: grammar and functional language

Students review the key language introduced.

Activity 44

- Do a couple of examples with the class to get the idea across, e.g.:
  That was a pretty exciting film. (pretty = adverb)
  This plum is too hard. I can't eat it. (hard = adjective)

Activity 45

- Students work in pairs for this activity. Start them off by saying something about yourself, e.g. "Every time I go to the doctor's, I feel nervous." "I'm really tired today. I'll probably not sleep at all tonight."

Activity 46

Possible answers:

a Look out! There is a lion behind you.
b If you do that again, I'll send you to your room!
c You're driving the wrong way!
d Never speak to me again like that!
e If you come any closer, I'll blow your head off!
f Don't look at me like that. I heard everything you said to her.

Review: vocabulary

Students check the vocabulary used in this unit.

Activity 47

- Give students some time on their own to think about appropriate animals and find associated vocabulary. Then as a whole-class activity, ask quick-fire questions along these lines:

T: So your favourite animal is a cat. What words can you use for it?
S1: *Purr. Catty.*
T: What does *catty* mean? Would you like to be called that?
S1 : …
T: Your least favourite animal is a rat, is it? What do rats do?
S2: *Squeal.*
T: What does *ratty* mean? Would you like to be called that?
etc.

Pronunciation

Students practise stressing words of more than one syllable correctly.

Activity 48

Students can try this activity then check their answers by listening to Track 17.

Answers:

a Stressed syllable in words of two syllables or more: 'turkey, 'catty, 'cocky, 'demonize, 'dog-eared, 'dogged, 'fairy, 'story, 'fishy, 'mousy, 'pigsty, por'trayed, 'ratty, sa'distically, 'sheepish, 'sociable, 'victim

b Vowel sound in the stressed syllable:
/ɪ/: fishy, pigsty, sadistically, victim
/æ/: catty, ratty
/ɒ/: cocky,
/ɔ/: dog-eared, dogged, story
/eɪ/: portrayed
/ɚ/: turkey
/ɛ/: fairy
/aʊ/: mousy
/i/: sheepish
/oʊ/: sociable

Activity 49

- [P] Students practice these in pairs, then listen to Track 18 to see if they are stressing these phrases correctly. Point out that the vowel sound of a short unstressed word (*of, a, the*) within a phrase becomes a schwa.

 Workbook Activity 16 *can be used at any stage from now on.*

Activity 50

- [I] Students can work on their own for this, but they can share their answers with the class when they are finished. They can then check their answers with the dictionary definitions and see how close they were.

Activity 51

- [SG] This game is best played in small groups. Either appoint a neutral student as judge or award groups points yourself.

 Workbook Activities 17–20 *can be used at any stage from now on.*

UNIT 4 Just for fun

Listening: things people do for fun

In this section, students listen to people talking about various leisure activities.

Activity 1

• Students look at the pictures and decide what these people are doing. Do the first example with the whole class.
  Answers:
  a train-spotting
  b angling / fishing
  c skydiving
  d potholing
  e golf

• Then ask if any student does any of these activities. If not, which one would they like to do? Ask them to give reasons for their choices, e.g. "Potholing is exciting." You can also ask students who did not choose this activity to say why not, e.g. "Potholing is dangerous."

Activity 2

• Students look at these people and decide which of the activities each of them does. Let them guess, then play Track 19 and let them check their answers. One listening should be sufficient at this stage.
  Answers:
  Danny: angling / fishing
  Carmen: potholing
  Jack: train-spotting
  Marcus: golf
  Ellie: skydiving

Activity 3

• [P] Now students listen again to Track 19, paying more attention to the details of what people say. Students can work in pairs for this.
  Answers:
  a Danny   b Carmen's husband
  c Carmen   d Carmen
  e Jack's interviewer f Jack
  g Marcus   h Marcus
  i Ellie   j Jack

Activity 4

• [I/P] Go over the first example with the class. Ask students to tell you who says this (answer: *Carmen's husband*). Then let them complete the activity either on their own or in pairs. To finish, they could listen to Track 19 and locate the other expressions they've found.

Answers:
a I've begged.
b I'm not addicted to it.
c I'll take your word for it.
d It's not for everybody.
e nerds
f the only downside
g You can't be serious.

Activity 5

• [P] Go round the class and listen to pairs working at this activity. Give help or make suggestions where necessary.

• When students have finished the activity, ask individual pairs to act out their question-and-answer conversation for the rest of the class. Cue pairs by naming one of the four characters, e.g.:
  T: Jack.
  S1: What does Jack do for fun?
  S2: He stands in a railway station and watches trains.
  S1: Is he a train-spotter?
  S2: Yes, he is.

> ▶ **Workbook Activities 1–4** *can be used at any stage from now on.*

Vocabulary: hobbies and activities

In this section, students focus on words associated with leisure activities.

Activity 6

• [P] Students continue working in pairs for this activity.
  Answers:
  a flower arranger   b golfer
  c mountain climber   d rock climber
  e stamp collector   f skydiver
  g angler   h potholer
  i beekeeper   j model maker
  k water-skier   l trainspotter
  m scuba diver   n skateboarder
  o snowboarder   p hillwalker
  q bird watcher

Activity 7a

• Draw up a table on the board and write the examples in the correct columns:
  Compound words   Others (e.g. verb + *-er* = noun)
  flower arranger   golfer

• [P] Now ask students to add words to the appropriate column, using the answers from Activity 6. Let them complete the table in the same way.

Answers:

Compound words	Others (e.g. verb + -er = noun)
flower arranger	golfer
mountain climber	angler
rock climber	potholer
stamp collector	
skydiver	
beekeeper	
model maker	
water skier	
trainspotter	
scuba diver	
skateboarder	
snowboarder	
hillwalker	
bird watcher	

Activity 7b

Answers:

a flower arranging   b golf (not "golfing")
c mountain climbing   d rock climbing
e stamp collecting   f skydiving
g angling / fishing   h potholing
i beekeeping   j model making
k water-skiing   l trainspotting
m scuba diving   n skateboarding
o snowboarding   p hill walking
q bird watching

Activity 8

- Go over the example with the class.
  In this activity much will depend on the resources available to students. If they have easy access to dictionaries and encyclopaedias, they will be able to complete this activity without much help from you. If not, you will need to give some additional clues.
  Note that many of these objects can be used in more than one activity.
  Possible answers:
  a stamp collecting
  b bird watching
  c snowboarding / water-skiing / stamp collecting
  d stamp collecting / model making
  e snowboarding / scuba diving
  f snowboarding / skydiving / rock climbing / potholing
  g stamp collecting
  h scuba diving / skydiving / beekeeping
  i all (but you could discuss which ones need more money and which are inexpensive)
  j fishing
  k bird watching / trainspotting
  l scuba diving
  m fishing
  n water-skiing
  o potholing
  p flower arranging
  q scuba diving, potholing

- [P] Students can ask each other to say why the object could be used for the activity they have chosen, e.g.:
  S1: Why do you need gloves for stamp collecting?
  S2: To keep your hands clean.
  S1: Why do your hands need to be clean?
  S2: To protect the stamps.

Activity 9

- [SG] This activity is suitable for small groups, because it gives students a chance to debate and discuss where to put the various expressions on the hate-love line. Draw the line on the board. Start off by trying to get a consensus on the first couple of examples, e.g.:
  T: "I am addicted to." Does that mean "I like it a bit?"
  S1: No.
  T: Is it stronger than that?
  S2: Yes.
  T: Much stronger?
  S3: Yes.
  T: So where should I put it on this line? Show me.
  (*Student points to or pin-points place on the line or writes "a" on the best place on the line.*)

Possible answers:
hate ---k--j--g--e--n--f--d--p-- m--i --l--b--o--c--a--h---Love

Activity 10

- [P] Students work in pairs for this activity. The first student picks an activity, say, potholing, and the second responds to it as in the example in the Student's Book, or this one:
  S1: Potholing.
  S2: I get a kick out of potholing but I'm really addicted to rock climbing.

Activity 11

- Look at the four pictures with the class. Elicit what these activities are called: rock climbing, flower arranging, beekeeping, water-skiing.
- Students in the group choose one of these people and other students interview him / her about his / her activity.
- Brainstorm some questions similar to those in the example, e.g.:
  Isn't ... dangerous?
  Is ... exciting?
  Don't you find ... difficult?
  Does it take a long time to learn how to ... ?
  Ask students to say which of the four people could best be asked each of these questions.
- When students have practiced their conversations, get each group to perform them to the rest of the class.

Workbook Activities 5 & 6 *can be used at any stage from now on.*

Speaking: making a presentation

In this section, students prepare a talk about an activity of their choice. They make notes, plan the talk, then deliver it.

Activity 12a

- Preparing, planning and delivering a talk is an important activity and needs a good deal of time and attention to detail if it is to be successful. Doing a talk activates a great deal of language which students have been presented with in this unit. It involves reading, writing, listening and speaking, and is thus a fully integrated language project.
- [P] Students work in pairs. This gives them an opportunity to help each other with the planning of the talk. Brainstorm the activities with the class. They may decide to choose one of the activities described already in this unit or go for something completely different—table tennis, embroidery, cooking, photography. The best results will be achieved if students talk about something they genuinely like doing, or would really like to try.

Activity 12b

- [P] In pairs, students go over these questions. The answers will form the basis of the plan of the talk. Again, students can help each other by asking further questions to ensure that there is sufficient detail in the talk. For instance, if the activity chosen is photography, the questioning could go like this:
  S1: (*quoting from the questions listed in the Student's Book*) What kind of person does this activity?
  S2: I don't know. Mostly men.
  S1: Don't women like taking photographs?
  S2: Yes, of course.
  S1: What about children?
  S2: No, I don't think so.
  S1: But children can start off with a simple camera, can't they?
  S2: Yes, I suppose so. But they have to be nine or ten years old.
  And similarly with the other questions.

Activity 12c

- [P] Answering the questions in 12b will help students plan their talks. In fact the answers can form the basis of the talk itself. The introduction ("what you're going to talk about and why") is probably the most important part. If the introduction is interesting, then listeners will be encouraged to pay attention to the talk. If not, they won't. Before letting students plan their talks in pairs, brainstorm the language needed to introduce the topic. Show them (or, better, try to elicit from them) different ways of beginning the talk. This can be presented in a multiple-choice frame, e.g.:

Today	I'd like to begin by talking about …
This afternoon	I'm going to start by describing …
Now	I want to talk about …

… something	I'm really addicted to.
… an activity	I love doing.
… a sport	I enjoy doing very much.

- Do the same with the other sections of the talk (what it is—how you do it, what it's like, etc.—and the conclusions) as necessary.

Activity 13

- [SG] For the delivery of the talk, students follow the plan outlined in the Student's Book. Allow the "observers" to write as critically as they like, but try to ensure that they do not use language which is too strong or in any way offensive. Monitor carefully so that the kind and harsh critics are accurate in their assessment of the language used.

Grammar: present perfect continuous (and simple)

In this section, students learn how to use the present perfect continuous and how to distinguish its use from that of the present perfect simple.

Activity 14

- Tell students that all the sentences (*a–g*) have a mistake in them. Get them to look at sentence *a*, and make sure they understand we don't use *since* with periods of time (e.g. *a long time*). Ask them how they would change the sentence (use *for* instead of *since*).
- [P] Students look through the sentences, identifying the mistakes. (You can also tell students that *rock climbing*, *cliff diving* and *freediving* will all be explained in the text on pages 43 and 44.)
- When they have finished, tell them they can look at **4A–4D in the Mini-grammar**. Do they want to change their answers?
  Answers:
  a <u>for</u> a long time
  b <u>didn't</u> see him
  c I've <u>only just</u> realized
  d I've <u>never tried</u> rock climbing
  e I've tried <u>cliff diving a couple of times</u>
  f I <u>watched</u> freediving
  g I have <u>already forgotten</u> the name

Activity 15

- Tell students to look through the four situations. Can they use the present perfect for all of them? Which is the one where the present perfect can't be used?
- Students make their choice. Tell them the correct answer and point out that we don't use the present perfect about a completed action in the past; we use the past simple.
  Answer: b

Activity 16

- Go over the example with the class. Then ask them which tense should be used in example *b*. Is it a past action that affects the present? (answer: *yes*)
[P] Students work in pairs to complete the rest of the sentences correctly.
  Answers:
  a has been skydiving
  b has made
  c 's been seeing
  d has asked; has agreed
  e has bought
  f has never jumped
  g has been going
  h hasn't enjoyed
  i has promised
  j has watched
  k has never been able

Activity 17

- [P] Students use the same sections of the **Mini-grammar, 4A–4F**, to help them decide whether these sentences are correct or wrong.
  Answers:
  a correct
  b wrong (I've had …)
  c wrong (I've seen …)
  d wrong (I've understood …)
  e correct
  f wrong (he's been going …)
  g wrong (this mountain has been here …)
  h correct
  i correct
  j wrong (… have you had)

Activity 18

  Answers:
  1 c
  2 a
  3 b

- [P/SG] Divide the class into three groups. Give each group one conversation to practice. Get pairs to act out their conversations to the rest of the class.
- Try to encourage students to be as imaginative as possible. Let them think up unusual or amusing continuations. A typical conversation for *3b* might go like this:
  A: Where have you been hiding recently?
  B: What? Oh, er, nowhere. I've just been working quite hard, that's all.
  A: Haven't you been playing tennis?
  B: Tennis? Well, yes, but only once or twice a week.
  A: Have you been watching the baseball on television?
  B: Yes, that's been really exciting. I've been watching it every afternoon.
  A: But you've been playing tennis, haven't you?
  B: Yes, but I've been playing in the evening.
  A: And you've been working very hard, of course.
  B: Of course.

> **Workbook Activities 7 & 8** *can be used at any stage from now on.*

Reading: looking danger in the face

Students skim-read three texts, choose one, then make notes on the most important points. Further questions focus on key vocabulary items.

Activity 19

- Tell students they are going to read three texts about dangerous activities. Get students to scan the texts. Which one is about cliff diving? (1) Which is about rock-climbing? (3) What is the other text about? (freediving)
- SG] Get students to work in groups of three. Each student picks one of the texts and reads it carefully. Then they copy the table and complete the column corresponding to their respective text. After this, each student will have one column filled in and the other two blank. The complete table should look like this:

	Text 1	Text 2	Text 3
a	Dustin Webster	Audrey Mestre	Leo Houlding
b	Orlando Duque	X	X
c	America	France 11/8/74	X
d	cliff diving	freediving	climbing snowboarding slack-lining
e	dives from very high	dives very deep without oxygen	enjoys taking risks
f	saw high divers aged 11	mother / grandfather spearfishers	father took him climbing
g	member of high diving team	set world record May 2000	X
h	lost the latest contest	died trying to set new record	not afraid to die

Activity 20

- [SG] Now students interview each other and collect the information they need to complete the table.
- Students can report back to the class on what they've been told. They should read out the answers they've been given. Other students who have studied that text can correct answers if they are wrong.

Activity 21a

- [SG] Students can stay in their groups to discuss this question. As important as the choice of activity are the reasons for the choice.

Activity 21b

- If students have difficulty in thinking about good questions, you may want to prompt them, e.g.:
  (to Dustin:) "Why do you do it if you're afraid?"
  (to Audrey:) "What would be your advice to young people interested in freediving?"
  (to Leo:) "How do you keep your balance when you go slack-lining?"

Activity 22

- Divide this activity into two parts. First, go over the example with the class, then ask them to identify the remaining parts of speech.
  Answers:

a verb	b noun	c adjective
d adjective	e noun	f noun
g noun	h noun; adjective	i adverb

- [P] Then ask pairs to suggest synonyms for these words. If students have dictionaries, let them use them.
  Possible answers:
  a launch = throw
  b piece = bit
  c frail = weak
  d vulnerable = able to be hurt / unprotected
  e thesis = piece of research
  f scuba diving = underwater swimming
  g apparatus = equipment
  h courage = bravery; disrespectful = rebellious
  i nonchalantly = calmly

Language in chunks

This section focuses on idioms and colloquial phrases used in the texts.

Activity 23

Answers:
a 5
b 6
c 7
d 2
e 4
f 1
g 3

Activity 24

- [P] Having worked out the meaning of the phrases in Activity 23, students ask each other these questions. Then each student reports back on their partner's answers.

Activity 25

- [I] Tell students to look for the four examples of present perfect continuous in the three texts on pages 43–44 and see who is the first to find them all.
  Answers:
  Text 1
  He has been high diving ever since.
  Text 2
  None.
  Text 3
  Mark's little boy has been climbing higher and higher and doing more and more dangerous things ...
  I've been traveling ...
  He's been climbing in and around Barcelona ...

Activity 26

- Students should use a variety of question forms, e.g.:
  Yes / No questions: *Has Dustin ever broken his leg?*

Open questions: *How long has he been cliff diving?*
Either / Or questions: *Did Dustin or Orlando win the prize?*

- Students should use as many examples of the present perfect tenses as possible in their comprehension questions.
- When students have written their questions, they should ask them of somebody who has read the same text.

 Workbook Activities 9–11 *can be used at any stage from now on.*

Functional language: asking for clarification / buying "thinking time"

In this section, students learn some crucial conversational skills. Asking for clarification and buying time are both important in spoken communication, for instance in negotiating.

Activity 27

- Read the conversation aloud with a student or ask a pair of students to do it.
- Ask students to read the question and see if they can find the answer in the conversation.
  Answers: She doesn't want to go to a party. A suitable word to fill the gap is *party*.
- Students check their answer by listening to the full version of the conversation on Track 20.

Activity 28

- The next three activities can be done in sequence. Students can work individually or in pairs to answer these questions.
  Answers:
  a ... what do you call it?
  b umm ...
  c Do you know what I mean?
  d Sorry?
  e Uh-huh? Yeah?
  f yes, but ...
  g Look, ...

Activity 29

Answers: 1 d   2 b   3 d   4 e   5 d   6 e   7 f   8 b
9 a   10 a   11 e   12 a

Activity 30

Possible answers:
a Excuse me?
b umm ...
c Pardon me?
d Sorry to interrupt, but ...
e Do you know what I mean?
f Well ...

 Workbook Activity 12 *can be used at any stage from now on.*

Pronunciation: intonation

In this section, students differentiate between rising and falling intonation.

Activity 31

- Students listen to Track 21 and decide whether the second speaker in every exchange is using a rising intonation (?) or a falling intonation (.). They copy the words and add the correct punctuation accordingly.

  Answers:
  a Yeah?
  b Excuse me?
  c Uh-huh.
  d Yeah?
  e Right.
  f Sorry?
  g Uh-huh.
  h Right.

Activity 32

- Having heard the difference between a listener who is asking for a speaker to repeat something and a listener who is simply confirming that he is listening, students get a chance to practice making the difference themselves.
- [P] Get one pair of students to act out the model exchange in front of the class. The key word here is *M'mmm?* which must be pronounced with a rising intonation if Student A is to respond. In pairs, students then work their way through the activity.

Extension

- [P] Now choose a pair of students. The first student makes statement *b*:
  S1: I've been looking for you everywhere.
  Ask the second student to pretend not to have heard or understood the speaker. He / She can choose what expression he / she uses to indicate this, e.g.:
  S2: Excuse me?
  This should cue the first student to repeat what he / she said, perhaps preceding the statement with *I said* ...:
  S1: I said I've been looking for you everywhere.
- Do the same with another pair, this time asking the second student to indicate that he / she wants the first speaker to go on. This conversation could go like this:
  S1: I've been looking for you everywhere.
  S2: Uh-huh.
  Then the first student has to think *why* he has been looking for the second student, e.g.:
  S1: We're going to be late for the party.
- [P] Let students practice making up similar conversations with statements *a–h*. Go round the class and listen. Then choose a few pairs to act out their conversations for the rest of the class. Encourage students to put a bit of feeling into their presentation, e.g. irritation, boredom, truculence, so as to give it a more realistic feel.

Writing: email interview

Students look at an email text, written in a mix of registers (traditional written register for the questions, informal register for the answers).

Activity 33a

- [SG] This activity is best done in groups. Students read the interview and express their opinions about Emma.

Activity 33b

- *Clubbing* may be unfamiliar. It means going out to nightclubs where you can dance and drink and listen to (loud) music.

Speaking and writing: speaking-like and writing-like

Students learn to tell the difference between language appropriate to speaking (speaking-like) and language appropriate to writing (writing-like).

Activity 34

- Look at the first two sentences with the class. Which sentence sounds like it comes from a conversation? (answer: *a*) Which seems more like something from a written statement? (answer: *b*)
- Now ask students if they can point to any differences in the language used in the two sentences.
  S1: In a), you've got *aren't they*? It sounds as if the person is speaking to someone else.
  S2: In b), *they are* sounds like it comes from something someone has written. In speaking, you'd say *they're*, wouldn't you?
- Now let students read the remaining sentences and decide whether they're speaking-like or writing-like.
- Go through the answers with the students. Make sure they realize that sometimes it's ellipsis that tells us that a sentence is speaking-like (e.g. *Fantastic, aren't they?* instead of *They are fantastic, aren't they?*), sometimes it's because the whole phrase is conversational (e.g. *See you later*), and sometimes it's the words and phrases themselves (e.g. *I'm like*). Writing-like language often uses fuller constructions (*I think they are fantastic*), more formal words (*I am not going to tolerate this any more*), or a combination of both (e.g. *It is worth investigating the new cafeteria*). Point out, however, that there is room for discussion on a number of these sentences (*e, f, i* ...). Sentence *e*, for instance, *I said that it was fine and he replied that it was OK*, could of course be heard in speech, and only seems more "writing-like" by comparison with the very colloquial version in sentence *d*.

  Answers:
  Speaking-like: a, c, d, f, h, j, k
  Writing-like: b, e, g, i, l

- [P] Students work in pairs to make up a short conversation (two or three sentences).

Activity 35

- Tell students they are going to write their own answers to the questions in the email. Elicit a few answers from the class, pointing out that they can use informal speaking-like language, as Emma Sanchez Moore did.
- [I/P] Students answer the questions. While they are doing this, go round the class helping where appropriate.
- Students compare answers. Who has the most surprising / interesting answers?

Activity 36

- Start by forming actual questions from the suggestions given here. Elicit these as much as possible from the class, e.g.:
  "What makes you happy / sad?"
  "Is there something that really annoys you / makes you happy?"
  "What quality do you look for in a friend?"
  "What kind of music do you like?"
  "Have you got a wish for yourself / the world in the future?"
- [P] Ask students to go on and write further questions that could be used in an interview.
  Possible questions:
  What's your favorite movie / TV program / book?
  Is there a movie star / musician / politician / writer you really admire? Why?
  If you could make one new law, what would it be?
  What are you reading now?
  What do you think you'll be doing in five years' time?

Activity 37

- Students "post" their questions to their partners or email them if this is possible.
- Partners can reply to these questions. This can best be done out of class time as a home task.

Workbook Activities 13 & 14 *can be used at any stage from now on.*

Review: grammar and functional language

In this section, students review the key language introduced in this unit.

Activity 38

- [P] Do the first example with the class. Then let students work in pairs to match the questions and answers.
  Answers: a 6 b 8 c 7 d 1 e 9 f 5 g 2 h 3 i 10 j 4
- [SG] This is best done in small groups where students have a chance to discuss who the participants may be. As the example indicates, there is usually more than one possible answer to each question and answer.

Possible answers:
a brothers and sisters; teenager and parent
b two friends; parent and adult child; teacher and pupil
c parent to child
d two friends; parent and son / daughter
e doctor / dietician and patient
f married couple; two partners
g two people involved in a mystery / a criminal activity
h teacher / counselor and pupil / student
i friends
j college lecturer and student

Activity 39

- [P] This is an open-ended activity. Here students should be given the maximum freedom to talk about themselves using some of the key grammar they've learned in the unit, such as the present perfect continuous.
- Do the activity yourself. If students get stuck with their activities, tell them what you've written. This could give them an idea.
  Possible answers:
  a I haven't been running for weeks.
  b I've always done all the cooking.
  c For the last few weeks, I've been reading *War and Peace*. It's brilliant!
  d I've only been kayaking once or twice but I'd really like to do it more often.
  e I went potholing once. Never again! I hated it.
  f I've never been to a bullfight.
- [P] Students work in pairs and compare the activities they've chosen to talk about.

Activity 40

- Work with students to rewrite the first few sentences. The result could be something like this:
  A: I've been thinking of taking up water-skiing.
  B: Excuse me?
  A: Water-skiing.
  B: What about it?
  A: I've been thinking of taking it up.
  B: Really?
  A: Yes, it looks quite exciting.
  B: Uh-huh.
- [P] Let students keep inserting signals to continue (*Really? Uh-huh.*), requests for clarification (*Excuse me? Pardon me? What do you mean?*) or attempts to "buy time" (*Umm ... What do you call it ...*) as appropriate.

Review: vocabulary

Students check the vocabulary used in this unit.

Activity 41

- Ask students to choose one of these occupations. Brainstorm words that name things you could use in this occupation, e.g.:
  bird watcher: binoculars, notebook, boots
  Which of these words are in the Word List?
- [I/P] Students then choose two other occupations and find the names of things they'd need for this occupation.

Pronunciation

In this section, students listen for individual sounds in a variety of words, including polysyllables.

Activity 42

- Students listen to Track 22 and count the sounds in these words.
  Answers:
  a 6: /æ/ /ŋ/ /g/ /l/ /ɪ/ /ŋ/
  b 9 /b/ /ɪ/ /n/ /ɒ/ /k/ /yə/ /l/ / ə / /z/
  c 6 /g/ /ɒ/ /g/ /ə/ /l/ /z/
  d 6 /n/ /oʊ/ /t/ /b/ /ʊ/ /k/
  e 8 /s/ /k/ /eɪ/ /t/ /b/ /ɔr/ /d/ /ɚ/
  f 5 /θ/ /i/ /s/ /ɪ/ /s/
  g 9 /t/ /r/ /eɪ/ /n/ /s/ /p/ /ɒ/ /t/ /ɔr/

Activity 43

- Get students to find a three-or four-syllable word that is stressed on the first syllable, then one that is stressed on the second syllable, finally one that is stressed on the third syllable, thus:
  <u>bee</u>keeper   bi<u>no</u>culars   appa<u>ra</u>tus
- Now play Track 23 and let students check their answers.
  Answers:
  Words stressed on the first syllable: *beekeeper, bird watcher, flower arranger, hillwalker, magnifying glass, mountain climber, nonchalantly, oxygen tank, potholer, rock climber, scuba diver, skateboarder, skydiver, snowboarder, stamp collector, trainspotter, water-skier, vulnerable.*
  Word stressed on the second syllable: *binoculars.*
  Words stressed on the third syllable: *apparatus, disrespectful.*

 Workbook Activity 15 *can be used at any stage from now on.*

Activity 44

- [P] Organize this according to the instructions in the Student's Book. Allow maximum freedom of expression. Encourage students to re-use some of the vocabulary, idioms and grammar they've learned in this unit, but remember that the focus here should be on fluency rather than accuracy.

Activity 45

- Tell students that they are going to design a questionnaire about either sports or hobbies. Elicit some of the questions they might want to ask (e.g. *How would you describe your interest in pop music? How often do you listen to it?* etc.).
- [P] Students work on preparing the questions. While they are doing this you can go round the class offering help where appropriate.
- Students now interview other members of the class, using their questions.
- Students report back the results of their survey to the rest of the class. Alternatively they can write up their results as a small report and hand it in to you for marking.

 **Workbook Activities 16–19** *can be used at any stage from now on.*

UNIT 5 Getting angry

Reading: what's anger all about?

In this section, students give their own views about anger and read a web page about the topic.

Activity 1

- This is a pre-reading warm-up. Get the whole class involved in the discussion of these four questions. The key questions are the last two and these form the basis for the web page article that follows.
- Students skim-read the article and find out if their opinions match those of the writer. They don't have to: this activity is basically to get students to think about the topic they're going to read about. In fact, if their views differ from those of the writer, so much the better: there will be more opportunities for genuine debate and discussion.

Activity 2

- Make sure students can locate the key phrase supporting statement *a*, "secondary to some other emotion," in the first paragraph of the article.
- [P] Students then work in pairs to find the other phrases that support these statements.
  Answers:
  a secondary to some other emotion
  b a way of displacing fear
  c if the limbic parts of their brains are stimulated
  d inheritance plays a part as does our upbringing
  e anger leads to an increased risk of heart attack
  f suppressing anger is bad
  g using anger consciously is a good thing
  h we should ... take a deep breath

Activity 3

- [SG] Divide students into groups of three. Each student follows his / her link to the Activity Bank. They should make notes on the main points of the articles they read there, as explained on the respective pages.

Activity 4

- [SG] It's best if students take it in turn to present what they've learned from the Activity Bank material to the other students. They should try to distinguish clearly between what was said in the article (fact) and whether or not they agreed with it (opinion).
- Get feedback from groups. Do most groups have the same opinions about what they've read or are there major differences?

Activity 5a

- Summarizing the information in these articles, especially the two articles students haven't read themselves but have only heard about, is not easy and is probably best done with the whole class sharing in the activity. Lead the discussion and make notes on the board as students speak. Don't expect a very precise summary of these arguments: two or three of the main points recalled from each article would be satisfactory.
- Question *5a* relates to Activity Bank 3 and the text on "anger types." Help students to produce their own language rather than the jargon of the article. Thus, *absolutist thinkers* could be described as "domineering, intolerant people," *situationally aggressive people* could be described as "people who get upset over certain things." The second category could be "people who want to succeed at all costs" and the third "people who are always angry but can't solve the problem that makes them angry."

Activity 5b

- This relates to Activity Bank 8 and differences between men and women.
  Possible answer:
  Anger expresses itself differently in men and women. For hormonal reasons, men can show more anger than women. For social reasons, women don't show their anger as readily as men. But modern ways of life mean people don't talk enough to each other. As a result, both men and women are becoming more frustrated and maybe more angry.

Activity 5c

- This relates to Activity Bank 15, which deals with controlling anger.
  Possible answers:
  Lower expectations.
  Understand the other person's point of view.
  Be assertive not aggressive.
  Watch out for things that frustrate you.
  Stop and take a deep breath if you feel yourself getting angry.
  Have calm and happy people around you.
  Imagine being angry, but don't act angrily.

Language in chunks

In this section, students focus on words and phrases associated with feelings of anger.

Activity 6

- [P] Students work in pairs for this activity. Do the first example with the whole class.
  Answers:
  a use your imagination
  b builds up over a long time
  c feel trapped
  d out of control
  e goes over the top
  f cuts you off

g take a deep breath
h on the surface
i shades of gray

Activity 7

- Brainstorm with the class suitable topics for arguing. They could be something trivial (missing an appointment, arguing about travel directions, the whereabouts of a key) or something serious (animal rights, global warming, banning smoking everywhere).
- Once you've decided on a topic, ask two students to act out a short argument about it. Imagine a couple in a car, the man driving and the woman navigating. You can supply the text if necessary, e.g.:
  A: We're going the wrong way! I said "Turn right."
  B: No, you didn't!
  A: Yes, I did.
  B: Well, I didn't hear you.
  A: How can you be so silly.
  B: Don't you call me silly!
- [I] Now students should write out the next stage, in which Students A and B discuss the argument they've just acted out. They should use phrases from the list in Activity 6.
  Possible answers:
  A: I went a bit over the top, didn't I?
  B: Yeah, you were really out of control.
  A: I should have taken a deep breath.
  B: You're right. But you know what? This was probably an argument about something else.
  A: What do you mean?
  B: Well, it was probably building up for a long time.

Activity 8

- [P] Students work in pairs to complete this table. They should rely partly on what they have read, but also on their own experiences. Encourage students to express their own views: there are no "right" answers here.
- [P] When pairs have completed their table, they should show it to other pairs and compare them.

▶ **Workbook Activities 1–3** *can be used at any stage from now on.*

Grammar: the third conditional

In this section, students learn to distinguish hypothetical conditions from real ones.

Activity 9

- Students match the sentences with the descriptions. Then they check their answers in **5A–5D in the Mini-grammar.**
  Answers:
  a 3
  b 2
  c 1

Activity 10

- Brainstorm the answers to these questions with the whole class. The first questions what students usually do (real), the second what they're going to do (possible), the third what they would do (hypothetical).
- [I/P] Each student writes similar questions and asks their partner to answer it. Each question should begin in the same way as the examples, i.e.:
  What do you do if ... ?
  What will you do ... ?
  What would you do if ... ?
- It might be helpful to write these beginnings on the board and ask students for various completions, e.g.:
  ... you've just missed a bus / train?
  ... the next time there's no bread in the house and the shops are closed?
  ... someone ran into your car?

Activity 11a

- Write a list of nouns from the story and ask students to sort them into *who ... ?* and *what ... ?* nouns, e.g.:
  Jesse, Jesse's uncle, surgeon
  helicopter, arm, hospital
- [P] Now let students ask and answer *who ... ?* and *what ... ?* questions for these nouns.

Activity 11b

- Students will need help to understand hypothetical conditions. First, ask students to read out the two *if* sentences from the text:
  If they hadn't recovered the arm in time, we wouldn't have been able to do the operation at all.
  This would never have happened if he had been in a designated swimming area.
- Ask students about the first sentence:
  T: Did they recover the arm in time?
  S: Yes, they did.
  T: So is Dr. Rogers talking about something that really happened or something that might have happened?
  S: Something that might have happened.
- Do the same for the other conditional sentence.
- Now ask students to analyze these conditional clauses. Write the first clause on the board and ask students to identify the various bits:
  If they hadn't recovered the arm in time, we wouldn't have been able to do the operation at all.
  if + past perfect
  would (not) + *have* + past participle
- [I/P] Now students write out an explanation of the grammar of the sentences, then check their answers with the information in **5E in the Mini-grammar.**

Activity 11c

- [P] Students work in pairs to produce more sentences like those in the examples. Give pairs a time limit and see who can produce the most sentences in the time.

Activity 12

- [P/SG] Students work in pairs. Choose a pair and ask them to act out the model conversation given here. They can also work in small groups with each student taking a turn at asking and answering questions.

Activity 13

- [I] Work out the first possible answer with the students. Write *If Jane hadn't passed her school exams* on the board and elicit completions from students. Students then work on their own.
  Possible answers:
  If Jane hadn't passed her school exams, she wouldn't have gone to college / she might still be living in the U.S.A.
  If she hadn't gone to college, she wouldn't have been introduced to Dave.
  If she hadn't met Dave, she might not be married now.
  If Dave hadn't broken up with his girlfriend, he might not have been pleased to meet someone new.
  If Jane hadn't been accepted on a course, they wouldn't have moved to Canada.
  If they hadn't moved to Canada, Dave would have been a lawyer.
  If Jane hadn't been accepted on a postgraduate course in Montreal, they / their children wouldn't have become Canadian citizens.
  They wouldn't have stayed in Canada, if Dave hadn't just got the main announcer's job on Channel 5.
  If Jane hadn't gone to college, she might have stayed single.
  If Dave hadn't gone to college, he would probably have stayed in the U.S.A.
  If Dave hadn't broken up with his girlfriend, he wouldn't have become a TV and radio personality.

▶ **Workbook Activities 4 & 5** *can be used at any stage from now on.*

Vocabulary: being angry

In this section, students look at the words we use when we talk about different kinds of anger.

Activity 14

Answers:
a Chris—I'm really fed up
b Denise—take it easy
c Karl—she drives me absolutely crazy
d Suzanne—caught off balance
e Olivia—sulky these days
  Emma—in a bad mood recently
f Peter—I lost it

Activity 15

- Ask students to find one synonym in the list for each of these words. Brainstorm this with the class.
  Possible answers:
  a angry—annoyed
  b fed up with—sick and tired of

c to drive somebody crazy—to get on somebody's nerves
d to get very angry—to lose it
e to relax—to calm down
f sulky—grouchy

- Then ask students to find at least one other word or expression for each of these words.
  Answers:
  a bad-tempered, cross, furious
  b sick and tired of (only)
  c to make somebody cross / angry
  d to lose your cool, to lose your temper
  e to keep your cool, to keep your head
  f grumpy, irritable, moody

Activity 16

- Get students to ask you the questions they have devised. Answer these questions about yourself. (Remember the rules!) Here are some examples:
  The last time I lost my cool was when I was kept holding on the phone for ten minutes.
  The last time somebody really got on my nerves was when I was listening to a politician on the radio.
- [SG] Then students ask each other these questions.

Activity 17

Answers:

	about	at	by	of	with
angry	✔	✔			✔
annoyed			✗		✗
cross	✗	✗			✗
fed up	✗				✗
furious	✗				✗
in a bad mood	✗				✗
mad	✗	✗			✗
sick and tired				✗	
to lose (your) temper	✗				✗

Activity 18

Answers:
a with; with
b with
c about
d about / at
e of
f with
g by
h with / at
i with
j with

Word Choice: *argument, fight, quarrel,* and *row*

Students learn to distinguish between these words.

Activity 19

- Students look at these notes. Explain anything they don't understand.

Activity 20

Answers:

a row
b arguments
c quarrel
d row
e argument
f fights
g quarrels
(other answers are possible)
Row, *fight*, and *quarrel* can all be verbs. From *argument* we get the verb *argue*.

Activity 21

• [P] Students work in pairs for this.
• One way of getting students to say what time of day they like is to draw four clocks on the board, indicating 12 o'clock, 3 o'clock, 6 o'clock, 9 o'clock. Then point to the clocks in turn and invite students to stand at the time they like best. Students at, say, 3 o'clock ask each other why they like that time of day. Then ask for feedback from the various groups.

 Workbook Activities 6 & 7 *can be used at any stage from now on.*

Speaking: investigation role-play

Here, students take part in a role-play of a police interview with a young person charged with a crime.

Activity 22

• [SG] This is the start of a major speaking activity. You will need to allocate a good deal of time to this and it may be best to spread it over more than one class lesson.
• Once all students have read the introduction in the green box at the top of page 55, divide the class into groups of five. Groups decide who is going to take which role. Each role-player consults the relevant Activity Bank section to find out about his / her role. Allow sufficient time for students to do this and answer any questions they may have about their role.
• It might be helpful before starting the role-play to go over each role and identify what are the key problems of anger each player faces, e.g.:
—suspect: getting angry with your lawyer
—police officer 1: getting angry with your partner
—police officer 2: getting angry with parents
—lawyer: getting angry with the suspect for antagonizing the police officers
—parent: getting angry with the police for blaming your child

Activity 23

• Let all groups rehearse the role-play, then choose one and ask them to play it out. Don't let it go on for too long. Three or four minutes should be enough. Ask the rest of the class to listen carefully then ask them for feedback. This should centre on where students carried out or failed to carry out their roles properly, e.g. police officer 2 didn't try to calm police officer 1 down or he / she did it inappropriately.

• Then get other groups to act out their role-plays. Involve the rest of the class in a similar kind of critique. At the end, sum up the role-play yourself and give each group notes on their performance.

Listening: keeping calm

Here students consider ways of preventing anger. They listen to an interview in which one participant tries to make the other angry.

Activity 24

• Brainstorm this with the whole class. If the students can't think of anything, tell them what you do to stop yourself losing your temper—taking a deep breath, counting to ten, imagining a peaceful scene, etc.
• Now play Track 24. Ask students to listen only for the information required here, i.e. do any of Dr. Khan's ideas match theirs?

Activity 25

• Students listen to Track 24 more carefully and complete the table. You may need to play the track more than once to enable students to get the information they need.
• When completed, the table should look like this:

Type of technique	Examples / What it means
a Relaxation	breathe deeply repeat relaxing phrase visualize a relaxing experience
b Cognitive restructuring	change the way you think understand why you're angry
c Silly humor	picture the person who's making you angry as funny

Activity 26

Answers:

Dr. Khan gets angry because Jay Reno makes fun of what he is saying.
He controls himself first by visualizing a relaxing experience (reading the paper in an easy chair), then by picturing Jay Reno as something funny and stupid.

Activity 27

• Go over the first example with the class. Then students listen to Track 24 again, complete the sentences and identify the speakers.
Answers
a point of (R)
b suppose it is (K)
c get rid of (K)
d of course not (K)
e say it to yourself (K)
f of good (J)
g Dead (J)
h getting angry (K)
i joking; joking (J)
j just nonsense (J)
k be telling (K)

Activity 28

Answers:

You can visualize a relaxing experience.
You can breathe deeply.
You can repeat a relaxing word or phrase.
You can picture something funny.
You can change the way you think.

 **Workbook Activities 8–10** *can be used at any stage from now on.*

Functional language: wishes and regrets

Activity 29

- [P] Students look at the pictures and identify what is happening in each picture.
  Possible answers:
  a The man is driving too fast.
  b The tramp is too poor to afford a big TV.
  c The bus is late and the man hasn't got an umbrella.
  d The swimming pool is empty.
- Now students discuss what these people might be thinking, probably wishing that things were different.
  Possible answers:
  a I wish he wouldn't drive so fast.
  b I wish I had a TV like that.
  c I wish ... the bus would come / it would stop raining / I had brought my umbrella.
  d I wish there was water in the pool.
- Then students listen to Track 25 and see if they were right.
  Answers:
  a I wish he wouldn't drive so fast.
  b I wish I was rich.
  c If only I'd brought my umbrella with me.
  d I wish they hadn't emptied the swimming pool.

Activity 30

Answers:
a I wish he would / wouldn't ...
b I wish I was / wasn't ...
c If only I'd / I hadn't ...
d I wish they had / hadn't ...

Activity 31

Possible answers:
a I wish I'd never met you!
b If only I could afford a new car.
c I wish I could understand the Welsh language.
d I wish I could like classical music like my friend does.
e I wish I hadn't left my address book at home.
f I wish I wasn't in the doghouse.
g If only I hadn't gone to their party.
h I wish my parents wouldn't keep asking me when I'm going to get a proper job.
i I wish people wouldn't swim in unguarded areas.
j If only people would stop criticizing wolves.
k I wish she wouldn't keep letting the cat out of the bag.
l I wish she hadn't told me what she thought of me.
m If only the government would do something about environmental pollution.

Activity 32

- [SG] Each student in the group picks a picture and writes a sentence about what the person or animal in his / her picture wishes he / she / it had done differently.
  Possible answers:
  a I wish I hadn't hit that policeman. / I wish I was at home.
  b I wish I were on that ship. / If only somebody could see me.
  c I wish I hadn't kicked the goalkeeper.
  d I wish I'd put on some sun cream. / If only I hadn't fallen asleep in the sun.
  e I wish I hadn't bitten that boy.

Pronunciation: /ʃ/ and /tʃ/

Activity 33

- Play Track 26. Students listen and decide which of the two words in each pair they hear.
  Answers:
  a cash
  b fuchsia
  c matching
  d share
  e cheap
  f chin
  g choose
  h watching
  i which

Activity 34

Answers:
a /ʃ/
b /tʃ/
c /ʃ/
d /tʃ/
e /tʃ/
f /ʃ/
g /ʃ/
h /ʃ/

- Students can use their dictionaries to help in their search for similar words.
  Sample answers:
  a chassis, cache
  b cheese, Manchester
  c ship, mashed
  d architecture, rupture
  e witch, pitcher
  f assure, sugar
  g beautician, atrocious
  h reaction, diction

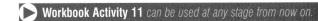 **Workbook Activity 11** *can be used at any stage from now on.*

Writing: designing leaflets

Students look at an example of an advertising leaflet and plan and design their own.

Activity 35a

- [P] Students try to summarize what *Aroma* offers in their own words. Try to get students to conduct a realistic conversation on this topic, e.g.:
  S1: Aroma is an organization that offers courses.
  S2: Language courses?
  S1: No. For instance, they teach Feng Shui, which is about placing furniture in your house.

Activity 35b

- [SG] You can brainstorm this with the class or set groups to give their opinions on these questions. There is no need to expect agreement on these topics: the more disagreement the better. But do ask students to defend their opinions and give reasons for them.

Activity 36

- [SG] Again, students are asked to give their opinions. There are no correct answers. Groups should discuss these questions. Ask groups to feedback their discussion to the class as a whole.

Activity 37

- [SG] Students continue to work in groups to do this activity. First, they must choose the institution they want to advertise. For instance, if they choose a gym, they complete the table with the information a leaflet advertising the gym should give. Their final table might look like this:

Questions / Topics to be decided	Notes / Decisions
What kind of place?	Gym
Name	Fit for life
Services	Gym - personal trainers available Pool Sauna Café
Names of staff	Ben, Tracey, Michelle, Matt, Judy
Address / Phone Number / Website	314 West 58ᵗʰ Street, New York, NY 10016 Tel: 212-968-4557 www.fitforlife.com

- Ask students to suggest what other information should appear in the leaflet. Here are some suggestions:
  —a cover picture: showing what? (people working out in gym? sex? ethnicity?)
  —qualifications / experience of instructors
  —cost per month / year (+ special introductory offers)
  —classes offered (over-50s, yoga, pilates, aerobics)

Activity 38

- [SG] Students need to spend some time on this activity, especially if they are working in groups. They need to make sure that their leaflet text follows what they've decided to include in the plan they drew up in Activity 37. Set a time limit for a first draft of the leaflet. Go round the groups and help where necessary.
- You may find it best to start this activity in the class, then allow students time to complete it out of class.

Activity 39

- [SG] Groups should choose their best draughtsman for this. Don't expect works of genius here: what you want is a clear statement of what the leaflet should look like, e.g. A4, but students can use other formats.

 Workbook Activity 12 *can be used at any stage from now on.*

Review: grammar

Students review the key language introduced in this unit.

Activity 40

- The story of Zenta is told in these pictures. First, ask students to put them in the right order, so that the story makes sense.
  Answers:
  6, 4, 2, 1, 3, 5, 7
- Then students answer these questions by referring to the relevant picture.
  Answers:
  a She went back to sleep.
  b She was stuck in a traffic jam.
  c Her boss got very angry.
  d He fired her.
  e She went to see a lawyer.
  f She fell in love with him.
  g They got married and had a big family.

Activity 41

- Go over the example with the whole class. Then ask students for a similar sentence to talk about the next picture. Sometimes one sentence can lead directly to another, e.g.:
  If she hadn't got stuck in a traffic jam, she wouldn't have been late.
  If she hadn't been late, her boss wouldn't have been angry.
- [P] Students produce similar sentences to go with the remaining pictures.

Activity 42

- [P] Students work in pairs. See which pair can come up with the most unusual or most amusing completion.
  Possible answers:
  a I could have taken a picture of you with egg on your face.

b I could reach the shelf where the chocolate cookies are.

c ... they gave all the staff a bonus today.

d I would have heard my winning number being called.

e Because they had an interview with my favorite singer.

f I would have been able to get some proper swimming gear.

Review: vocabulary
Students check the vocabulary used in this unit.

Activity 43

- Draw this line on the board. Choose a few words from the Word List and ask students where they should be placed on it. Write these words (or get students to write them) on the right place on the line, e.g.:

not angry---very angry
  moody   bad-tempered   cross   annoyed   furious

- [P] Now students work in pairs to place the remaining adjectives on the line.

Possible answers:

not angry-------------------------------------- very angry
moody   bad-tempered   cross   annoyed   furious
sulky   grouchy
             grumpy
             irritable

Activity 44

Answers:

a grumpy

b irritable

c sulky

d moody

e cross

f annoyed

g sulky

h furious

Pronunciation
Students identify the stressed syllables in polysyllabic words and say them aloud.

Activity 45

- Ask students to make up four sentences (including the example started in the book) using phrases from Word Plus. Write them on the board. Ask where the stressed syllables are and mark them, e.g.:
On the 'surface, things seemed O'K, but we were 'rather an'noyed.
She's 'really in a 'bad mood to'day.
I'm 'sick and 'tired of your com'plaints.
You're 'really getting on my 'nerves.

- [P] Get each student to write three more sentences and mark the stressed syllables in the same way. Students then show these to their partners who try to read them following the stresses their partner has written.

 Workbook Activity 13 *can be used at any stage from now on.*

Activity 46

- Go over the example with the class. Ask students to choose another phrase from Word Plus and together with them develop a story about how you found yourself using it, e.g. *My boss was in a really bad mood last week. In fact, she really lost her cool. She was almost out of control.*

- [P] Now pairs work together to develop another story along these lines, using as many as possible of the phrases from Word Plus.

 Workbook Activities 14–17 *can be used at any stage from now on.*

UNIT 6 Looking forward

Vocabulary: seeing and believing (multiple meanings in words and phrases)

This section introduces students to the idea of words having more than one meaning.

Activity 1

- Look at the first group of sentences, *a1–a4*, with the class. Does *see* mean the same in the first two sentences? There is the "ordinary" *see* (= perceive through the eyes) of sentence *1*; *see* in sentence *2* means something more *like perceive through the mind, understand*.
  Ask students to look at the remaining two sentences in this group. Does *see* mean the same in each sentence? In sentence *3*, *see* means *find out, observe*, but not necessarily through the eyes (it could be through the ears). In sentence *4*, the meaning is literal, and *see* could be replaced with *watch*.
- [P] Students work in pairs to find what *see* means in the sentences in groups *b* and *c*. They should suggest synonyms for *see* in each sentence.
  Possible answers:
  b1 understand
  b2 perceive
  b3 imagine
  b4 experienced
  c1 meeting
  c2 met
  c3 examining
  c4 (*seeing a lot of each other* =) in each other's company a lot
- Students do the same for *believe* in group *d*.
  Possible answers:
  d1 trust
  d2 think
  d3 accept
  d4 have faith (= some people think reincarnation really happens)

Activity 2

Answers:
a a1
b a3
c c4

Activity 3a

- [P] Students use the synonyms they found in Activity 1 for this.

Activity 3b

- If students have trouble coming up with ideas, you could suggest *head, foot, course, bear, mean*, etc. If you are teaching a monolingual class, you could also ask students to think of words in their own language which have more than one meaning.

Activity 4

Draw the line on the board and ask students to place the first two sentences on the line. Then get pairs to place the remaining sentences correctly on the line.
Possible answers:
disbelief

> I don't believe you.
> I think that's ludicrous.
> That's totally out of the question.
> I'm rather cynical about your claims.
> I'm going to take that with a pinch of salt.
> I'm fairly skeptical about all this.
> I doubt what you are saying.
> I'm not so sure about this.
> I'll give you the benefit of the doubt.
> I'll take it at face value.
> I'll take your word for it.
> I'll take it on trust.
> I accept what you say.

belief

Phrase with *give*: d
Phrases with *take*: e, g, h, j

Activity 5

- [SG] Ask students to look at these sentences quickly. Take a head count of who believes each statement.
- Brainstorm further suggestions. If necessary, suggest a couple yourself, e.g.:
  —*By 2200 there will be no more schools. People will learn all they need from the Internet.*
  —_____ *(name of country) will win the World Cup in the next ten years.*
- Ask students to write down two similar predictions.

Activity 6

- [P] Now students make their predictions to their partners who respond with expressions of belief or disbelief, e.g.:
  A: If global warming continues, _____ (name of country) will be under water by 2020.
  B: I think that's ludicrous. I don't believe that global warming will affect us.

Activity 7

Answers:
a	believe	i	Seen
b	believe	j	saw
c	see	k	see
d	see	l	believe
e	seen	m	see
f	see	n	believe
g	believe; believe	o	see
h	see		

Speaking and writing: spoken vs written phrases

This section continues the examination of speaking and writing styles begun in Unit 4.

Activity 8a

- Go through the sentences from Activities 4 and 7 with the class. Ask them to pick out the informal, colloquial uses.
  Answers:
  Activity 4: g, h
  Activity 7: a, b, c, f, g, h, k, l, m, o
- Then they find the more formal uses.
  Answers:
  Activity 4: b, d, e, j
  Activity 7: d, e, i, j, n

Activity 8b / 8c

- [P] Ask students to read the two questions. Let them compare answers with their partners.
- Discuss the answers with the students.
  Answers:
  b You are more likely to hear informal English in conversation than in print.
  c The more formal phrases sound more like written English than the informal colloquial ones.

Activity 9

- [P] Students work in pairs to produce a short conversation. Ask pairs to act out their conversations for the rest of the class.

▶ **Workbook Activities 1 & 2** *can be used at any stage from now on.*

Listening: the paranormal

Students give their views on the paranormal then listen to a conversation between a believer in the paranormal and a skeptic.

Activity 10

- [P] First let students discuss the meaning of the words in the box in pairs, using a dictionary if these are available. Then check with the whole class that they know the meaning of these words and explain those that they don't know (*ESP* = extrasensory perception; *UFOs* = unidentified flying objects). Which of these terms are linked to talking about the future? See what the class thinks. The obvious answers are: astrology, fortune-telling, palmistry, tarot. See whether students can come up with any others.

Activity 11

- [P] Pairs share their opinions. Get feedback from pairs. Then let pairs compare their responses to those of other students. You could take a count of the most popular of these beliefs.

Activity 12

- Students listen to Track 28 and decide on the answer. One listening should be enough for this, as students aren't listening for detail here, but only for the gist. **Answer:** The woman is the believer (she reads her horoscope all the time and believes there are some phenomena that can't be explained), the man is the skeptic.

Activity 13

- Now students listen to Track 28 again, this time more carefully. More than one listening may be necessary.
  Answers:
  a 6   b 3   c 5   d 2   e 7   f 1   g 4
- [SG] Students can debate this in groups. Which point of view is the most popular? Or are there students who think there is something to be said for both sides?

Activity 14
Answers:
a pizza
b restaurant
c paranormal
d saying
e began / started
f incident
g could
h knowing
i rational
j believe
k cynical
l fun
m answer

Activity 15
Answers:
a It's all made up.
b It's all made up.
c It's all junk.
d There's an explanation.
e They're not lying, but they're susceptible to suggestion.
f If the suggestion is repeated often enough, people start to believe it.

Activity 16

- See if students can complete these sentences without listening to Track 28 again.
  Answers:
  a don't believe in
  b complete nonsense
  c How am I
  d out there
  e that one out
  f would you
  g where's the fun
  h depends

Activity 17

- [SG] Ask students to think about the pretend horoscope. What was the man trying to show? (That anyone could make up a horoscope that other people would believe.) Tell students to think about their partners. How much do they know about them—their likes and dislikes, their hopes and fears, their family, their travel plans? This should help them to write their pretend horoscope.
- When students have completed their horoscopes, choose two or three and ask them to read what they've written to the rest of the class. Ask the class to guess who the horoscope was written for.

 Workbook Activities 3–5 *can be used at any stage from now on.*

Functional language: speculating

Here students learn the language we use when we're speculating about the future.

Activity 18

- Play Track 29 once only. Ask students what the two people are talking about. What are the two teams called?
- Then play it again, perhaps more than once, and let students fill the gaps in these sentences.
  Answers:
  a do you think about
  b hard to tell
  c That's true
  d the chances
  e far as I can
  f what you mean
  g ideas on
  h You're right
  i never know
  j do you think
  k haven't a clue
  l you ask me
  m not convinced

Activity 19

Answers:
Asking for speculation
  What do you think about ... ?
  What are the chances ... ?
  Any ideas on ... ?
  What do you think ... ?
Speculating
  It's hard to tell.
  As far as I can see ...
  You never know.
  I haven't a clue.
  If you ask me ...
Accepting / Rejecting speculation
  That's true.
  I see what you mean.
  You're right.
  I'm not convinced.

Activity 20

- [P] Elicit the first two examples from the class. Then let students work in pairs to write these expressions under the correct headings.
Answers:
Asking for speculation
  Do you think ... ?
  What do you reckon?
  Do you suppose ... ?
  Do you have any idea about ... ?
  Is there any chance that ... ?
Speculating
  If you ask me ...
  It's hard to say for sure, but ...
  I reckon ...
  I wouldn't be surprised if ...
Accepting / Rejecting speculation
  Not a chance!
  You may be right there.
  You must be joking!
  Do you really think so?

Activity 21

- [P] Students work in pairs for this. Ask each pair to choose a different question and debate it as in the example. Pairs can then act out their conversations for the whole class.

Activity 22

- [P] Here are some examples of how the expressions studied in Activities 19 and 20 can be used with these topics:
a A: <u>Do you think</u> you'll go to college?
   B: <u>It's hard to say for sure, but</u> I'd like to.
b A: <u>Do you suppose</u> it's going to be a nice day?
   B: <u>Not a chance!</u> Look at those clouds.
c A: <u>I wouldn't be surprised if</u> Amir won today.
   B: <u>Do you really think so?</u> Have you seen the other boxer?
d A: <u>I reckon</u> I'm going to do well in this test.
   B: <u>You may be right there.</u> You've been working hard the last few weeks.
- Go round pairs and see how they're getting on. Try to ensure that students get a good balance between accepting and rejecting speculations.

 Workbook Activity 6 *can be used at any stage from now on.*

Speaking: interview and role-play

Here students take part in a role-play of an interview with a fortune-teller.

Activity 23

- [SG] Students in groups ask each other these questions. The group leader makes a note of the responses. Ask groups to feed back these responses. Is there any unanimity within the groups? Are there any students who think that fortune-telling is a lot of nonsense? As always, ask students to justify their opinions by citing evidence.

Activity 24

- Before students begin working in groups, brainstorm some questions with the whole class. Write a couple of these questions on the board, e.g.:
  Will I get married?
  Will I make a lot of money?
  Will I pass my exams?
  Of course, the kind of questions students want answers to will depend greatly on the age, marital status and general interests of your students.
- [SG] Groups continue with this and agree on six questions about the future they want answers to. They should also guess the kind of responses a real fortune-teller will make. Remember that since the future is unknowable, these predictions are likely to be very general, e.g.:
  You will go on a journey.
  Someone you know has an important message for you.
  You will argue with an old friend.
  I see a big change in your life in the next six months.

Activity 25

- [SG] Divide the class as indicated: there should be more customers than fortune-tellers. This probably works best with the students remaining in groups, one of whom is the fortune-teller. This should be a fun activity. Don't forget to join in yourself. Who the best fortune-teller is will depend on which one satisfies his / her customers best. After a while, students swap roles.
- Ask groups which of their members proved the most successful fortune-teller.

Reading: what kind of future?

Here, students read some predictions about the future after making some predictions of their own.

Activity 26

- [P/SG] This is a warm-up exercise, a preparation for the text students are about to read. Predictions about medicine usually relate to cures, e.g. for AIDS. Predictions about the universe are obviously much more wide-ranging, from increased pollution on earth to the possibility of encounters with life-forms outside our solar system. Students work in pairs or small groups and draw up their own predictions. Ask a few groups what they predicted. Then ask the class to speed-read the article to find out if any of their predictions are included.

Activity 27

- Now students read the text more carefully. They have to find a suitable title for each paragraph. This is an important comprehension skill in that it demands that students understand the main point of each paragraph and are able to trace the development of the discussion.

Answers:
a 7
b 4
c 6
d 1
e 3
f 5
g 8
h 2

Activity 28

Answers:
a because he said that we had reached the limits of what we could do with technology (wrong), but also that his statement would sound silly in five years' time (right)
b mapping the human genome; extraction of stem cells
c The doctor operated by remote control.
d because it's too cold and dry
e by warming it up and planting trees to make oxygen
f within the next 80 years

Activity 29

Answers:
a looks forward to
b most important / top
c making a plan of
d rebuilding
e unrealistic
f dead, lifeless
g avoiding / getting around

Language in chunks

Students use some of the phrases and idioms found in the reading text.

Activity 30

Answers:
a a long way off
b warm up
c by that time
d dismiss ... as
e scoot around
f tend to
g spewing out

Activity 31

- First, students distinguish between the different forms of the *will* future used here.
  Answers:
  a *will* + *be* + *-ing* form of the verb = future continuous
  b *will* + *be* + *-ing* form of the verb = future continuous
  c *will* + infinitive of the verb = future simple
  d *will* + *be* + *-ing* form of the verb = future continuous
  e *will* + *have* + past participle of the verb = future perfect

- At this stage, students just focus on the difference in meaning between the sentences.
  Answers:
  Sentences *a*, *b* and *d* describe something which will be in progress or commonplace in the future.
  Sentence *c* describes something which will definitely happen at some point in the future.
  Sentence *e* describes something <u>completed</u> by a certain time in the future.

Activity 32
- [SG] Groups discuss these predictions. Group leaders give feedback on what their group has decided. Which predictions are thought to be most likely? Which least likely?

Activity 33
- [SG] Students continue in groups to discuss these questions. Again, review what groups think. Which is the most popular wish? Get students to say why they would like to do these things.

 Workbook Activities 9–12 *can be used at any stage from now on.*

Grammar: future perfect and future continuous

Having been introduced to these tenses, students now study them in more detail.

Activity 34
- Read the instructions for this activity carefully with students. Make sure students understand the four different functions described here.
- Go over the example. Do students agree? Then let students decide which of these four functions the remaining sentences demonstrate.
  Answers:
  a 3
  b 3
  c 1
  d 2
  e 3
  f 3
  g 4
  h 2
- When they have completed this exercise, students look at **6A–6D in the Mini-grammar** and change any answers they think are wrong. Point out that sentence *b* is an example of function 2, 'plans for the future which are fixed and decided', used in the context of politely asking whether something has been decided.

Activity 35
- [P] In some responses to these questions, both tenses can be used, but the likeliest responses are as follows.
  Answers:
  a He'll be playing tennis. / He'll have finished work.
  b I'll have been studying English for two years in September.

c I'll be visiting my grandparents.
d I'm sure they'll be enjoying themselves.
e I think things will be getting better—so I guess I'm an optimist.
f I hope I'll be living in another country. / I hope I'll have finished my degree.

Activity 36
- [P] Here students can discuss the differences between these sentences in pairs. These differences are often rather subtle and difficult to explain. Go over the first example (*a1* and *a2*) with the class.
  T: When would you ask someone "Will you stay the night at our place?"?
  S1: I don't know.
  T: When you say that, do you want the person to stay?
  S2: Yes, I do.
  T: So what are you doing when you say this?
  S2: I'm inviting him to stay.
  T: That's right. Now what about when you ask "Will you be staying the night at our place?"? Are you inviting your friend?
  S3: No.
  T: So what do you want to know?
  S3: I want to know *if* he is staying the night.
  T: That's right.
- Ask students to suggest the context for this conversation. For example, the second conversation could be at a party at your house, where it's very late and you'd like to know if your guest is staying or not. There are no right answers to these questions: the important thing is for students to use their imagination and for the rest of the class to decide if the answers are plausible or not.
  Possible answers:
  b Husband to wife; perhaps the letter is a letter of complaint – to a school, a local council, a company, a shop.
     1 is asking about the intention of the person to finish.
     2 is asking about the completion of the letter— asking for perhaps the time it will be finished by.
  c Employer to employee in a job interview; perhaps the employee is going to get a pay raise?
     1 and 2 are very similar in meaning.
  d A couple planning on visiting friends: they don't want to disturb the baby's routine.
     1 is stating what will be happening at a certain time in the future.
     2 is saying what the person thinks is happening at the time of speaking.
  e A scientist reporting to a university department head or the head of a company that is sponsoring the research.
     1 emphasizes when the research will be completed.
     2 states what will be happening in October if all goes according to plan.

Activity 37

- Do the first sentence with the class. Ask students to suggest the appropriate tense for this exchange.
  Answers:
  1 'll be arriving
  2 'll be
  3 I'll have gone
  4 'll leave
  5 will've been coming
  6 'll be eating
  7 Will ... be staying
  8 'll go
  9 'll be working
  10 won't have had
  11 won't have put

 Workbook Activities 13 & 14 *can be used at any stage from now on.*

Pronunciation: strong and weak forms in contracted sentences

Students learn the different usage of strong and weak forms of auxiliary verbs like *have*.

Activity 38

- Students listen to Track 30. On first listening they note the stressed words and mark them in these sentences accordingly.
  Answers:
  a working
  b married
  c finished
  d arrived
  e living
  f put
- Play Track 30 again. This time students listen to see how *have* is pronounced.
- [P] Students talk briefly about what they have heard.
- Play Track 30 again, stopping each time to make sure they have heard the speakers correctly.
  Answers: *Have* is pronounced /əv/ in all the sentences except *e*, where it is pronounced /həv/.

 Workbook Activities 7 & 8 *can be used at any stage from now on.*

Activity 39

- [P] Choose a pair and get them to act out the example conversation, adding further questions and answers of their own using future tenses, e.g.:
  A: What will you be doing at this time next year?
  B: I'll have finished college and I'll be working.
  A: Where will you be working?
  B: I'll be working in a lawyer's office.
  A: Will you still be going to English classes?
  B: ...
  [P] Go over the rest of these questions with the class. Ask students to imagine the occasion and the relationship between the speakers.

Possible answers:
a two friends, or a parent to a son / daughter
b a job interview, with an employer talking to a job applicant
c two friends talking in a café
d a teacher talking to a student
e a parent talking to a son / daughter about their work / study.
f a parent or a school tutor to a teenager

Writing: planning compositions

Here students make notes and plan a short text describing a day in their lives in a future world.

Activity 40

- Students start this writing activity by looking at a student's notes on life in 2050.
- Take the first set of notes (*Home*) and work these up into sentences with the class. Decide whether you're going to write in the first person (*I will be living on Mars*) or in the third person (*People will be living on Mars*). What are the advantages and disadvantages of each approach? (*I* is more personal and so perhaps more interesting; *they* is more objective and so perhaps more convincing.) Suppose students decide on a first-person approach, how will they convert these notes into full sentences?
  T: Read the first note. What does it say?
  S1: "Living on Mars."
  T: Okay, so how do we make this into a sentence? What do we need to add?
  S2: "I."
  T: Yes, "I." What else? Remember we're talking about the future.
  S3: "I'll be living on Mars."
  T: Good. "I'll be living on Mars.: That's the first sentence.
- [I/P] If necessary, do the same for the remaining sentences in the first section (*Home*). Then ask students to write up the rest of the paragraph, and to compare it with a partner's. Students then compare what they have written with the paragraph in Activity Bank 18.

Activity 41

- [I/SG] Students first work individually, then discuss their ideas in groups. A group leader should make notes of their discussion similar to those given in Activity 40, e.g.:
  school—no schools; lessons given by internet; website; self-correcting; teachers out of work
  Groups should agree on these notes and use them as the basis for their work in the next activity.

Activity 42

- [I] After describing the general way of life in 2050, students write a text giving details of their daily routine, using the ideas they noted and discussed in

Activity 41. For the daily routine part of it, a diary form is possible here, e.g.:

0800: Get up. Robbie the Robot has made tea and toast. The toast is burnt—again. I must speak to him.

[SG] Discussion: this would best take place within a small group. Circulate among the groups and at the end of the discussion, choose two or three texts that students can read out. The rest of the class decide how plausible these predictions are. You could add your own predictions and ask the class to assess them.

 Workbook Activities 15 & 16 *can be used at any stage from now on.*

Review: grammar and functional language

Students review the key language introduced in this unit.

Activity 43

Answers:
1 e
2 b
3 d
4 g
5 a
6 c
7 f
8 h

Activity 44

Answers:
a will be created
b will exceed; will be able
c will have; will use
d will feed / will be fed; will have read
e will become; will believe
f will be eating; will be
g will have joined

Activity 45

- [P] Before letting pairs practice, demonstrate a conversation about one of the predictions from Activity 44 with students. You can cue their responses to illustrate the different types of speculation, acceptance and rejection which are possible, e.g.:
  T: 'The majority of text will be created by speech recognition.' What do you think? (*Agree.*)
  S1: I wouldn't be surprised if that were true.
  T: (*Disagree.*)
  S2: I'm not convinced.
  T: (*Strongly disagree.*)
  S3: Not a chance! You must be joking!
- Let the class decide which of these predictions are most plausible. Which do they think is the most unlikely? Take a vote.

Review: vocabulary

Students check the vocabulary used in this unit.

Activity 46

- Get pairs to choose their most useful phrases. They should make their own choice but there's no harm in you choosing your top five and allowing students to compare your list with theirs.

Pronunciation

- Here students focus on word and sentence stress.

Activity 47

- Students check their answers against Track 31.
  Answers:
  a ex'tinct
  b 'fanciful
  c 'ludicrous
  d 'skeptical
  e recon'structive
  f 'shortcutting

Activity 48

- Students listen to Track 32 and decide where the stress is in these phrases. Do the first example with the class then let students do the remaining examples on their own or in pairs.
  Answers:
  a 'pinch of 'salt
  b 'face 'value
  c 'benefit of the 'doubt
  d 'eye to 'eye
  e 'take it on 'trust

Activity 49

- Follow the same approach here.
  Answers:
  a 'totally   'out   'question
  b 'scarcely   be'lieve   'eyes
  c 'don't   'see   'not
  d 'see   'do
  e 'Let's   'see   'goes
  f 'later

Activity 50

- Encourage students to look back over the whole unit, including the conversation about the paranormal (Track 28) and evaluate the various speculations that have been made. The important thing here is for students to express their own views, whether skeptical or believing. Try not to impose your own opinions.

 **Workbook Activities 17–20** *can be used at any stage from now on.*

UNIT 7 Out of the blue

Vocabulary: colors

Here students are introduced to words and ideas associated with color.

Activity 1

- [P] Pairs work together through questions *a–d*. After a few minutes, ask students to say what the most striking features of the painting are: its bright colours? its geometric pattern? As before, when students give their opinions of the painting, they should give reasons, e.g.:
  T: Do you like the painting?
  S1: Yes, I do.
  T: Why do you like it?
  S1: It's very colorful. And I like the patterns.
- Get groups to feedback all their responses to questions *a–d*. Compare these opinions: is there a general consensus about the painting or not?

Activity 2

- Colors are indeterminate: they fade into one another. It is often difficult to say if something is green or blue, yellow or orange. So we often use words like *dark*, *light* to modify color words. First ask students to use these modifiers to describe shades of color. It would be helpful here to bring in objects which exemplify these colors, e.g. a dark blue T-shirt, a light brown brush, a pale yellow flower.
- When they have chosen color-word phrases, students should organize these under the headings *strong*, *strong / weak*, *not strong*, in a table which might look like this.
  Suggested answers:

Strong	bright red
	brilliant orange
Strong / Weak	light blue
Not strong	faded gray
	pale green
	dull brown
	muddy yellow

Activity 3

- [SG] Students can use classroom objects and pictures for this. Or you can give them colorful pictures or photographs for them to talk about. Students show their pictures to the rest of the group and describe the color of objects in them. Other students ask questions about the colors in the picture, e.g.:
  S1: What color is that boy's shirt?
  S2: It's bright red.
  S1: What about his shoes?
  S3: They're a kind of faded white.
- Note the use of further modifying phrases like *a kind of* or *a sort of* to describe colors more precisely. You might like to teach these here.

Activity 4

- Students look at the picture and decide which colors describe these people's clothes.
  Answers:
  1 lime-green
  2 scarlet
  3 cream
  4 khaki
  5 mustard
  6 beige
  7 coffee-colored
  8 golden brown

Activity 5

- You could start students off by talking about some of your own things. If you have photos of them, so much the better.
  T: I've got a really nice car. It's bright red. I like red. It's a very cheerful color … My favorite room in my apartment is the kitchen. The walls are pale blue. That's a very calming, restful color.
- [P] Now students ask each other about the color of things listed here. Invite them to follow you by saying what they think about particular colors. This will prepare them for talking about the links between colors and feelings in the next activity.

> **Workbook Activities 1 & 2** *can be used at any stage from now on.*

Activity 6a

- [P] This activity is a preparation for reading a text about color word associations. Let students discuss which words are associated with these emotions or situations. For a contrast, make a note of color associations in your own culture, if it is different from that of your students, e.g.:
  anger—*red*
  cold—*white*
  cowardice—*yellow*
  death—*black*

Activity 6b

- Brainstorm these questions with the whole class. The responses you get will greatly depend on whether your class is monocultural or multicultural.

Activity 6c

- Brainstorm as before.

Activity 7

- In this text, students are introduced to the metaphorical uses of color words. See if students know any such expressions—*blue in the face, red-handed, white as a sheet*—already. Write these on the board.

- Ask students to look at the picture. What is the man on the left doing? Why?
- Now students read the text and fill the gaps.
  Answers:

a red	b black	c white
d green	e red	f red
g red	h yellow	i blue
j black	k blue	l black
m blue	n blue	o green

Activity 8

- There are two separate parts to this activity—completing the phrase and matching it to the correct meaning. Ask students to complete the phrases first and check that these are correct. Then ask students to match these phrases (a–o) to the meanings (1–15).
  Answers:
  a cold 10
  b mood 3
  c he / she is painted 1
  d blue 15
  e yellow 5
  f as ink 2
  g as a sheet 9
  h envy 4
  i red-handed 14
  j green light 11
  k red 6
  l blue in the face 7
  m the town red 8
  n blue murder 12
  o red 13

Activity 9

- [I] Students can prepare this story at home and read it out to the class later. Tell students to focus on something that happened to them that other students might find interesting. An amusing or frightening or exciting incident—something that can be described in a few lines—is what is required.

Reading: color effect

In this section, students read a text about the importance of color in our everyday lives.

Activity 10

- This is a pre-reading warm-up activity. First ask students to look at the title of the text. What's odd about it? Why are we surprised to think of a police station being painted pink? What color do we expect it to be? Why?
- Then ask students to look at the paragraph summaries a–e and ask them to speculate as to what the paragraph might be about. Here are some possibilities:
  a the importance of color in everything we do
  b the colors of rooms can affect the way we feel
  c how color affects the brain
  d what your favorite color says about you
  e when choosing a color, we should take into account our eye color

- As with all such speculative pre-reading activities, it doesn't matter if students get the 'right' answer or if their predictions turn out to be true. The object of this exercise is to get students thinking about what the possible contents of these paragraphs might be and so prepare them better to understand what they're about to read.
- Now students read the text quickly and match the summaries a–e to the paragraphs 1–5.
  Answers:
  1 c 2 d 3 b 4 e 5 a

Activity 11

- [P/SG] Students discuss these questions in pairs or small groups. As with similar texts where new and somewhat controversial ideas are described, students may divide into those who accept what the text says, dismiss it out of hand, or agree with some of the ideas but are skeptical of others. See how many students fit into each of these three groups.
- Students who are interested in discovering more can take the test by visiting www.colorquiz.com

Activity 12

- Here students focus on what the writer is actually saying in this text and decide on which completion is the best in each case.
  Answers:
  a 2 b 2 c 3 d 1 e 2

Activity 13

Answers:
a derive
b elicits
c complement
d nurturing
e conventional
f chilling out
g vibrations
h contract
i adamant
j inadvertently

Language in chunks

Students look at phrases and idioms associated with colors.

Activity 14

Answers:
a affects us
b look for different ways of
c causes a strong reaction
d polite, well-behaved
e is entitled to

Activity 15

Answers:
a Brilliant sunshine has a bad effect on me.
b Interior designers are seeking new ways of combining colors.

c The color red elicits a strong psychological response in bulls.

d When their grandmother comes to tea, the children are always on their best behavior.

e No one has the right to order me about.

Workbook Activities 3–6 *can be used at any stage from now on.*

Speaking: making joint decisions

In this section, students exchange ideas on colors in rooms and justify their opinions.

Activity 16a

- [SG] Students look at the picture of the room, which is empty. Ask them to look at the pictures of the items and decide which six items they will choose to put in the room. Here is the list:
  a table
  4 chairs
  2 armchairs
  a sofa
  a bookcase
  3 pictures or 3 posters
  a television
  a stereo with external speakers
  a coffee table

Activity 16b

- [SG] Having chosen their six items of furniture, students now decide on colors for those items, but also for the rug, drapes, walls and ceiling. They should discuss reasons for their choices and be prepared to explain them to others, saying for instance "I would like the sofa to be pink, because it's a romantic color." Go round the groups and help the discussion where necessary.

Activity 17

- Groups then describe and explain their decisions to the rest of the class.

Listening: the new house

Here, students learn the language we use when talking about jobs to do around the house.

Activity 18

- This listening task is to be done in three distinct steps (Activities 18, 19 and 20). Students first listen to Track 34 to pick out some details of the conversation. Ask students to look at the questions *a–e*. Then play Track 34 once and see how many of these questions students can answer. Only play the track again if students are unable to answer the questions.
  Answers:
  a New York   b London   c turbulent / bad
  d Carol = captain (just moved into a new house) ; Mark = co-pilot (respectful, likes painting rooms)
  e She's not looking forward to it because she's just moved into a new home and there's so much to be done.

Activity 19

- Go over the blank table with students. Make sure they understand what the three categories are. Then students listen to Track 34 again more carefully. When completed, the table should look like this:

What part?	Problem	Who'll fix it?
a downstairs	2 windows need replacing	builders
b roof	needs fixing	builders
c outside	needs painting	painters
d rooms	need painting	Carol and Bob
e house	a new heating system needed	heating engineers

Activity 20

- Now students listen to the next part of this conversation (Track 35). Ask students who the main speakers are on this track (Carol and Bob). What is Bob asking Carol about? (Furnishing and painting their new house.)
  Answers:
  a (light) beige—paint for outside of house; black (sofa); (dark) green—sofa
  b at the house
  c what color to paint the house (she says it isn't a good time)
  d in the furniture warehouse
  e He wants to know if he should buy a black or a (dark) green sofa. Carol tells him to decide for himself.
  f She's not happy about it, probably because she realizes that it's going to be hard work fixing the house up. That's why she suggests going back to New York.

Language in chunks

Here students focus on some of the idiomatic phrases used in the recorded conversation on Tracks 34 and 35.

Activity 21

- Ask students to read the questions. Can they answer them from memory or do they need to listen to the tracks again?
- Students have to identify the speakers and explain the key phrases. Do these activities separately.
  Answers:
  a Carol: She doesn't want to go home, but she has to.
  b Carol: We haven't got enough money for any more.
  c Bob: I want you to say what you want.
  d Carol: If light beige is nice, let's have it; if not, we won't.
  e Carol: The plane is going to go up and down a lot.
  f Mark: I'm glad the bad weather is over.
  g Carol: This is irritating me. What do you want?
  h Carol: I don't know (*strong*). Please stop bothering me.

Workbook Activities 7–12 *can be used at any stage from now on.*

Grammar: *needs doing; have something done*

In this section, students learn how to use the structures *need doing* and *have something done* in the context of repairing and servicing things.

Activity 22

- Students look at the pictures and decide what needs doing in each case. Do the first example with the class, then let students decide about the remaining pictures in the same way.
  Answers:
  a The man's hair needs cutting.
    The man's shirt needs changing / ironing.
    The man's pants need changing / mending / cleaning.
    The man's shoes need cleaning.
  b The tire needs changing
    The door needs respraying.
    The windshield needs replacing.
    The bumper needs repairing.
  c The roof needs fixing.
    The gate needs fixing.
    The grass needs cutting.
    The door needs painting.
- Sections **7A–B in the Mini-grammar** deal with this grammatical form. Students should refer to it after completing this activity and decide if their answers are correct.

Word Choice: *fix, mend, repair* and *service*

Here students study the different uses of these words.

Activity 23

- Students go over these notes. Offer any help or explanation that's needed. You could in particular highlight the constructions *have something done, get something done, something needs doing, something needs to be done,* used with these four verbs.

Activity 24

- First students have to decide which verb is to be used in each sentence (*a–i*). Then they have to choose the appropriate form. Brainstorm the choice of verbs with the whole class. Sometimes more than one verb is possible.
- Then students decide on what grammatical form is appropriate for each sentence.
  Possible answers:
  a servicing
  b fix
  c repair
  d mending
  e serviced
  f fix / repair
  g fix
  h fixed / repaired
  i mending

Activity 25a

- This text illustrates the difference between saying that you're doing things for yourself and saying that you're having other people do things for you.
- Ask students to look at the picture and describe Bruno. What do they think Bruno is going to do first?
  Answers:
  a mend his shirt (himself); hair cut and dyed, car serviced, new production designed (others)

Activity 25b / c / d

- [P] Students work in pairs to answer these questions about this text. They need to look closely at the grammatical forms used.
  Answers:
  b when the person (agent) is an important piece of information in the sentence
  c after the past participle
  d *have* + something + *done* + (adjective) + by somebody
- **Mini-grammar 7C and 7D** deals with this grammatical form. Students should refer to it after completing this activity and decide if their answers are correct.

Activity 26

- Go over the example with the class. Then students decide what the other people in the pictures are going to have done.
  Possible answers:
  a Ruth's going to have her dresses cleaned.
  b Alistair's going to have his portrait painted.
  c John's going to have his hair cut.
  d Carol's going to have her eyes tested.
  e Mike's going to get new tires fitted.

Activity 27

- Go over the relevant section in the **Mini-grammar (7D)** with the class. Answer any questions students may have about it. Then students find the appropriate word (*get / have*) for each sentence. They must of course use the correct tense / form.
  Answers:

a get	b get	c had	d had
e have	f get	g get	h get
i have	j had		

▶ **Workbook Activities 13 & 14** *can be used at any stage from now on.*

Activity 28

- Brainstorm some verbs that might be used for each of these categories, e.g.:
  house—*paint, decorate, sell*
  clothes—*repair, clean, replace*
  hair—*wash, cut, style*
  bicycle—*service, repair, clean*
  car—*wash, service, replace*
- Then let students decide what form these verbs should take in sentences about these things. Start them off:
  T: House.
  S1: I'd like to have my house painted.
  T: Car.
  S2: I'd like to have my car washed.

Activity 29

- Ask students to say what a nightmare is. What kind of day do they think a *nightmare day* is? Now they read about Caroline and her unfortunate experiences. First, they match the two halves of each sentence.
  Answers:
  a 2 b 7 c 5 d 4 e 3 f 1 g 6
- [P] Students can work in pairs to answer the remaining questions.
  Answers:
  - The sentences describe bad experiences that happened to her.
  - The construction is the same, but the meanings are different: they are all events (largely) outside her control.
- [P] Students discuss if these experiences or similar ones have ever happened to them. What kind of nightmare experiences have they had?

Functional language: taking something to be fixed

Students listen to a conversation between a car owner and a car mechanic and study the functional language used.

Activity 30

- Ask students to look at the pictures and describe them briefly, e.g.:
  S1: Picture *a*: A woman is sitting in her car and a man is looking at the engine.
  They should describe the other pictures in the same way.
- Students listen to Track 36. One listening should be enough for them to say which picture is correct.
  Answers:
  Picture c

Activity 31

- Students read the questions *a–c* and listen to Track 36 again to find the answers to them.
  Answers:
  a engine noise (rattle); gear-change click
  b Charlie
  c 4 o'clock

Activity 32

- Play Track 36 again if necessary.
  Answers:
  a in … second
  b a strange noise … engine
  c move … makes … loud
  d leave … with
  e collect it
  f have … checked
  g have … ready
  h that sound
  i back at

Activity 33

- [P] Students work in pairs for this. Sentences *a–r* are remarks that might be made during the course of a discussion between a customer and a service provider, for instance a mechanic or a shop assistant. Do one or two examples with the whole class then let pairs assign each sentence to the relevant table.
  Answers:
  Customer: b, c, d, e, h, i, j, k, l, q, r
  Service provider: a, f, g, m, n, o, p

 Workbook Activities 15 & 16 *can be used at any stage from now on.*

Pronunciation: /s/, /z/, and /tʃ/

Students learn to distinguish between similar consonant sounds.

Activity 34

- Ask students to find an example of each of these sounds in the words given here, e.g.:
  /s/—cour<u>se</u> /z/—depend<u>s</u> /tʃ/—<u>ch</u>ecked
- Students now place the remaining words under the appropriate heading. They can check if they were right or wrong by listening to Track 37.
  Answers:
  /s/—course, outside, perhaps, said, us
  /z/—depends, noise, promises, suppose
  /tʃ/—change, Charlie, checked, switch

Activity 35

- [SG] Divide the class into three groups. One group chooses a letter for all groups to work on. See which group can produce the most words. Set a time limit of one minute for this. Here are some common words for each sound:
  /s/ – *writes, sound, face, sky, miss*
  /z/ – *reads, razor, raise, freeze, ages*
  /tʃ/ – *church, reach, China, itchy, watch*

Activity 36

- Take a couple of these items and brainstorm their likely problems with the class, e.g.:
  T: A watch. What can go wrong with a watch?
  S1: It stops.
  T: What else?
  S2: It shows the wrong date.
  T: Anything else?
  S3: The strap breaks.
- [P] Now students work together to think of things that can go wrong with the other items. Here are some possibilities
  car—*flat tire, alarm, doors not shutting properly, overheating*
  bicycle—*puncture, brakes don't work*
  stereo—*damages CDs, poor sound, speakers not working*
  mobile phone—*can't turn off, ring tone wrong, poor reception*

printer—*pale print, paper sticks, ink leaks*
laptop computer—*won't start, crashes a lot, CD drive not working*

Activity 37

- [P] Students work in pairs for this. Either let students choose which item they want to talk about or assign items to pairs, but make sure that all the items listed here are covered by one pair or another.
- [P] Pairs write a short conversation and act it out for the rest of the class. There should be at least one conversation for each item.

Writing: instructions

Students look at the language of instructions for working various appliances.

Activity 38

- [SG] This is a preparation for an activity on writing instructions. Students discuss these questions. Which of these items do students find most difficult to work? Do students find instructions useful or difficult to understand? Groups should exchange experiences.

Activity 39

- Ask students to look at the pictures. What are these instructions for? (answer: *setting up an electronic notebook*.) Now focus on the first picture (*a*, the battery pack) and ask students to find the instruction that matches that picture (instruction *2*).
  [P] Now students work in pairs to match the remaining pictures and instructions.
  Answers:
  a 2
  b 5
  c 4
  d 3
  e 1

Activity 40

- [P] Students should look at the two lists (verbs and nouns) and try to recreate the instructions that went with the pictures. They should work in pairs and attempt to write the appropriate instructions together.

Activity 41

- [SG] Students work in groups for this. Groups should choose a task (recording a message, using a washing machine, etc.). Try to have all tasks covered. If necessary, assign tasks to groups.
- In part *a*, students set out the vocabulary needed to describe the task and to write instructions. For example, recording a message might include instructions such as the following:
  press button, speak close to microphone, press START to begin, STOP to end

- Having listed the steps to take in the right order (part *b*), students write a set of instructions for their task. It should follow the style of the Sony Notebook instructions in Activity 39.

> ▶ **Workbook Activities 17 & 18** *can be used at any stage from now on.*

Review: grammar and functional language

Students review the key language introduced in this unit.

Activity 42
Answers:

a do	b doesn't	c needs
d does	e course	f Interesting
g watch	h should	i going
j have	k forgot	l think
m cleaning	n work	o few
p want	q latest	r problem
s cut	t going	u have
v taking		

Review: vocabulary

Students check the vocabulary used in this unit.

Activity 43

- Brainstorm examples of each category of color word with the class. Write *warm / lukewarm / cold* on the board. Divide the class into two groups. Ask students from one group to call out a word and students from the other group to call out a category, e.g.:
  G1 STUDENT: Mustard.
  G2 STUDENT: Warm.
  Then ask Group 1 students if they agree or disagree with this categorization. They should give reasons for their opinions, e.g.:
  G1 STUDENT: I agree. Mustard is a warm color.
  T: Why?
  G1 STUDENT: Because mustard is hot, isn't it? Also, the color is a bit like gold. And that's warm.
  or
  G1 STUDENT: I don't agree. Mustard isn't a warm color.
  T: Why?
  G1 STUDENT: Well, I think it's a dull color. It's not bright, so it's kind of lukewarm.

Pronunciation

Here students focus on the difference between two English diphthongs, /eɪ/ and /aɪ/, and learn when the schwa sound /ə/ is used.

Activity 44

- Give an example of words in the lists which contain these sounds, e.g.:
  /eɪ/—*beige*   /aɪ/—*light*
- Brainstorm a couple more examples from the class, e.g.:
  /eɪ/—*faded, pale*   /aɪ/—*white, lime*

- [P] Now pairs of students add as many more words as they can to each column. See which pair finds the most words.
- Now students listen to Track 38 and see if there were any words on the list that they missed. If they can think of any other words that contain these vowel sounds, they should add them to the list.
  Answers:
  /eɪ/—beige, faded, pale, vibrations, sake, painted, behavior, face, make, ways
  /aɪ/—bright, derive, lime, vibrations, slightest, idea, white, light, like, ride, psychological, right

Activity 45
- Follow the same procedure for the schwa sound. Basically the schwa is used to replace the full form of vowels when the syllable in which the vowel appears is unstressed.
- Go over the example with the class and ask students for more examples of the schwa sound from the list, e.g.:
  afford, complement, adamant, scarlet, the right to
- Now students listen to Track 39 and check their answers.
  Possible answers:
  as black as he is painted, I haven't the slightest idea, to make a decision, out of the blue, on your best behavior, to paint the town red

Activity 46
- This is an interesting game which can be played towards the end of a lesson. As well as being fun, it also provides a review of some of the topics introduced in this unit and reviews some of the most useful language associated with them.
- Have students write the phrases from Word Plus on different pieces of paper.
- [SG] Students get into small groups. In each group, everyone puts their pieces of paper in a "fish bowl"—or in a pile anyway.
- A students starts talking about one of the topics in the Student's Book. When another student says "Now!," the first student has to reach into the "fish bowl" and take one of the pieces of paper. Then he or she has to use that phrase in their conversation immediately.
- The conversation passes on to the next student. Again, when someone calls "Now!," the speaking student has to get a piece of paper and use the phrase in their conversation before handing the conversation on to someone else. Here is an example:
  S1: I don't mind traveling by airplane—except that sometimes it's not very comfortable.
  S2: Now!
  S1 (*picks out the phrase* "as white as a sheet"): ... but some people get really scared. They go as white as a sheet when the plane takes off.
  S3: Yes, that's true, and ...

Workbook Activities 19–22 *can be used at any stage from now on.*

UNIT 8 Food for thought

Reading: what we eat

In this section, students read a variety of texts about healthy and unhealthy food.

Activity 1

- Ask students to look at the title of the unit. Can they tell you what the expression means? Explain that in English when we say 'that's food for thought', we mean that someone has given us something to think about. In this case, it is a play on words as the unit is also about food.
- [SG] This is a pre-reading exercise which prepares students for the texts on healthy and unhealthy food. Groups should work together to discuss their views on these foods.
- Begin by going over these foods with the class. Ask students to name the different foods. Ask further questions about the food shown in the pictures, e.g.:

  T: Look at the second picture. Is the fish cooked or is it raw?

  S1: I don't know. It could be cooked or it could be raw.

  T: Have you ever eaten raw fish?

  S1: No, never.

  T: Would you like to eat raw fish?

  S1: No, thanks.
- Go over the other foods in the picture. Ask students to identify the food and say whether they like it or not. They should also say which of these foods is good for you, which is bad for you. Do they find that the food they like is good or bad for them?
- Now students answer questions *a–f* about these foods. *Comfort food* means food that is delicious but not very good for you if you eat too much of it too often—e.g. cookies and chocolate. It's the kind of food people eat to cheer them up.
- In order to prevent feelings of guilt, it might be worth pointing out that even hamburgers and sweets are only bad for you if these are the *only* things you eat.

Activity 2

- Students skim these four website extracts (*1–4*) on pages 81 and 82 and match them with the descriptions of the websites (*a–d*).

  Answers:

  a 3   b 4   c 2   d 1

Activity 3

- Students read these texts (*1–4*) more carefully and decide which website is in favor of these beliefs.

  Answers:

  a Dr. Mercola

  b vegans

c Greenpeace

d Monsanto

e vegans / Dr. Mercola (he says "for certain health conditions")

f Monsanto

g Greenpeace

Activity 4

- [P] This is a vocabulary exercise. The first match is done for you. Do another example with the class if necessary. Then pairs try to match the remaining words with the appropriate synonyms or definitions.

  Answers:

  a 4   b 5   c 8   d 6   e 9   f 3   g 1

  h 7   i 11   j 2   k 10
- [SG] Conclude this part of the unit by dividing the class into four groups, one for each website. Ask groups to defend their position, using the arguments in the texts and any others they may think of for themselves. Groups can then debate the issue of what is and is not healthy food with each other.

Language in chunks

Students look at some idiomatic words and phrases used in talking about food.

Activity 5

- Check first that students know the meaning of words like *debilitating, stave off, devoid*, etc. They can use their dictionaries for this.
- Do the first example with the class. What does *debilitating* mean? "Making weaker." Which of the words in the list can be described as debilitating? *Condition*—yes, *illness*—yes, *sickness*—yes, *disease*—yes, *wave of rejection*—no. Go through the rest of the list in the same way. Then let students match the remainder of these words.

  Answers:

  a condition, illness, sickness, disease, hunger

  b terrorism, hunger, disease, fat, animal products, poverty, living longer, dying earlier

  c wave of rejection, hunger, terrorism, poverty

  d hunger, illness, poverty

  e destroying, winning, producing, living longer

  f emotion, protein, fat, animal products, vitamins

  g sickness, disease, terrorism, poverty, dying earlier, living longer

Activity 6

- Students choose phrases they have made in the previous activity to complete these sentences. The first one is done.

  Answers:

  a global poverty

  b devoid of animal products / fat

c linked to living longer
d a debilitating illness / condition / sickness / disease
e intent on winning
f stave off hunger
g associated with dying earlier

Activity 7

- [P/SG] Students work together to produce more sentences which relate to some of the ideas put forward in the texts. See how many of these phrases they can use in a sentence, e.g.:
  AIDS is a debilitating disease which is linked to global poverty.
  Animal products are associated with obesity, which is a serious condition in some countries.
- Groups should read out their sentences to the rest of the class. Which sentences are the most interesting?

Activity 8

- Get students to list these articles—*a / an*, *the*, 0 article. Write these headings on the board. Ask students to read the first sentence and tell you under which heading to write each noun or noun phrase:

a / an	the	0 article
	consumption	animal fats
		proteins
		heart disease

- Now students do the same for the nouns in the remaining sentences.
- Set a time limit for this. Ask students to find at least one example of each type of article from the texts.
  Answers:

	a / an	the	0 article
a		consumption	animal fats
			proteins
			heart disease
b	risky process		genetic engineering food
c	diet	dangerous effects	animal products
d		genetic manipulation	agricultural products

Activity 9

- [SG] Students discuss these five questions in groups. The first two questions relate to students' own eating habits. If they eat foods that they know are bad for them, why do they do it? Possible answers are: because they taste good, because everyone else does. The remaining questions are more philosophical. Students may not be able to decide on their answers yet: it may be a good idea to return to these questions at the end of this unit.

 **Workbook Activities 1–5** *can be used at any stage from now on.*

Vocabulary: food and drink (idioms)

This section focuses on the metaphorical uses of food words.

Activity 10

- Go over the pyramid with the class. Ask students to think of one example to go in each category, e.g.:
  fat and sugar—*cookies*
  dairy products—*milk*
  meat and fish—*chicken and tuna*
  vegetables—*cabbage*
  fruits—*oranges*
  bread, cereals, rice, pasta—*corn*
- [I/P] Students then copy the pyramid and complete it with as many food items as they can, then compare their list with their partner.

Activity 11

- [P/SG] Students, in pairs or small groups, discuss these questions. Students compare what they eat with what they should eat. Most of us don't avoid all foods which are said to be bad for us.
- For the third question, ask students to say how important food is to them. Ask them to place their responses on a line like this:
  very important   quite important   not important
  ⟵——————————————————————⟶

Activity 12

- Like color words in Unit 7, many food words are used metaphorically and appear in common idioms. See how many of these idioms students know. You could do the first two phrases with the class, then let students work individually or in pairs.
  Answers:

a cake	b bread	c milk
d mustard	e pancake	f eggs
g apple	h fruit cake	i bacon
j beans	k pie	l egged
m tea	n bread	o hot cakes
p cucumber	q beans	r cake

Activity 13

- Students discuss these questions. If you're teaching a multicultural, multilingual class, then students can compare idioms from different languages.

Workbook Activities 6 & 7 *can be used at any stage from now on.*

Speaking and writing: when words are used

Students look again at the differences between written and spoken language.

Activity 14

- Ask students to glance quickly over these entries. What words do the dictionary-makers use to indicate how the words are used? (*informal* = spoken).

Activity 15

- [P] If students have dictionaries which give clues as to usage, e.g. *formal / informal*, students should be able to find three examples of both spoken and written English. If not, they will need your help to decide how these words are normally used.

Listening: where people like to eat

In this section, students listen to people explaining where they like eating out.

Activity 16

- [P/SG] Students look at the pictures and decide where they would like to eat (*a*, fast-food outlet; *b*, posh restaurant; *c*, informal buffet-style restaurant; *d*, simple café; *e*, romantic bistro). They give their partners their reasons, then switch roles.

Activity 17

- Ask students to look at one person and guess where he / she would prefer to eat, e.g.:
  T: Where would Julia prefer to eat?
  S1: In the restaurant.
  T: In which restaurant?
  S1: The nice one in picture *b*.
- [P] Students work in pairs to decide where they think the other people in the photos would prefer to eat. Then they listen to Track 40 and check their answers.

Activity 18

- This involves a more careful listening to Track 40.
  Answers:
  a Martin   b Naomi   c Jed   d Chris   e Julia

Activity 19

- [P] Students draw up a table to match speakers and what they say about these various categories. Students listen again to Track 40 and complete the table for the first speaker (Chris). Then play the track again and let students complete the table.
  Answers:

Food	Service	Atmosphere	Price
C home-cooked	friendly	feels at home	cheap
Je not delicious	polite, fast, first class	no surprises; clean, hygienic	great value
Ju great food	great service	luxurious, delightful surroundings	not important (probably expensive)
M good		romantic, soft lighting, small intimate tables, no loud music	
N plenty of it, variety, plain, fresh	self-service		cheap – eat what you want for one set price

- [P] Students compare their table with their partner's. If there is a disagreement over any of these answers, play Track 40 again to see who's right.

Activity 20

- This simulation requires a good deal of preparation. It may be best for students to prepare notes first, then do a presentation of their ideas in another session. First students need to decide on what are the most important features of a good restaurant. Brainstorm these and write them on the board, e.g.:
  food   drinks   service   décor   price
  location   opening times
- What questions need to be answered under each heading? Pick the first heading (food) and get students to outline the key questions, e.g.:
  —What kind of food? Meat, fish, vegetarian? Or specializing in one kind of food—pizza, curry, hamburgers, sandwiches, pies?
  —What kind of cooking? Italian, Asian, other national cuisines? Or a mixture?
- [SG] Groups list similar questions under their other headings and answer them. Each group should then prepare a short presentation on their restaurant. Which restaurant is likeliest to succeed? Groups vote on each other's proposal.

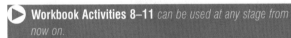

Workbook Activities 8–11 *can be used at any stage from now on.*

Functional language: making a complaint

Here students focus on some of the language used in making a complaint, typically in a restaurant or shop.

Activity 21

- First students reconstruct the conversation by putting the sentences in order. The conversation starts with line *i*, *Excuse me*. Ask students what the customer is doing here. (answer: attracting the waiter's attention)
  Answers:
  1 i   2 c   3 f   4 e   5 b   6 j   7 a   8 h
  9 g   10 d
- Students check their answers by listening to Track 41.

Activity 22

- Each of these sentences demonstrates a function associated with complaining. Three different categories are given here. Ask students to find an example of each category, e.g.:
  Starting to make a complaint: a, c
  Reasons for the complaint: b
  Ways of dealing with a complaint: d
- [P] Then students place the remaining sentences under the correct headings.
  Answers:
  Starting to make a complaint: a, c, h, k, n, q
  Reasons for the complaint: b, e, g, i, l, p, r
  Ways of dealing with a complaint: d, f, j, m, o

Activity 23

- [P] Pairs decide which adjectives can be used to complain about these foods. An example is given for the first food, *soup*. Ask students to think of others that could be used, e.g. *salty, cold, spicy, awful*.
- Pairs continue with the other foods. Some words can be used for more than one kind of food. Which is the most common word?

  Answers:
  a salty, awful, spicy, cold, bland
  b salty, awful, gritty
  c burnt, stale, awful, bland
  d undercooked, tough, overcooked, burnt, raw, awful, cold
  e undercooked, overcooked, raw, salty, awful, cold
  f undercooked, tough, overcooked, burnt, greasy, raw, salty, awful, cold
  g stale, greasy, awful
  h undercooked, tough, overcooked, burnt, raw, salty, awful, spicy, cold, bland

Activity 24

- Ask students to read through the three situations. Elicit from them the kind of language which they might use in such a situation. Offer feedback.
- [P] Students choose a situation and start rehearsing a conversation for that situation. They can write it down if they want to. While they are doing, this you can go round the class offering appropriate feedback.
- Listen to some of the pairs with the whole class. Let the students know when / if they have produced good dialogues, and offer constructive feedback where there are problems.

 **Workbook Activities 12 & 13** *can be used at any stage from now on.*

Speaking: restaurant jokes

Students match beginnings and endings of jokes about restaurants and rate them for humour.

Activity 25

- Take a vote on whether students find the joke funny. Are there any other funny ways the waiter could reply to this complaint?

Activity 26

[P] This is a jigsaw reading / listening exercise. Students refer to the relevant pages in the Activity Bank. Each student has one part of the joke, but not the other part. A has the first line, e.g. *a*, "Waiter! There's a fly in my soup!"
Can B find a funny reply from his / her set of "second lines?" It should be *7*, "Don't worry, the spider on the bread will get it."

- [P] Pairs go through the rest of these lines and try to match the two parts of the jokes.

  Answers:
  A's jokes / B's replies: a 7, b 6, c 1, d 2, e 3, f 5, g 4
  B's jokes / A's replies: a 4, b 3, c 7, d 5, e 2, f 1, g 6

Activity 27

- [P/SG] Students discuss these questions and compare their responses to those of other groups. Ask for volunteers to explain the jokes. See if groups can think of any other restaurant jokes.

Grammar: using articles

Students continue to study the use of definite, indefinite and zero articles in front of nouns.

Activity 28

- Ask students to read Sections 8C–D of the Mini-grammar. (There is a good deal of material in this and it might be best if you ask students to do this as a homework task before doing this activity.) They will need to understand this before they are able to complete this activity. To make sure, go over these sections of the Mini-grammar with the whole class beforehand.
- [P] Do the first two lines with the whole class:
  T: There's no article before *breakfast*. Why?
  S1: We don't use the definite article before the names of meals.
  T: But in the next sentence we have *the breakfast*.
  S2: That's because we're talking about one particular breakfast.
  T: What about *cereal* and *toast*?
  S3: We don't normally use articles in front of uncountable nouns.
- [P] Students work in pairs to find reasons for the use or non-use of articles in the remaining sentences. If students have difficulty in finding reasons, refer them back to the notes in the Mini-grammar.

  Answers:
  a breakfast: name of meal; the breakfast: one particular meal; cereal, toast: uncountable nouns
  b food: uncountable noun
  c the mango: one particular mango
  d vegetables: vegetables in general
  e people: people in general
  f the cook book: one particular book
  g the restaurant: one particular restaurant
  h animal fat: uncountable noun

Activity 29

Answers:
a no article   b the   c no article   d the / no article
e the / no article   f no article   g the / no article
h no article   i no article   j no article
k the   l no article

Activity 30

- [P] Students go back to the Mini-grammar to find the reasons for the use or non-use of articles here. Help by going over the first couple of sentences, e.g.:
a *the violin*—definite: the violin is a musical instrument
b *an apple*—indefinite: single countable noun
   the apples—definite: specific apples (the ones bought at the market)

- [P] Students continue discussing the reasons for the use or absence of the articles in these sentences. Let pairs compare their answers.
  Answers:
  a musical instrument
  b *an apple*: single countable noun
     the apples: specific objects
  c before a superlative
  d uncountable noun
  e *a chocolate bar*: singular, countable noun
     the fridge: specific object (the one in my kitchen)
  f *the cherries*: specific noun (the ones on offer at the market)
     a pound: quantifying expression
  g a class of objects (formal use)
  h plural noun in general
  i we know what is being referred to (a specific object and a specific person)
  j before names of professions
  k unique concepts
  l *a dish*: single, countable noun
     the Hungarians: to refer to a group of people

Activity 31

- [I] This activity is intended to sum up the use of articles outlined in the previous activities. Students work on their own for this.
  Answers:

a a	b a	c the
d no article	e no article	f no article
g no article	h no article	i an
j a	k no article	l a
m an	n the	

Activity 32

- Ask students to go through this list quickly. Who knows these places? If students say they do, ask them to say something about the place, e.g. where it is or what it's famous for.
- Now ask students to decide which of these places need the definite article.
  Answers:

Acapulco	Angkor Watt
the Bermuda Triangle	Buckingham Palace
Colorado	the Eiffel Tower
the Grand Canyon	the Golden Tower
Harvard University	the Hilton Hotel
the Igacu Falls	Krackow
the Kremlin	Madagascar
the Mississippi river	Mount Vesuvius
the province of Buenos Aires	
Narita Airport	the pyramid of Cheops
the state of Sonora	the Statue of Liberty
the Taj Mahal	the Temple of Heavenly Peace, Kyoto

Pronunciation: weak and strong *the*
Students learn to distinguish between the normal pronunciation of *the* and its pronunciation when the following noun is emphasized or begins with a vowel.

Activity 33

- Ask students to read these sentences aloud. How is *the* pronounced in each sentence? Is it pronounced /ðə/—with a schwa, or /ði/—the full, stressed form? Try to get agreement among students on how *the* is pronounced in each of these sentences.
- Students listen to these sentences read on Track 42 and see if their pronunciations were right. They practice saying the sentences again.
  Answers:
  We use the full form /ði/ when we want to stress the importance of the noun that follows and also when the noun that follows begins with a vowel.
  a weak
  b strong (for emphasis)
  c strong (before a vowel)
  d weak
  e weak
  f strong (before a vowel)

 Workbook Activities 14 & 15 *can be used at any stage from now on.*

Writing: describing graphs and tables
Students learn to interpret tables and graphs and convert the information into writing.

Activity 34

- Ask students to take a quick look at the table. What is it? (answer: a kind of survey.) What's the subject? (answer: people's attitudes to GM food.) Check at this stage that students now what *GM* means (genetically modified).
- Now students read the report and match its three parts to the headings (*a–c*) given here.
  Answers:
  a = part 3   b = part 1   c = part 2

Activity 35

- [I/P] Students write up Table 2 in the same way, using the introductions to each paragraph given here. Students can work in pairs or individually for this.

Activity 36 / Activity 37

- Brainstorm suitable questions with the class. Try to find topics relating to food, e.g. "It would be better if we all become vegetarians," "Obesity is a bigger risk to health than smoking" or "The government should ban the advertising of sweets and fizzy drinks on television."
- Let each student choose a topic and use it to ask the rest of the class their question(s), following either the Table 1 model or the Table 2 model. Check that the reports follow the format of the report on Table 1. When the tables and reports are completed, students

pair up to check each other's work. Students can finally report back on their findings.

- Finally, ask students if there are any drawbacks to such surveys. For example, to what extent do respondents give the answers they think the questioner wants? This is a particular danger when reporting on your own behavior. Thus, in surveys people normally claim to eat a healthier diet than they actually do. Are there any other dangers about relying on information gathered in this way?

 Workbook Activities 16 & 17 *can be used at any stage from now on.*

Review: grammar and functional language

Students review the key language introduced in this unit.

Activity 38
Answers:

a the	b the	c a
d a	e no article	f the
g no article / the	h the	i no article
j the	k the	l the
m the	n the	o an
p the	q no article	r the
s the		

Activity 39
Answers:

a 3 b 5 c 8 d 1 e 4 f 2 g 6 h 7

Activity 40
- Ask students to look at this picture. Ask them to list what's wrong with the room—there's no bulb in the lamp, the room is dirty, the phone doesn't work.
- Think about the kind of complaint that the guest could make to the manager. How could the manager respond? He / She could apologize, but might also point out that there aren't any other rooms available in the hotel and there might not be any other rooms in any other hotel in the city.
- Now students work out a conversation between the guest and the manager and rehearse it.

Review: vocabulary

Students check the vocabulary used in this unit.

Activity 41
[P/SG] Pairs or groups discuss their preferences. Go round the class asking students to explain their preferences, e.g.:

T: What's your favorite expression?
S1: *A piece of cake.*
T: Why do you like that phrase?
S1: Because it means that something is easy and I like things that are easy. And I like cake!
T: Can you name something that is *not your cup of tea*?

S2: I don't like people who are very aggressive. They're not my cup of tea at all.
T: Who is *the apple of your eye*?
S3: My husband / My goddaughter.
T: What is *a piece of cake* for you?
S4: Doing sums / Playing a computer game.

Pronunciation
Here students decide how many syllables there are in words they have learned.

Activity 42
- Ask students to look at the Word List and find an example of one word to go in each of the five columns. Say that they should also mark where the stress falls in these words, e.g.:

One syllable	*bland*
Two syllables	*aw̲ful*
Three syllables	*a̲dvocate*
Four syllables	*mille̲nnium*
Five syllables	*subs̲tantiated*

- [P] Now students write all the words from the list under the correct heading and mark where the stress falls. Then they listen to Track 43 and check.

Answers:

One syllable	bland	burnt	raw
	stale	tough	yield
Two syllables	aw̲ful	cons̲ent	enha̲nce
	gre̲asy	gri̲tty	ri̲sky
	sa̲lty	spi̲cy	ur̲ging
Three syllables	a̲dvocate	cu̲ltivate	nu̲merous
	obje̲ction	overco̲oked	
	underco̲oked		
Four syllables	mille̲nnium		
Five syllables	subs̲tantiated		

Activity 43
- This makes for an enjoyable game to round the unit off. Follow the instructions given in the Student's Book. Set a time limit of three minutes and see which team has the most words. If there are arguments as to whether a word is acceptable, you make the decision.

Activity 44
- [P] Each partner should choose one of these scenarios, *a* or *b*. Make sure students know what these expressions mean. For example, *putting all your eggs in one basket* is not usually considered a sensible thing to do. Why not?
- Similarly, *spilling the beans* usually means passing on some information which is not meant to be made public. Ask students to think of cases where *spilling the beans* has been a good thing and other cases where it was not such a good idea.
- Then students can talk about occasions in their own lives where they did either of these things and describe the consequences of their actions.

 **Workbook Activities 18–21** *can be used at any stage from now on.*

UNIT 9 First impressions

Listening: *Café Talk*

In this section, students listen to a group of friends discussing what attracts people to each other.

Activity 1

- [P] This is a pre-listening exercise which prepares students for the conversation which follows. Students in pairs discuss these questions. Get feedback from them. Ask students to compare pairs' responses. Is there a consensus or is there a wide variety of opinions?
- In the last phase (comparing answers with the rest of the class), there are opportunities here to use the expressions of agreement and skepticism students met in Unit 6, e.g.:
  - S1: When I meet someone for the first time, I always look at their eyes.
  - S2: Their eyes? You must be joking. I always look at their body. I hate skinny people.
  - S3: No, I agree with [S1]. The eyes tell you a lot about what a person is like.
- Find out if male and female students differ in what they look for, especially when thinking about people of the opposite sex. Ask students if they can make any generalizations about this.

Activity 2

- Students look at the picture and try to answer the questions. These questions are all speculative—i.e., students can only guess the answers—but they help students focus their attention on what they're going to hear.
- Then play Track 44 and ask students if their guesses were correct.
  Answers:
  a Greenslade
  b Sally
  c a psychologist

Activity 3

- Students read the summaries then listen to the track again. Which summary is the best?
  Answer: c

Activity 4
Answers:

a Mitch	b Mitch	c Seb
d Sally	e Greenslade	f Seb
g Greenslade	h Sally	i Mitch
j Sally	k Sally	

- What is the basic pattern of this conversation? Who is trying to put forward a point of view about what attracts people to each other? (Greenslade). Who is

skeptical? (Seb and Mitch). Who is inclined to believe Greenslade and stop the others from laughing at him? (Sally). Ask students to list the skeptical remarks, the "lay-off" remarks, the believing remarks.

Pronunciation: attitude

Activity 5
Answers:

a	That's not true.	Disbelief.
b	But it's true.	Listen to me. I know it sounds funny, but …
c	I read it in a book.	Don't be surprised if I read books.
d	Who says this?	That's unbelievable.
e	You're not still talking?	Surprise.
f	Why should I apologize?	Sneering.
g	I've heard this before.	Boredom.
h	Because if you had a dog, then you'd look like it.	Making fun of Greenslade.
i	You do like him.	Triumph.

- Sometimes you can tell a speaker's attitude by the stress he / she places on certain syllables. For example, in "Yeah, right," the extra emphasis on *right* suggests sarcasm. The same thing happens with *OK* in Greenslade's "I read, Seb, OK?"

Activity 6

- [SG] Divide the class into groups of four. Each student takes on the role of one of the speakers (it doesn't matter if you can't get an exact gender match). Play Track 44 again. Students pay particular attention to "their" character. Then they try to copy the way he / she speaks his / her remarks.

Activity 7

- [SG] Students stay in these groups and continue to work on this conversation. Each group practices acting it out. Which group comes closest to the speakers on Track 44? End this section by playing the track one more time.

▶ **Workbook Activities 1–3** *can be used at any stage from now on.*

Vocabulary: physical description (connotation)

In this section, students learn the language used to describe how people look.

Activity 8

- [P] Students work in pairs to decide where to put these adjectives. Here is how the completed table might look.

Possible answers:

Chin	large, pointed, protruding, receding, square, strong, weak
Eyes	appealing, bright, dark, deep-set, kind, mean, shiny, wide
Hair	curly, dark, fine, long, receding, shiny, soft, straight, thick, thinning, wavy, wiry
Mouth	generous, large, small
Nose	large, long, pointed, snub, straight, turned-up

- How many of the phrases *a–e* are familiar to students? Elicit as many answers as possible. Students can, of course, work out the meanings, e.g. that a bald patch is a part of a man's head where no hair grows.
  Answers:
  a short spiky hair
  b no hair on part of his head
  c coloured / dyed strands of hair
  d hair made wavy or curled by the hairdresser
  e bits of hair added

Activity 9

- Ask students to look at the pictures and make a comment about each of them. Now ask them to look at the first picture and go over the example.
- Ask students to describe the other people in the same way.
  Possible answers:
  a He's got a long nose, a wide, generous mouth and a strong chin.
  b She's got dark skin, hair extensions and a small nose. Her mouth is large and her eyes are appealing.
  c He's got a short nose and a small mouth. His eyes are small and deep-set and he's got receding hair.
  d She's got a long nose, a small mouth and wide eyes. She's also got long dark hair, which is very straight.

Activity 10

- Explain the words "connotation" and "overtones" (= the ideas suggested by a word, rather than its actual meaning). Here some words have a positive meaning. Ask students to find one from each group, e.g. a) *lean*, b) *muscular*, c) *good-looking*.
  Now ask students to find one word with a negative meaning from each group, e.g. a) *skinny*, b) *pudgy*, c) *scruffy*.
- [P] Then students, in pairs, sort the remaining adjectives into positive and negative. Ask them also to list neutral adjectives, i.e. adjectives which can be either positive or negative.
  Answers:
  a negative: emaciated, puny, skinny
  positive: lean, slender, slim
  neutral: slight, thin, underweight
  b negative: chubby, flabby, obese, pudgy
  positive: muscular, voluptuous, well built
  neutral: not thin, overweight, plump, stout

c negative: a bit of a mess, hideous, plain, scruffy, ugly, untidy
positive: attractive, beautiful, cute, elegant, good-looking, gorgeous, handsome, pretty, smart, well dressed

Activity 11

- Ask students to find examples of both types of word or phrase—qualifying (making things not quite so strong) and intensifying (emphasizing an extreme quality). Then they list the phrases used here.
  Answers:

a little	absolutely
kind of	extremely
rather	fantastically
	incredibly

- [P] Students work in pairs. See which pair can come up with the most interesting or convincing phrases, e.g.:
  absolutely gorgeous   a little untidy   rather slight
  Note that there are some possible combinations which don't in fact work, e.g.:
  a little elegant   absolutely slim

Activity 12

Possible answers:
Amélie is kind of slender / rather skinny.
Gandalf is rather handsome / a bit of a mess.
Bridget is a little plump / incredibly flabby.
Rocky is fantastically well built / absolutely hideous.

Activity 13

- Have students think of people that the rest of the class is likely to know (e.g. TV personalities, sports stars, politicians, etc.). Give them time to do this. They can write the name of the person they have chosen and then jot down some notes about how they might describe them.
- [SG] One student (S1) picks a famous person and tells another (S2) who he / she is thinking of. Then the first student describes what this person looks like and the rest of the group tries to guess who he / she is talking about. S1 says whether their guess is right or wrong.

 Workbook Activities 4 & 5 *can be used at any stage from now on.*

Reading: hair

Students read a text and discuss public perceptions of blond and dark hair.

Activity 14

- This is a warm-up activity in preparation for reading a text about women's hair colour. One of the women is blond, the other has dark hair. The theory is that many people perceive blonds as being more attractive, but less clever than brunettes.

- Ask for a show of hands to see how many students thought Stephanie, the "clever" woman, was the dark-haired woman in photo *a* and how many thought she was the blond woman in photo *b*. Was the theory proved correct in this case?
- Ask students to give reasons for their choice.

Activity 15

- [SG] As a pre-reading task, groups discuss questions **a**, **b** and **c** then feed back their answers to the rest of the class. Make a note of these opinions then explain that students are going to read an article about blonds.
- Students read the article *The new blond bombshell* on page 93 and check their opinions against what the writer reports. Do they agree?

  Answers:
  The article on page 93 states that:
  a there are more dyed blond women than natural blonds in the world.
  b it seems that blonds are thought more attractive than brunettes.
  c it might <u>not</u> be an advantage for women to be blond.

Activity 16

- [SG] This is a jigsaw reading activity. Each student looks at a different Activity Bank section and gains different information from it. Each student has questions which he / she can answer from his / her text and other questions which can only be answered by students who have read the other texts.
- This activity may take a little while to set up and may even be a little confusing at first. Explain carefully how the dialogue between students is to be organized and go round groups checking on how they are coping with the activity.

Activity 17

- Having completed Activity 16 and compared notes with their partners, students should have clear answers to the question asked here. Together, they fill in the table.

  Possible answers:

Advantages	Disadvantages
better social life, as they are considered more attractive and more feminine	worse career prospects (more likely to be rejected, lower salary), as they are considered less intelligent, less mature and less capable, because blondness gives a child-like appearance

Activity 18

Answers:
a applicant   b résumé   c equally qualified
d reject   e appointed   f salary   g PA

Language in chunks

Here students look at idiomatic phrases used in the article they have just read.

Activity 19

Answers:
a make use of
b harm your professional future
c It's almost unbelievable
d make much difference
e really tried
f when they were asked about it

Activity 20

- [P] Students work in pairs and say something about themselves, using one of these phrases, e.g.:
  "I'm not very good at maths, but I don't think that will damage my career prospects."
  "The fact that she was a blond didn't play a major part in my decision to employ her."

Activity 21

Answers:

golden-haired	freckle-faced	darker-haired
blue-eyed	brown-eyed	dark-eyed

 Workbook Activities 6–8 *can be used at any stage from now on.*

Grammar: adjectives and adjective order

Students focus on adjectives, particularly two-word adjectives and how to order adjectives when there are more than one.

Activity 22

- Students try to answer the questions by themselves by looking at these sentences and trying to work out the rules from them. At first they will probably make guesses which don't cover all cases. Help them to refine their rule so that it applies to all cases:
  S1: We use *and* when there are three adjectives.
  T: What about *a yellow and green tie*? There are only two adjectives there.
- When student have established rough and ready rules, tell them to look at Section **9A of the Mini-grammar**. Are their rules correct or do they need some modification?

Activity 23

- Having established rules for the use of *and* between adjectives, students now apply these rules. Do the first sentence with the class. What's wrong with it? (The *and* is unnecessary.) How should it be corrected? (Replace the *and* with a comma.)
- Students correct the remaining sentences in the same way.

  Answers:
  a He had dark, thinning hair.
  b They are coming to stay for the next two days.
  c He looked handsome, elegant, and rich.

d He behaved like a silly young fool.

e She painted a successful, happy, voluptuous woman.

Activity 24

- This text is designed to showcase the range of hyphenated, two-word adjectives that can be found in English. It's important to point out that the excessive use of such adjectives, as in this text, is unusual and not to be recommended.

- Students read the text and then describe the two people. Ask them to find other words for as many as possible of the two-word adjectives used here. Help students to find alternatives, e.g. *busy* for 'time-consuming', *rich* for 'well-off', *attractive* for 'good-looking', etc.

- Students try to find equivalents for all of the two-word adjectives used in the text. They can check their findings against the information given in **Section 9B of the Mini-grammar.**

  Answers:

  The following adjectives fall within the 9B typology:

  1 good-looking, long-standing, badly designed

  2 well-off, built-up, all-out

  3 world-famous, duty-free, bullet-proof,

  4 time-consuming, self-centred, air-conditioned,

  There are other ways of making two-word adjectives, and the following examples fall within these categories:

  adjective + noun + -(e)d ending: *two-faced, red-haired, big-headed,*

  noun + noun: *part-time*

  adjective + adjective: *shocking-pink*

Activity 25

- This activity practices the adjective + noun (+ -*ed* ending) pattern of adjective formation.

  Possible answers:

  auburn / gray / red-haired (actress); brown / curly / fair / straight-haired (boy)

  absent / high / narrow-minded (professor)

  cut-price (shoes)

  long / short-sighted (person with glasses)

  brown / white-skinned (girl); hard-skinned (fruit)

  short / bad-tempered (dog)

Word Choice: *seem, appear,* and *look*

Activity 26

- Go over these notes with students. Check that they are understood and explain any problem areas.

Activity 27

- [P] Students put what they have learned in the previous activity into practice. Go over the example then let pairs complete the remaining sentences with the appropriate forms of the correct verbs.

Answers:

a appeared

b appeared

c looked

d seems

e look

f appears

g looks

h seems

i appear

Activity 28

- Ask students to read the phrases. Get them to tell you how many adjectives there are in each one (e.g. four in *a*, two in *b*).

- Ask students to give you examples from the sentences of adjectives which describe color (black), origin (Mexican), opinion / judgment (gorgeous), size (big), material (knitted), purpose (hunting), shape (square), description (big-hearted).

- Now ask them to put the bullet-pointed headings in the right place in the diagram to show the normal order of adjectives before a noun. Put the diagram on the board and have students come up and fill it in. If you miss out some adjectives (i.e. some categories) the diagram still gives you the answer.

- When students have done the activity, tell them to look at **9B–9C in the Mini-grammar** to see if they want to change their answers. Remind them that we don't normally put a list of four or more adjectives before the noun.

  Answers:

  size or shape / description + opinion / judgment or size + shape / description or color + color or origin + origin or material + material or purpose + noun

Activity 29

- Demonstrate this with a student. Mention something you have in your room and get the student to ask you to describe it, e.g.:

  T: I've got a nice picture on the wall.

  S1: Can you describe it?

  T: It's a beautiful little French painting of a boat.

- [P] Now students work in pairs to hold similar conversations about things they have in their room or in their house. One student notes the adjectives and nouns the other uses and passes this list to another pair for them to put them in the right order.

Workbook Activities 9 & 10 *can be used at any stage from now on.*

Functional language: taking ourselves to be fixed

Students learn the language used in consulting professionals (beauty salon or barbers, doctors, dentists).

Activity 30

- Students listen to Track 46 and look at the pictures. Which picture shows the place where the conversation takes place?
  Answer: b, the barber's
- Now students see if they are right by listening to Track 47.

Activity 31

- Students listen to Track 47 more closely and answer these questions.
  Answers:
  a a couple of months ago
  b coffee, sugar and cream; coffee, cream, one sugar
  c It's a bit messy.
  d It should look smarter / neater.

Activity 32

- Go over this explanation of some of the functional language used in meetings between professionals and patients / customers. Some phrases are quite direct, e.g. *I'd like a haircut, please*; others are more indirect, e.g. *I was thinking of …, I was wondering if …* Ask students "When would you use each of these phrases?"
- Students practice using these phrases, substituting other examples. Ask students to think of alternatives to some of the things asked for in section *d*, e.g.:
  I'd like a shampoo, please.
  I was thinking of having my hair dyed.
  I was wondering if you could give me advice about losing some weight.
- Students should practice altering the professionals' responses in the same way, e.g.:
  I recommend taking some exercise.
  I think you'd better use an electric toothbrush.
  I think we could give your hair a more natural look.

Activity 33

- Students refer to Activity Bank 13 for suggestions as to what words they could use in these situations.

Activity 34

- Now students work in pairs, one acting the role of professional, the other the role of customer / patient. Students then switch roles. Try to ensure there's a balance between the three professions mentioned. Pairs can act out their role-plays for others.
- For variety, students could pretend to be irritable customers or tired professionals. How would people show that in the language they use?

 **Workbook Activity 11** *can be used at any stage from now on.*

Writing: Résumé

Students learn how to present information about themselves in applying for a job.

Activity 35

- Students look this document over quickly. What is it for? (To give information about someone who is applying for a job.)

Activity 36

- [P] Pairs compare the two Résumés. One student looks at Neil's Résumé, the other looks at Nigel's. How many similarities between the two Résumés can pairs find? See which pair can find the most similarities. Here are a few:
  —They attended the same school (Oak Park College).
  —They both enjoy sports.
  —They both had part-time jobs at McDonald's.

Activity 37

- [P] Students look at the two Résumés more carefully and answer these four questions. The answer to question *d* is a matter of opinion, which students can debate. How impressed are they by the hobbies of the two job applicants? Ask students to say which of their hobbies and interests they would include in their Résumé.
  Answers:
  a Neil: Speedo Sports Store
     Nigel: Features Editor, *Times* Newspaper
  b Schools attended, Qualifications gained, Employment record, Hobbies and interests, Additional information (why I'd be good at this job), References
     Neil leaves out qualifications because he hasn't got any.
  c They start from the most recent.

Activity 38

- [I] Now students have a chance to write their own Résumé. Encourage them to be as creative as possible—that is, they can imagine they have more experience than they actually have. First they have to decide what job they are applying for. Ask them to consider what qualifications they would need for a range of jobs, e.g. sales manager, mechanic, journalist, teacher.
- Students will have more chance to exercise their imagination if they choose a fictitious character. But even here it's important to think up qualifications that are appropriate to a particular job. Thus, a journalist should have some experience of writing and interviewing people; a mechanic must have some knowledge of cars and some evidence of solving mechanical problems.
- This is one of those tasks which are probably best prepared in class and then completed as a homework task.

 Workbook Activity 12 *can be used at any stage from now on.*

Speaking: the interview

Students learn how to conduct a job interview and in particular how to present themselves most effectively.

Activity 39a

• [P] Pairs work to decide which of these topics are appropriate. Some, e.g. *1*, are obviously important. Others, e.g. *2*, are obviously irrelevant. But other topics, e.g. *5*, are not so clear-cut. As always, students should give reasons for their choice of answers.

Answers:
The most relevant topics seem to be 1, 3, 5 and 6.

Activity 39b

• Now students consider the form questions about these topics might take. Exemplify this with the first topic. How might an interviewer ask this question? Give students alternatives and ask them to choose one, e.g.:

"Why do you want this job?"
"Could you tell us why you want this job?"
"Please tell us why you want this job."
"I wonder if you'd be so kind as to tell us why you'd like this job."

Students discuss the appropriacy of these questions. Which are too direct, which too indirect?

• [P] Now students find the right questions to ask about the other appropriate topics. They should also think of any other questions which an interviewer might reasonably ask. Here are a few examples:

"How do you think you get on with other people?"
"What would you say your weak points are?"
"What was the thing you liked best / least about your last job?"

Activity 40

• [SG] This activity is the start of a role-play where students try their hand at interviewing and being interviewed for jobs. First, students pick the job they want to apply for. Try to ensure that there's a good spread of applicants for each job.

• Follow the suggestions (a–c) in the Student's Book. In drawing up their Resumé, students need to look at the job requirements and make sure that what they have to offer matches what the employer wants. Students work together to decide on who the interviewers / interviewees are going to be and how they are going to handle the interview.

Activity 41

• Students role-play the interview as suggested in the Student's Book.

Review: grammar and functional language

Students review the key language introduced in this unit.

Activity 42

• Remind students that "not making the sentence ridiculous" means using no more than three or four adjectives.

Answers:
woman: an elegant, traditionally-dressed Japanese woman
guitar: an old, brown, cracked Spanish guitar.
cloth on table: a beautiful Thai silk cloth
car: a shiny new Swedish car
old man: a short-sighted, absent-minded old professor

Activity 43

• [P/SG] Go over the model conversation with the class, then think of an object yourself and describe it in the same way. Students ask "yes / no" questions about it, e.g.:

T: It's a blue metallic thing with wheels.
S1: Is it a car?.
T: No, it isn't.
S2: Can you drive it?
T: No, you can't.
S3: Can you ride it?
T: Yes, you can.
S3: Is it a bike?
T: Yes, it is.

• [P] Now students work in pairs or small groups and take turns in asking and answering questions about objects in the same way.

Activity 44

Answers:
a help
b see
c appointment
d luck
e name
f like
g in
h how
i want
j you
k like
l What?
m climb
n examine
o want
p something
q chest
r aren't
s see
t next

Review: vocabulary

Students check the vocabulary used in this unit.

Activity 45

- [P/SG] Students discuss this in pairs or small groups. Take a vote on the most / least popular words.

Pronunciation

Students check the pronunciation of some of the key words used in this unit.

Activity 46

- Ask students to supply one example for each sound listed here, e.g.:

/ʃ/	/ʒ/	/tʃ/	/dʒ/
extensions	0 words	chubby	damage

- Now students look for other words in the Word lists which contain these sounds. Then they listen to Track 48 and check their answers.

  Answers:

/ʃ/	/z/	/tʃ/	/dʒ/
extensions	0 words	chubby	damage
shiny		patch	generous
			gorgeous
			large
			major
			pudgy
			reject

Activity 47

- Students read through items *a–c*. Tell them to find the odd one out in each case. Remind them it could be something to do with sounds or stress.

  Answers:

  a voluptuous (because it has one more syllable than the others)

  b square (all the other words have the /i/ sound)

  c thick (all the other words have the /aɪ/ sound)

 **Workbook Activity 13** *can be used at any stage from now on.*

Activity 48

- [P] Students go through this task in pairs. When they have finished, ask each pair to report on *one* of the characters they have been working on.

▶ **Workbook Activities 14–17** *can be used at any stage from now on.*

UNIT 10 Heavy weather

Reading: *The Storm*

In this section, students read a narrative description of a storm and how people reacted to it.

Activity 1

- [SG] This is a pre-reading exercise which prepares students for the text which follows. Groups guess from these words what the topic of the text might be. Is it about food (espresso machine and pasta)? Or movie-making (reel of film, editors)? Or gardens (flower beds, frogs, water)? As with all such pre-reading activities, the aim is not for students to get the "right" answers, but to get them to think about what the possible subjects of the text they are going to read might be.
- Students read the text quickly and see if their guesses were correct.

Activity 2

- [P] Students read the text more closely. Allow enough time for this. The sentences given here form a summary of *The Storm*, but they need to be put in the right order.
  Answers:
  a 12   b 9   c 6   d 5   e 4   f 8   g 10   h 3
  i 2   j 7   k 11   l 1

Activity 3

- [I] Ask students to select and write down words and phrases from the text which tell you how Eleanor felt about the evening. Here are some examples:
  exciting   a terrific dinner   really beautiful
- (P) Ask the students to think of a meal they have enjoyed and tell each other about it, using similar expressions.

Activity 4

- [I] Ask the students to read the definitions *a–i* and find the words in the text that match them.
  Answers:
  a thunder   b roast   c intersection
  d staged   e flooded f streaming
  g soaked   h waded   i fabulous

Activity 5

- Ask the students to refer to the text and write down the answers to questions *a–j*.
  Answers:
  a ... because they liked the way it moved under their feet.
  b ... because they couldn't get home.
  c ... because the water was six inches deep in the room.
  d ... because he'd had to walk through the rain.
  e ... because there wasn't enough meat for everyone.
  f ... because dirt from the garden was flowing into it.
  g ... because the thunder and the rain were so loud.
  h ... because there was no electricity.
  i ... because they can compensate for low levels of light.
  j ... because when the electricity came on all the appliances in the house started up again.

Language in chunks

Students look at some of the idiomatic phrases used in the reading text.

Activity 6

- [I] Ask the students to read the text and write down the appropriate phrases.
  Answers:
  a carpet looked like it was floating; kids thought it looked like a water bed
  b to make it home
  c turned on *La Bohème* full volume
  d Now and then
  e we had bananas flambé by candlelight
  f they can compensate for the low level of light

Activity 7

- Elicit the six phrases from the students and see if anyone can give you a sentence for each one. You may have to give them suggestions for context (e.g. a power cut, a romantic dinner, etc.).
- Get students to suggest situations such as the ones above or others you may want to concentrate on.
- [P] Students write sentences. While they are doing this, go round the class offering help where appropriate.
- Students read their sentences out to the class. Give appropriate feedback.

Activity 8

- Ask students if they have noticed that the text is written in American English, and if so what told them this was the case.
- [SG] Students look through sentences *a–e* to try and see what makes these examples of American English.
- Go through the sentences with the class.
  Answers: a The phrase *started out the bedroom door* would be written as *started to come from the bedroom door*. b Words like *realize* and *apologize* are often written with a "z" in American English, whereas they are usually written with an "s" in British English. c The word *gotten* is an American English past participle, not used in British English. d *Backyard* and *yard* would be called *back garden* and *garden* in British English. e *I guess* is an American English equivalent of *I think*.

Activity 9

- Before tackling this exercise, brainstorm the different kinds of past tense with the class. Choose a common intransitive verb, e.g. *go*, and ask for sentences in as many past tense forms as possible. The result should be as follows:
  They went to school.—past simple
  They were going to school.—past continuous
  They had gone to school.—past perfect
  They had been going to school.—past perfect continuous
- Now students look for examples of these tenses in the reading text and list them under these past tense headings. Here are some examples:

Past simple	*got*
	started
	looked
	thought
	was
	arrived
Past continuous	*was floating*
	was running around
Past perfect	*had taken*
	had been stuck
	had gotten out
Past perfect continuous	*had been ... preparing*

- Ask students to say which is the most common tense in this narrative (past simple).

Activity 10

- To help students, brainstorm some key moments from the story and ask students to jot them down, e.g.:
  storm—house flooded—roads blocked—people forced to stay in house—14 for dinner—Francis makes pasta—loud music—lights go out—romantic candlelight—people sleep anywhere
- Now students use these notes to deliver a spoken summary of Eleanor's story. Choose a student to start. If he / she falters or gets something important wrong, ask another student to continue.

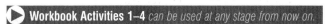
Workbook Activities 1–4 *can be used at any stage from now on.*

Speaking: consensus-reaching and role-play

Students practice discussing plans and ideas and reaching agreement.

Activity 11a

- Ask students to look at the picture and see if they recognize any of the dinner party guests (Queen Victoria, Shakespeare, Cleopatra).
- Ask the students individually to think of and write down the names of two people they would like to invite for dinner, then divide the class into groups of five.

Activity 11b

- [SG] The students then discuss their chosen guests in groups of five. Each group decides which five guests they want to invite from their lists. This should involve negotiation and debate, with each individual either defending their choice or making concessions, e.g.:
  s1: I've chosen Beyoncé. What about you?
  s2: I've chosen Shakira.
  s3: And I've gone for Britney.
  (*T suggests that they should choose one of these three singers.*)
  s1: Not Britney, okay?
  s2: I agree. So it's either Beyoncé or Shakira. What do you think?
  s3: I'd go for Beyoncé. She'd be more interesting than Shakira.
  s1: So it looks like Beyoncé. All right?
  s2: Yes, all right. Now what about our next choice? The point of these discussions is to get students to put forward an argument, defend their choices, but be prepared to make concessions.
- One spokesperson from each group reads out the five names. Is there any overlap between groups' choices or are all the choices different?

Activity 12a

- [SG] Still in groups of five, ask the students to consider the seating plan, explaining, perhaps with a diagram, what a seating plan is. What do they have to consider? Should like-minded people, say, pop stars or writers, sit together, or is it better to mix up people from different worlds?
- What kind of food is best? What kind of food would your guests like or not like? Is it better to serve food where each guest has his / her own plate with the food already on it? Or is it better to have food to which guests can help themselves and dishes you can pass around? Students can discuss the pros and cons of these alternatives, and write a menu. Compare the menus from each group.

Activity 12b

- [I] Brainstorm good / bad topics and list them on the board, discussing why they are, or are not, appropriate. Try to get students to strike a balance between topics that are 'safe' but not very interesting (the weather, your last holiday) and topics which are tricky but interesting (politics, animal rights, discipline in schools).

Activity 13

- [SG] The groups should by now have a range of interesting guests and (hopefully) a list of interesting topics. Groups join forces to role-play each other's guests. Set a time limit (say, five minutes) for a dinner-party conversation. Each role-player should make at least one contribution to the conversation.

Grammar: narrative (past simple, past perfect simple, past continuous, past perfect continuous)

Students look at the different kinds of past tense forms which they have encountered in the reading passage.

Activity 14a

- [I] Ask students to look at these pictures and write in the correct phrase from the box on each day.
  Answers:
  Monday: working out in the gym
  Tuesday: attending a long meeting
  Wednesday: arguing with her colleagues
  Thursday: visiting her parents
  Friday: driving too fast
  Saturday: watching sports on TV
  Sunday: partying till late the night before

Activity 14b

- [P] Go over the example with the class, then pairs produce similar questions and answers about the rest of Martha's week, e.g.:
  S1: Why was she stopped by the police on Friday?
  S2: Because she'd been driving too fast.

Activity 15

- Ask students to look at these pictures. What nearly happened to the woman in the first picture? To the man in the second picture?
- Now students look at this story and choose the better alternative to fill each of these gaps. Then they refer back to **10A–D in the Mini-grammar** to see if they want to change any of the choices they've made.
  Answers:
  a walked   b had been working
  c had only finished   d ~~gotten~~ had
  e called   f asked
  g had gone   h drove
  i had been talking   j nearly killed
  k was   l continued
  m felt   n was driving
  o noticed   p fell off
  q had braked   r had seen (*saw* is possible too)
  s just missed / had just missed   t woke up
  u had been having (*had had* is possible too)
  v looked   w was
  x had been (*was* is possible too)

Activity 16

- Go over the model answer. Students should refer to **10E in the Mini-Grammar** to decide how to join these verbs in a sentence.
  Answers:
  a Mary woke up, got out of bed, looked out of the window, and saw the tiger.
  b Sally was sitting at her desk talking on the telephone and drawing pictures on her notepad.
  c They had been there all day studying the pictures and deciding what to do with them.

d He took the ball from a player on the opposing team, ran past a defender, and shot the ball into the back of the net.

e She was writing a letter, listening to music, eating a cookie, and drinking a cup of coffee.

g They had been at the dinner table for an hour, laughing and enjoying each other's company, and talking about their vacation.

Activity 17

Possible answers:
a The frying pan is on fire.
b A man is delivering pizzas.
c They are drinking wine.
d They are waving goodbye.

Activity 18

- [SG] Tell students they are going to try and come up with a story that links all the pictures. Remind them of their answers to Activity 17.
- While students are discussing the pictures, go round the class giving help where appropriate.
- Ask one of the groups to tell their story. The other students should listen and see (a) if the story is the same as theirs, and (b) what they think is good and not-so-good about what they are hearing.
- Ask other students to comment on what they have heard, and to offer alternative versions of the story if they want. Give feedback, but remember that their story-telling fluency is as important as strict grammatical accuracy here.
  Possible version of the story: When the doorbell rang, Di and Vince opened the door to greet Jon and Judy who they had invited around to dinner. They went into the dining room and started to talk happily about the things that interested them. That was when Di smelt something burning. She rushed into the kitchen to find the frying pan on fire. The dinner was ruined. She apologized to her guests and, because there was no alternative, she called up a pizza delivery company. And so, instead of having Di and Vince's special dinner, the four friends had pizza—and a very good evening.

 Workbook Activities 5 & 6 *can be used at any stage from now on.*

Vocabulary: weather words

Here students look at words and phrases associated with the topic of this unit.

Activity 19

- [P] Students discuss where to put the words and phrases. When completed, the table should look like this:

	Least severe / Most severe	Associated verbs
rain	light shower, heavy shower, downpour, torrential rain	fall, pour, drizzle
snow	light snowfall, heavy snowfall, blizzard	fall, settle
sun	sunshine, strong sunshine, blazing sun	scorch, shine
wind	light breeze, breeze, strong breeze, strong wind, gale	blow, howl, roar, whistle

Activity 20
- Students choose the correct form of the verbs they have put into the table.
  Answers:
  a fell b pouring c blowing d roaring
  e drizzling f whistling g shining h settle
  i scorch j howling

Activity 21
- Students read this text quickly. If students don't know any of these words, they can use their dictionaries.
- [P] Students try to describe the weather in Tikan. What is the key word here? (Predictable.) How would they describe the summer weather / the winter weather? Now compare it to the weather in their country. Is it predictable? How does it differ from the weather of Tikan? Does it resemble the weather in Tikan in any way?
- [SG] Groups discuss these questions. Get feedback. Are there any constants, e.g. does everyone like warm, sunny weather? Does anyone like cold weather? As always, students should give reasons for their answers.

Activity 22a
- [P] Students look at the photo of the young woman. Ask them to say what they think of the dress she is wearing. What word would they use to describe it—*interesting, ridiculous, exciting, dramatic, silly*?
- Explain that the woman's name is Mary and she is a dress designer. Tell students that they are going to read a story about her.
- Students read the story and find the first example (*sunny*). What does *sunny* mean here? (*sunny* = "happy"). Ask students to say why *sunny* is associated with happiness.
- Then ask students to find the remaining weather words and say what they mean.
  Answers:
  showered = gave generously *gales* = strong bursts
  blazing = burning *thundered* = shouted
  stormed out = left in a temper
  thunderstruck = amazed
  thunderous = very loud *storm* = strong outbreak

Activity 22b
- [P] When pairs have written their sentences, ask them to read them out to the rest of the class.

 **Workbook Activities 7 & 8** *can be used at any stage from now on.*

Listening: *Stormy Weather*
Students read about a famous jazz singer then listen to one of her most famous songs.

Activity 23
- Ask students who their favourite singer is—man or woman. Explain that they are going to read about and listen to a very famous singer of the past called Billie Holiday.
- Students read the mini-biography and answer the questions.
  Answers:
  a Lester Young
  b Billie Holiday
  c many singers
  d Billie Holiday
  e Billie Holiday
  f Lester Young
  g Count Basie
  h a black victim of lynching

Activity 24
- Play Track 50 as many times as necessary for the students to write down the answers to the questions.
  Answers:
  a She's a TV continuity girl.
  b the music of the golden age of jazz ('30s–'50s)
  c because her grandfather played jazz records to her when she was young
  d her voice, the way she puts over the lyrics of a song
  e a songwriter
  f a woman who has broken up with her lover

Activity 25
- Play Track 50 again and focus the students' attention on the song.
- [P] Students discuss the song and exchange views. The teacher could help by suggesting words used to describe music, e.g. *blues, jazzy, tuneful, sweet, boring, sentimental, old-fashioned, moody*, etc. How do their views compare with the views of other pairs?

Activity 26
Answers:
a sun b sky c man d together e gloom
f everywhere g together h weary i away
j met k away l pray m walk n sun
o gone p man q together

Activity 27
Answers:
a what everyone likes
b as a child

c kind of
d her voice didn't go very high or very low
e communicates the words
f moves me
g I suddenly got very sad
h I'll just sit and do nothing

 Workbook Activities 9–11 *can be used at any stage from now on.*

Speaking and writing: shortening things

Activity 28a

- Divide these shortened sentences into those which are missing verbs and those which are missing pronouns. Ask students to find one example for each heading and say what the missing words are, e.g.:
  missing verbs—*(Do you have) any favorite kind of jazz?*
  missing pronouns—*(I) don't know why*
- [P] Now students write the other shortened sentences under these headings.

Activity 28b

- An apostrophe normally indicates that one or more letters are missing. Ask students to find an example of a normal word with an apostrophe, e.g. *can't, don't*. These are words that are used in everyday speech (and also sometimes in writing).
- But there are other words here which have apostrophes to indicate missing letters. Ask students to find examples of these (*rainin', mis'ry*). What are the missing letters in these words? (*g, e*)
- Now ask students to think why the songwriter chose to omit these letters. (Sometimes the letter is omitted because of the rhythm of the music and sometimes because of the dialect the singer is using.) Listen to the song again. Does the singer pronounce these missing letters?

Activity 29

- Students look through some of these scripts and find as many examples as possible of the kind of shortening of sentences that is illustrated in Activity 28.

Activity 30

- [P] Students role-play a conversation similar to that on Track 50, using the kind of sentence-shortening illustrated in Activity 29. Point out that this kind of shortening is not usually done in written English.

 Workbook Activity 12 *can be used at any stage from now on.*

Functional language: conversational gambits

Students learn how to structure a conversation, including interrupting, changing the subject, backing up another speaker's argument.

Activity 31

- Students try to complete the dialogue with one of the phrases listed here. Do the first example with the class: *a Yes, and what's more …*
- Then students try to fit the remaining phrases into the correct slots in the conversation.
  Answers:
  a Yes, and what's more …
  b Yes, and one shouldn't forget
  c On another topic altogether
  d Wait a minute, I'd just like to say …
  e I don't want to interrupt, but

Activity 32

- Ask students to find one phrase to go in each cell of the table.
- [P] Then ask them to fit the remaining phrases into the correct cells. When finished the table should look like this:

Reinforcing	on top of that (b) what's more (a) and as if that wasn't enough (c) and that's not all (c) furthermore (a) in addition (a) moreover (a)
Balancing	looking at it from another angle (b) one shouldn't forget (a) we should remember (a) yes, but on the other hand (c) yes, but there again (c)
Changing the subject	by the way, talking of (c) incidentally (b) moving swiftly on (c) on another matter altogether (b)
Interrupting	could I just say something? (b) excuse me (b) hold on a minute (c) I don't want to interrupt, but (b) if I could just get a word in edgewise (c) if I might just come in here (b) wait a minute (b)

- Ask students to decide which of these phrases are more likely to be used in conversation (informal) or in writing (formal) or either (neutral). The table above shows (a) more formal, (b) neutral, (c) less formal phrases.

Activity 33

- [SG] Demonstrate this simulation with one of the topics. Ask all students to write a sentence expressing their opinion of the weather (and referring in particular to the idea of global warming).
- Start with the example. Go over that, then ask students to write a sentence that demonstrates the other functions listed in the table students have just completed, e.g.:

Balancing—*One shouldn't forget that the weather is always changing.*
Changing the subject—*Talking of weather, we had terrible weather on our holiday this year.*
Interrupting—*Wait a minute. Have you any evidence that the weather is getting worse?*

- Now students work in groups to act out a conversation on some of the other topics listed here.

 Workbook Activities 13 & 14 *can be used at any stage from now on.*

Pronunciation: intonation

Students learn how intonation can be used to indicate how speakers feel about a proposal or an idea.

Activity 34

- Do the first example (a) with the class. How does the man sound in his first response? (He sounds reluctant, cautious.) Is he going to do what he's asked to? (He might, but possibly he won't.) Make sure students understand that it's because of the intonation he uses.
- Tell students they are going to listen to items *b–h*. They should say whether they think the man is going to do what the woman asks.
- Play Track 52. Students note down the answers.
- Let students compare their answers in pairs.
- Go through the items on Track 52 one by one.
  Answers:
  b He's not going to help. (falling intonation, low pitch)
  c He might help. (rising intonation at the end, high pitch)
  d He probably won't help. (sounds angry, falling intonation)
  e He might help. (sounds weak, high pitch, no definite fall)
  f He's trying to get out of it. (sounds reasonable, but low pitch and rise suggest he's very reluctant)
  g He might help, but he needs a reason. (genuine information question, marked pitch variation, rising intonation)
  h He probably won't help. (definite statement, low fall)

Activity 35

- Tell the students they are going to say the man's part and try to speak in the same way as he did.
- Play Track 53. Students should say the responses *a–h* when they hear the beep. Stop the audio. They will then hear the man again so that they can compare their efforts with his.

Writing: diaries

Students look at the style and content of personal diaries.

Activity 36

- [SG] Groups discuss these questions. If necessary, help to start the discussion by giving some possible answers to these questions.

Possible answers:
a To remember what they did
b Important events, personal observations
c Yes—many times!
d (Take your pick)

Activity 37

- [P] Students choose the best description for the diary.
  Answer: b

Activity 38

- [SG] Students work in groups of three, each student taking one of these dates and answering questions about it.
  Answers:
  April 15th
  a Mole's boss   b Mole
  c His bicycle was stolen.   d sarcastic
  May 24th
  a because of a dog that may be dangerous.
  b on the surface, friendly
  c that the dog will bite his face
  d related to what he thinks will happen if the dog bites him
  May 25th
  a Oxford
  b ride on the tops of buses, walk along looking upward and ask the way
  c sending them the wrong way
  d (*open-ended*)

Activity 39a

- [P] Brainstorm this from the whole class. Get a selection of things students did yesterday and write them in note form on the board, e.g.:
  —late for college
  —burned the toast
  —had coffee with Leïla
  —missed the last bus
- How could these notes be expanded into full sentences? Get students to work this out, e.g.:
  —Yesterday I was late for college.
  —I didn't have breakfast because I burned the toast.
  —In the afternoon I had coffee with my friend Leïla.
  —I stayed so long that I missed the last bus.

Activity 39b

- [P] Now students write about things they wished had happened yesterday. Encourage them to indulge their fantasies, e.g.:
  —Yesterday I beat Tiger Woods at golf.
  —I won $500,000 in the lottery.
  —Beyoncé asked me for a date.
  —Someone gave me two tickets for the Cup Final.

Activity 39c

- Staying in pairs, students decide on a famous character and try to imagine his / her day. Then they write a diary entry similar to the fantasy entry they've just completed.

 Workbook Activities 15–18 *can be used at any stage from now on.*

Review: grammar and functional language

Students review the key language introduced in this unit.

Activity 40

- This activity reviews the different forms of the past tense used in this unit. Students draw up a table and write each verb in this story in the appropriate row. When completed, the table should look like this:

Past simple told said was were had finished would thought took off reached got pulled stopped passed went down detached came hit passed swore
Past continuous was walking
Past perfect had tried had been had bought hadn't stopped hadn't made it up
Past perfect continuous had been walking

- Then students should find the sentences that have one subject with more than one verb.
  Answers:
  1 he was walking along a street ... thinking, smoking
  2 he took off his gloves, reached into ... got a pack ... pulled out
  3 ice detached itself ... and came crashing down
- Students see how much of the story they can remember. Although correct tense usage is important, the point of this exercise is to see whether students can recall the main points, i.e. the gist, of the story.

Activity 41

- [P] First, get students to produce a variety of requests, e.g.:
  "Could you help me ... ?"
  "I wonder / was wondering if you could help me ... ?"
  "Is there any chance you might help me ... ?"
- Then ask for a similarly varied set of responses. Remember that these responses should indicate *by their intonation* that the speaker is not very keen to help. Here are some examples:
  "Well ..."
  "Sure ..."
  "I don't know ..."
  "That depends ..."
  "I'm a little busy right now ..."

Review: vocabulary

Students check the vocabulary used in this unit.

Activity 42

- [P] This is a development of Activity 21b, where students were asked to say what their favorite weather was. Here, however, students have to be more specific about the weather they like. They also have to say what they like to do in this kind of weather—walk, dance, sunbathe, swim, ski? They talk in similar terms about weather they don't like. Suppose you don't like

cold, wet weather. What do you do in such weather—go to the gym, play tennis at your local sports centre, watch television, play computer games, read? Students share their ideas on these subjects with their partners.
- [P] In the same way, students share their word preferences with their partners.

Pronunciation

Students check the pronunciation of some of the key words used in this unit.

Activity 43

- Go over the example with students. Ask them to find another vowel, say /əʊ/, and find words that have this sound in their stressed syllable, e.g.:
  show, blow, snowfall, roast, soaked
- Now students look for words in the Word lists which contain other vowel sounds, for example, /eɪ/ or /aʊ/, and make a list of all the words that contain this sound. Then they listen to Track 54 and check their answers.
  Answers:
  /eɪ/ as in *day*: *blazing, gale, staged, waded*
  /əʊ/ as in *show*: *blow, snowfall, roast, soaked*
  /iː/ as in *see*: *breeze, stream*
  /aʊ/ as in *how*: *downpour, shower, howl*
  /ɔː/ as in *saw*: *fall, pour, roar, scorch*
  /ʌ/ as in *fun*: *flooded, sunshine, thunder, thunderstruck*
  /e/ as in *pet*: *heavy, settle, torrential*
  /aɪ/ as in *might*: *light, shine*

Activity 44

- Get students to give you one word for each of these sound clusters to start the table off.

a	b	c	d	e
/bl/	/br/	/dr/	/zəl/	/fl/
blazing, blizzard, blow	breeze	drizzle	drizzle	flooded

f	g	h	i
/kr/	/kʃ/	/str/	/pr/
crossed	intersection	stream, strong, thunderstruck	protest, presents

- Finally, students listen to Track 55 to check their answers.

Activity 45

- [SG] Students should make up their own story about a weather situation, and write it down. This may be true or fictitious.
- Groups present their story to the rest of the class. Which is the most interesting? Which is the most believable?

Workbook Activities 19–22 *can be used at any stage from now on.*

UNIT 11 Famous for 15 minutes?

Reading: reality TV

In this section, students read about the phenomenon of reality TV.

Activity 1

- [P] This is a pre-reading exercise which prepares students for the text which follows. Three different types of reality TV show are introduced here. Students read the texts and complete them with words from the box.

  Answers:

a criticized	b eliminated
c deal with	d betraying
e reveal	f humiliated

- Ask students if they have seen any reality TV shows similar to the ones described here.

Activity 2

- [SG] Students discuss these questions and make their decisions. Outline a possible scenario to give students an idea of what they might do, e.g.:
  - a the army
  - b the contestants have to pass a series of survival tests
  - c the winner would be the one who performed best in the test.
- [SG] Now let students draw up a similar scenario for one of the other areas of life suggested here.

Activity 3

- Ask students to read Julie Marsfield's *Opinion* column and complete the table with the information they find there. When completed, the table should look like this:

a	b	c	d
Shows that go into someone's home	Shows that put people into an unusual situation	Shows where people talk about their personal problems	Shows where people go on dates with strangers
The Osbournes	*Joe Millionaire The Real World Pop Idol Survivor*	*Jerry Springer Judge Judy*	*Blind Date Elimidate*

Activity 4

- Students now go on to read the article more closely and answer series of comprehension and vocabulary questions about it.

  Answers:

a F	b T	c F	d T	
e T	f F	g F	h T	i T

Activity 5

Answers:

a making money from something
b the number of people who watch TV shows
c feature / have in the central role
d keen
e invented and made
f likely to cause arguments
g dangerous, embarrassing
h occasions when they are seen by the public

▶ Workbook Activities 1–3 *can be used at any stage from now on.*

Language in chunks

Students look at some of the idiomatic phrases used in the reading text.

Activity 6

Answers:

a to reveal all
b jumped at the chance
c no qualms about
d no limits as to
e were reassured
f With the growth of
g one by one

Activity 7

- [P] Have students look back at the text to find the four verbs from the box. They should try to work out what they mean.
- Go through the answers with the class.

  Answers:

  get along with = like / tolerate each other
  give away = offer for free
  look at = consider
  take off = become successful or popular
  Other phrasal verbs:
  deal with   open up

- Ask the class if they find these verbs easy to understand, and if not, why not. Ask them to say why they think the verbs might be difficult to understand. Explain that the difference between these verbs and other verbs in the text is that we often can't guess the meaning of phrasal (or multiword) verbs, even though we know, separately, the meaning of each word (e.g. *get*, *along* and *with*).

Activity 8

- [I/P] Having read about reality TV shows, students give their opinions about some of the issues raised in the article. They can either work individually or in pairs for this.
- When the tables have been completed, take a poll of the class. Find out how many would be willing to go on a reality TV show. Ask students to give reasons for their choice.

Vocabulary: fame and notoriety

Students look at words associated with negative and positive ways of talking about fame.

Activity 9

- Ask students to say what kind of words these are (nouns). You may need to explain some of them, or get the students to look them up in the dictionary. Then students decide which of these nouns have a related adjective or verb. Do a couple of examples with the class to get them started.
  Answers:

	Adjective	Verb
celebrity	celebrity	to celebrate
eminence	eminent	–
fame	famous / famed	–
infamy	infamous	–
legend	legendary	–
notoriety	notorious	–
renown	renowned	–
star	star	to star
stardom	star	to star
superstar	–	–

- Ask students to think about which of these adjectives express a positive attitude towards fame, and which express a negative attitude towards fame. This is an issue which will be dealt with further in Activity 11.

Activity 10

Possible answers:
a notoriety
b celebrity
c name
d fame
e eye
f name
g headlines
h name
i VIP (celebrity) ... well known
j famous

Activity 11

- [P] Ask students to look at these sentences and pick out an example of each of these categories, e.g.:
  neutral—*world-famous*; negative—*notoriety*.
- Now students look through the rest of the sentences and decide which expressions fit into which category.
  Answers:

a neutral	b negative	c neutral
d neutral	e neutral	f neutral
g neutral	h neutral	i negative
j neutral	k neutral	

Activity 12

- [SG] If you have pictures of people who come into these categories, show them to students to start them off. Groups can pool their knowledge and see how many names they can come up with in each category. These can be living or dead people. Here are some current examples:

a Nigel Kennedy, Vanessa Mae
b Beyoncé, Sting, Bono
c Tiger Woods, Hisham El Garrouj, David Beckham
d Colin Powell, Wesley Clark

- Which of these people could be described using neutral or positive words, and which using negative words? Students choose a person from their list and ask students from other groups to describe him / her:
  S1: David Beckham.
  S2: He's a world-famous footballer.
    Colin Powell.
  S1: He's a celebrated army general.

Activity 13

- [SG] All of these people are, or have been, famous. Groups discuss these people and answer the questions about them. Additional questions might be:
  "Which of these people are singers?"
  "Which are film stars?"
  "Is any of these people a politician?"
  "Is any of these people a scientist?"
- See which group knows most people. Which group knows most about them?

Activity 14

- Ask students to look at the words and phrases in the box. Which do they understand and which are unclear to them?
- Help them with explanations, e.g. *a dime a dozen* = "very common and very cheap," *in your face* = "very obvious, right in front of you," *(it's) open season* = "anything is permitted."
- Students read through the comments of the stars and identify which words and phrases go in the blanks.
  Answers:
  a in your face
  b a dime a dozen
  c drawbacks ... compensations
  d heroes ... villains
  e image
  f pressure
  g taking it as it comes
  h go to my head
  i open season

Workbook Activities 4 & 5 *can be used at any stage from now on.*

Grammar: phrasal verbs

Students learn how two- or three-part phrasal verbs function in sentences.

Activity 15

- Students look at the sentences (*a–h*) and match them with the meanings (*1–8*). While they are doing this, go round the class helping where appropriate.
- Go through the answers with the students.

Answers:
a 4   b 1   c 6   d 3
e 8   f 2   g 5   h 7

- Now ask students to look at **11A–11C in the Mini-grammar** to see if they identify which type of verb (1 or 2) the verbs are. Make sure students understand the difference between transitive (the verbs take an object) and intransitive (they don't take an object).
- Go through the answers with the students. Make sure they understand that a transitive verb (e.g. *pull down*) can be used both actively and passively (as in example *b* here) and that objects can be made up from gerunds (e.g. *solving the problem*).
  Answers:
  Type 1: took off, blew up, work out, break up
  Type 2: pulled down, turned down, let down, put off

Activity 16

- [P] Students work in pairs to match words and meanings. Do the first example with the class.
  Answers:
  a 8   b 2   c 7   d 5   e 6   f 3   g 4   h 1
- [P] Students sort these verbs into Type 1 and Type 2 verbs.
  Answers:
  Type 1: come by, speak up
  Type 2: work out, pick out, bring up, point out, take in, write off
- [P] Follow the instructions here. See how many pairs match the phrasal verbs and synonyms correctly.

Activity 17

Answers:
a comes by   b pick ... out
c brought ... up   d speak up
e work out   f took ... in
g write ... off   h pointed out

Activity 18

- Go over these sections of the **Mini-grammar (11D and 11E)**. Type 3 = inseparable verbs, Type 4 = inseparable three-word verbs.
- Students write the verbs in this activity under the correct heading.
  Answers:
  Type 3: look for, fall for, take after, look after
  Type 4: put up with, look forward to

Activity 19

- [I] Have students match the verbs (*a–f*) with their meanings (*1–6*).
- Go through the answers with the students. Point out that *take after* (*d5*) is generally used to talk about people and their parents, grandparents, aunts and uncles.
  Answers:
  a 4   b 1   c 2   d 5   e 6   f 3

Activity 20

Answers:
a ran into
b got along with
c looking down on
d paying ... back
e check up on
f look into
g came across

Activity 21

- [P] Students discuss these sentences and agree on how to complete them, e.g.:
  "At work / school, I'm not prepared to put up with ... bullying / laziness / being late."
  "I'm looking forward to ... the holidays / Christmas / a pay raise."
  "In my family, people say I take after ... my father / my mother / my aunt / my uncle" OR "I don't take after anyone."

Activity 22

- [SG] Divide the class into small groups and carry out the activity as suggested in the Student's Book instructions.

 Workbook Activities 6–9 *can be used at any stage from now on.*

Functional language: checking and confirming

Students learn about the different functions of questions in conversation.

Activity 23

- Ask students to look at the picture. Who are these people? What are they doing?
- Now students listen to Track 56 and find out if their answers were correct. Ask a few simple questions—how many people are speaking? how many men / women?
- Then students listen to the track more carefully and fill in the spaces in the script.
  Answers:
  a right? [2]
  b Does that mean ... ? [3]
  c doesn't it? [1]
  d yeah? [2]
  e aren't we? [1]
  f is this gonna (going to) [3]

Activity 24

- Ask students to find an example of each question type in the Audioscript, e.g.:
  Type 1—*doesn't it?*
  Type 2—*yeah?*
  Type 3—*Does that mean we only have ten days?*
- Students match the rest of the questions on the track to the appropriate type.

Answers (see also the notes for Activity 23):
1 And it starts at 7, doesn't it?
  And we're doing ten songs, aren't we?
2 Friday, right?
  And we're playing for an hour, yeah?
3 Does that mean we only have ten days?
  So, is this gonna make us famous?

Activity 25
Answers:
a 2 b 1 c 2 d 3 e 1 f 2 g 3
h 1 i 3 j 1 k 2

Activity 26
- Ask students to read through the sentences. Let them ask you about any words they don't understand.
- Tell students they are going to practice the question types they looked at in Activities 23–25. They should use as many different kinds as they can.
- [P] Students practice their conversations. While they are doing this, go round the class offering help where appropriate.
- Listen to a few of the "conversations" with the whole class, giving appropriate feedback.

Workbook Activities 10 & 11 *can be used at any stage from now on.*

Activity 27
- [P] Students work in pairs to talk about the information in Activity Bank 21. First, Student A asks B about the information in the posters, etc., and then they swap roles.

Pronunciation: intonation in tag questions

Activity 28
- Students listen to Track 57. Ask whether the speakers' voices are going up or down when they ask these questions. Ask students to look at what the speakers are saying. Is there any pattern to whether they use a particular intonation? What does a falling intonation indicate? (Generally, certainty: you just want to have what you think confirmed.) What does a rising intonation indicate? (Generally, uncertainty: you don't know if what you've said is correct or not.)
- Students listen to the track again and decide which speakers want confirmation of what they know and which are genuinely unsure of the answer.

Activity 29
- Students listen to the speakers again and try to copy their intonation.

Activity 30
- Students first add the correct question tags to these statements.
  Answers:
  a isn't it?   b is he?
  c don't they?   d do they?
  e haven't you?   f have they?

- [P] Students practice this conversation in pairs, concentrating on getting the intonation of the tags right. Then they listen to Track 58 and see how well they did.
- Finally, pairs try to improve their performance. Which pair can come closest to the intonation of the speakers on the track?
- Note here that many non-native speakers of English use *isn't it?* as the question tag for any statement, e.g.:
  She's beautiful, isn't it?
  They're hungry, isn't it?

Listening: Diana's story
Students listen to the story of Diana, a young woman from India, and make notes about what they hear.

Activity 31
- This is a pre-listening exercise, a warm-up for the listening text that follows. Students look at the picture of Diana and speculate about her, e.g.:
  S1: She looks Indian.
  S2: Or Pakistani?
  S3: Of course, she might be from Britain.
  S1: Yes, she might.
  S2: Do you think she's a film star?
  S1: No, she just looks ordinary.
  S2: But she is beautiful, isn't she?
  S1: Yes, she is.

Activity 32
- Ask students to read these questions quickly. Apart from guessing the answer to the first question, they will probably not be able to answer them. That's all right. But these are the questions they should have in mind when they're listening to Diana's story.
- Now students listen to Track 59 and find the answers.
  Answers:
  a Hyderabad
  b Her parents split up.
  c She knocked on people's doors.
  d 7.30
  e because she felt sorry for Diana
  f You can succeed if you really try.

Activity 33
- Brainstorm suggestion as to what Diana went on to become, e.g.:
  a film star
  a singer
  a writer
  a politician
- Students listen to Track 60 and find the answer (a beauty queen).

Activity 34

- Students listen to Track 60 more carefully and make notes on these questions as they listen.
  Answers:
  —What Diana was afraid of: she was afraid of tripping because she was wearing high heels.
  —The number of people: millions.
  —How she felt: numb.
  —What she did: she kept the crown near her bed so that she would see it when she woke up in the morning.
  —What happened: she couldn't stop grinning.

Activity 35

Answers:

a something you're very nervous about, almost afraid to face

b We're scared, amazed or very emotional. The woman Diana quotes uses a Pakistani English version (leaving out *on end*), meaning she is really amazed and emotional.

c a lot of effort

d stumble or make mistakes in your speech

e no

f fantastically happy

g ordinary

h take care of or accompany someone (usually a child or a young woman)

i the place at the front of an aeroplane where a pilot sits

Activity 36

- [SG] Students work in groups for this. One member of the group starts telling the story, then hands over to another. Then the whole group performs their version of the story for the rest of the class.

Activity 37

- [P/SG] Students discuss these questions in pairs or small groups and compare their responses to those of other groups. There is a good opportunity for a debate here, as many people hold strong opinions about beauty competitions like the one Diana won.
  S1: I think beauty competitions are awful. Girls walking up and down for men to stare at. It's degrading.
  S2: Nonsense. It's just a bit of fun. Anyway, everyone likes to look at a beautiful woman.
  S1: Why don't they have beauty competitions for men?
  S2: But they do.
  S1: Well, if you entered …
  T: Thank you, I think we'll stop there for the moment.

Workbook Activities 12–15 *can be used at any stage from now on.*

Speaking: decision-making (making a star)

Students get information about different pop groups and decide which one is worth backing.

Activity 38

- [P] Students look at the pictures of these groups. Ask them to find words or phrases that sum up their first impression of how these groups look, e.g.:
  "These guys look kind of dirty."
  "He looks boring."
  "I'm not into rap—too aggressive."
  "These girls are country singers—I like country music."

Activity 39

- [SG] Now groups discuss these acts in more detail. Give each group one act to promote and leave one group to study the pros and cons of all the groups—they will be the record producers at the next stage of the activity. What are the good points about their act they need to push? Are there any criticisms they need to defend their act against? Suggest that each group draw up a list of pros and cons for their act. They should take their ammunition from the information set out in Activity 38.

- Now go on to the record producer role-play outlined here. The record producer group interviews the 'managers' of the six acts featured here. Both groups should make full use of the various tag, checking and confirming questions presented earlier in this unit. Here is a sample interchange:
  The Brainstormers
  MANAGER: The Brainstormers are a terrific band. They really rock. They're tough and rebellious—just what the kids want today, right?
  RECORD PRODUCER 1: Maybe, but the kids don't buy records these days. Their parents buy records and they don't like grungy rockers, do they? They want something with a tune, don't they?
  MANAGER: But that's just it. The Brainstormers are like the new Rolling Stones, don't you think?
  RECORD PRODUCER 2: But the people who buy records want the old Rolling Stones, OK? Let's have the next act.

Writing: researching for writing

In this section, students learn how to find information about a person and how to use this information to write about him / her.

Activity 40

- [I/P] Students work in pairs for this activity. Each student completes this table with their responses. Then students compare their answers. How similar / different are their responses?

Activity 41

- First, students find the information about Jackie Chan. How is this information organized in headings *a–k*? (Out of its order in time.) How is this information presented in the text? (In the order in which these events occurred.)

- When they have found the information they need about Jackie Chan, students number the items of information in the order in which they appear in the article.
- This information can be presented in an information table. Draw up the framework for such a table and ask students to complete the first row. When completed, the table should look like this:

	Topics	Information	number
a	Date of birth	1954	2
b	Early career	stuntman	8
c	How famous	famous all over the world	11
d	What he learned	how to perform stunts	7
e	What he thought of school	hated it	5
f	Position today	biggest Hong Kong film star in Hollywood	10
g	What made him famous	adding comedy	9
h	Where he studied	China Drama Academy	6
i	Where he was born	Hong Kong	1
j	Where he went to school	Hong Kong	4
k	Who his parents were	cook / housekeeper	3

Word Choice: *at the moment, at present, at this moment in time, at this time, currently, these days, today*

Activity 42

- Go over these notes with the class. Explain any difficulties.

Activity 43

Possible answers:
a At the moment
b At present
c These days
d at the moment
e Today
f currently
g At this moment in time
h At present
i At the moment

Activity 44

- Students should write out the headings *a–k* used in the activity about Jackie Chan, i.e. date of birth, etc. They should then write the information presented here against the correct heading. Are all the Jackie Chan headings needed here? If not, which can be omitted?

Possible answers:
a 2/2/77
b wrote songs aged 8; first record deal aged 13
c worldwide
g personal style, with many influences
i Barranquilla, Colombia
k father Lebanese; mother Colombian
Headings d, e, f, h and j could be omitted.

- Now students work up these notes into a short biographical paragraph about Shakira similar in style to the biography of Jackie Chan in Activity 41. This can be set as a home task. Students can then bring their biographies to class and read them out.

Activity 45

- [SG] Each group should choose a celebrity. First, they need to discuss and debate who this should be. There's plenty of scope for argument, concession and negotiation here. Groups should compile notes that can be used in writing a biography of their celebrity.
- Then students use these notes to write a biography. This is a major writing task and students should be given adequate time to produce their biographies.

 **Workbook Activities 16 & 17** *can be used at any stage from now on.*

Review: grammar and functional language

Students review the key language introduced in this unit.

Activity 46

- [P] Students refer to earlier activities before completing this revision exercise.
  Answers:
  a put up with
  b to look for
  c fall for; break up
  d take after
  e brought up
  f turned down
  g looking forward to
  h picked out
- [SG] Groups discuss these statements. What do they think of them? Whether they agree or disagree with these opinions, they should give reasons for their opinions. They can also cite examples of famous people to back their case.

Activity 47

- [I/P] Students work on their own to complete this list of the drawbacks and compensations of fame. Then they compare their list with that of their partner. The examples give each student a start.
- The final table could look like this (but there is scope for more features in each section).

Drawbacks
lack of privacy   media speculation   people want you to fail   everyone wants you to do something for them

Compensations
money   being recognized   being a role model popularity   hanging out with other celebrities

Review: vocabulary

Students check the vocabulary used in this unit.

Activity 48

• [P] Students work in pairs to draw up a list of words and expressions they could use here. The example can be used to start students off.

Pronunciation

Students check the pronunciation of some of the key words used in this unit.

Activity 49a

• Here, students copy and complete the table with words containing the vowel sounds /ʊ/ and /uː/.
Sample answers:

/ʊ/—pull	/yu/—dispute
reassured	euphoria
put	humiliate
look	

Activity 49b

• Demonstrate this game with students. Do the example, then choose another phrasal verb, e.g.:
T: der DER der der
S1: *Get along with*?
T: No.
S2: *Look forward to.*
T: Yes. Can you do *get along with*?
S1: der der DER der
T: That's right!

Activity 50

• Students complete the dialogue with words and phrases from the list, adapting them slightly if necessary.
Answers:
a put up with
b a dime a dozen
c image
d star
e criticized
f in his face
g open up
h betraying
i reveal
j puts me off
k eliminated

 **Workbook Activities 18–21** *can be used at any stage from now on.*

UNIT 12 Writing and writers

Vocabulary: writing, books and authors

In this section, students read about different authors and about how to become an author.

Activity 1

- [P] This is a pre-reading exercise which prepares students for the text which follows. Students read about a number of different authors and look for similarities between them.
- First, ask students to look at the photos of these authors and make some guesses about what kind of books these authors write. They can also guess what these authors did before they wrote the novels they are famous for.
- Now students read about these authors and complete the descriptions with words from the box.
  Answers:
  a prolific   b best-selling
  c twists   d prize-winning
  e background   f acclaimed
  g characters   h adapted
  i plot

Activity 2

- [SG] Students find similarities between these writers. First, they are all novelists. Students should think of different types of characteristics, e.g nationality, type of novel written, gender, popularity. Which of these seem the most important? (Type of novel?) Which is least important? (Gender?) Here's a possible way of grouping writers.
  Possible answers:
  American—King, Grisham, Tan, Walker
  Thriller writers—King, Grisham
  Multicultural—Smith, Tan, Walker, Allende
- There are, of course, other ways of grouping these writers. Encourage groups to find other links and to explain these to the rest of the class.
- [P] What kind of novel do students like to read—thrillers, horror stories, stories of family life, romances?

Activity 3

- [SG] Ask students to discuss these questions. The first question is the easiest—most people would like to write a book—but what kind of book? A novel (then what kind of novel)? A biography (of whom)? A travel book (where)?
- Now students read about how to write a book and get it published. Return to the questions after they have read the text.

Activity 4

Answers:
a characters, plot, twists, draft, themes, narrative structure
b to pen, to author
c prolific, acclaimed, best-selling, prize-winning, respected
d research, basic outline, draft, first version, editing process, completed manuscript
e author, publisher, editor
f autobiography, novel, travel book, poetry, horror, romance

- Encourage students to add as many words to the word map as they can.

Activity 5

- Some English words can be used as both nouns and verbs. Sometimes these words are differentiated by stress. For example, 'research is a noun, re'search is a verb.
- Now students read this text and fill the spaces with verbs derived from nouns.
  Answers:
  a authored   b penned   c outlined
  d draft   e twisted   f plotting

Activity 6

- This activity can be done in class or set as a homework task. Tell students to look in their dictionaries and find words that are listed as both nouns and verbs. Explain that this usually means two different entries for the same spelling—so that should give them a clue.
- [P/SG] Students look through their dictionaries. To make sure you get a range, have some of them start at the beginning, while others start at the end. Still others start somewhere in the middle, going forwards, and others start in the middle going backwards. While they are doing this, go round offering help where appropriate.

Activity 6a

- [P] Tell students to write sentences using their words as both nouns and verbs. Set a time limit for this.
- Find out who has written the most sentences.

Activity 6b

- [P] Students now read their sentences to another pair and also tell them which word to focus on. The other pair says whether it's a noun or a verb.

 **Workbook Activities 1 & 2** *can be used at any stage from now on.*

Reading: the blurb

Students read blurbs—summaries of books which are intended to attract readers to buy the book.

Activity 7

- First, ask students if they know what a blurb is. If not, ask them to scan these sentences and see if they can find what the word means.
- Ask students if they read books (apart from textbooks like this, of course). How many students read for pleasure? What kind of books do they read? Conduct a straw poll to see how many of the class are readers and what kind of books they read.
- [P] Assuming that some at least of your students read, ask them to check the way people choose what books, magazines or newspapers to read. Which of these apply to them? Pairs compare their responses. What do the rest of the class think?

Activity 8

- Students read the text of this blurb. Help the class by asking questions about the content of the blurb, e.g.:
  T: What does this blurb contain?
  S1: A summary of the novel.
  T: Is it a summary of the whole novel?
  S2: No.
  T: Why not?
  S3: Because if it was a summary of the whole novel, you wouldn't need to read it.
  T: So what is it a summary of?
  S1: The beginning of the story.
- In the same way, ask about the rest of the blurb. "What does it tell you about?" (The author.) "What else is there?" (Reviews of the book.) "Are they good reviews?" (Yes.) "Why are they printed here?" (To make you want to read the book.)

Activity 9

- Now students read the blurb more carefully and say who did these things.
  Answers:
  a Will's father
  b Marcus's Mum
  c Will
  d Marcus
  e Marcus's Mum
  f Nick Hornby
  g Will
  h Marcus

Activity 10

- [SG] Students discuss the book and say whether they think they would like it. They should give reasons for their opinions. If they don't like the sound of *About a boy*, ask them what kind of book they would rather read—a thriller, a romance, a science fiction story? Or would they prefer a factual book—historical, technical, travel?

Activity 11

Answers:
a the large area of land near an island
b unfashionable
c very happily
d huge
e sports shoes
f what someone used to do or be
g gives us
h certain
i trying hard

▶ **Workbook Activities 3–5** *can be used at any stage from now on.*

Language in chunks

Students look at idiomatic phrases used in the text they have just read.

Activity 12

Answers:
a 3   b 2   c 7   d 5   e 4   f 1   g 6

Activity 13

Answers:
a settled down   b to face up to
c from a mile off   d figure of fun
e awe-inspiring   f relate to
g didn't mind admitting it

Activity 14

- [SG] First students identify the relative clauses, and then the relative pronouns—*which, where, who.*
- Then students need to think about why we use different relative pronouns.
  Answers:
  We use different pronouns to refer to different kinds of things.
  We use *which* to refer to a thing (*song*); we use *where* to refer to a place (*apartment in London*); we use *who* to
  refer to a person (*mother*).
- Now ask students to go back to the text of the blurb and find other relative pronouns. What or who do they refer to?
  Answers:
  There is one more example of a relative clause with a pronoun:
  someone who knows what kind of running shoes he should wear (in which *who* refers back to *someone*).
  If students ask, you can explain that *who* in ... *who Kurt Cobain is* is not a relative pronoun, but an interrogative pronoun.
  There is also a relative clause with the pronoun omitted: [*that*] *every man struggling to face up to his responsibilities will relate to.*

Activity 15

- This is a jigsaw reading activity. Two students read different texts and so have different sets of information.

- Students choose one of these blurbs. When they have done this, ask students to sit with someone else who has read the same blurb.
- [P] Students prepare a summary of their blurb with their partner. As far as possible, students should rely on their memory of what they have read.
- [SG] Now students work with other pairs who have read the other blurb. They listen to their description of their blurb and make notes. They then write up a blurb based on what they have heard and written down.
- Now students read the other blurb—the one they haven't read yet. How does it compare with what they have written? What are the differences—are they matters of fact or of style? How different is the language of their reconstruction of the blurb and the language of the blurb itself?

Listening: books and movies

Students listen to an extract from the book *White Teeth* and consider the differences between a novel and an adaptation of a novel for the screen.

Activity 16

- [P] Students work in pairs to discuss these questions. Many movies are based on books, but here students should be thinking of famous books which were made into movies, e.g. *The Lord of the Rings* and books featuring Harry Potter or James Bond. Sometimes people think that the book is better than the film, others prefer the movie to the book. What do students think? Were they ever disappointed by a movie of a book they enjoyed?

Activity 17

- [I] Explain that *White Teeth* is set in London but has a cast of characters drawn from different countries and diverse ethnic backgrounds. Students read the summary of the story of the book and answer the questions.
  Answers:
  a Archie and Samad
  b Clara
  c Archie and Clara's daughter
  d Alsana
  e twin sons of Samad and Alsana
  f Samad
  g Magid
  h Archie

Activity 18

- Students read these scenes from the screenplay for *White Teeth* and think about the relationship between the characters.
  Possible answers:
  Millat and Magid are brothers so they argue with each other. Samad and Archie are friends—they help each other when there's trouble.

Activity 19

- [SG] Suggest that students act out these scenes. Groups decide who is going to play which part. Students should be given time to study their part and rehearse it. Each group can present their version of these scenes to the rest of the class.
- [SG] Ask groups to think about how these scenes will be presented on film. For example, in the first scene, do we see the scene from the point of view of Archie or Samad? Do we start with a long shot of Samad approaching Archie and then move to a close-up of the two men? Groups can discuss what should appear on the screen and make sketches of what the screen will look like for each scene.

Activity 20

- [SG] There are a number of differences between a novel and a screenplay. These questions focus on the most important. Students listen to the extract from the novel and compare it to the scenes they have just acted out.
  Answers:
  a Scene 25: In the book, Archie does not explain about the children until Samad has seen the children in the back of the car.
     Scene 27: Irie waking up and starting to cry.
  b Archie's explanation of why he had to bring the other children, the children calling Samad "Daddy" instead of "Abba."
  c ARCHIE: That's what friends are for, Sam, but I have to tell you something.
     IRIE: I want to go home.
     MILLAT: Shut up about your stupid plants!
  d SAMAD: I won't forget what you do for me tonight, my friend.
     MILLAT: Will he come back? It would be cool if he didn't come back.
     SAMAD: And then when we get there, Magid— Magid—
     ARCHIE: Come on. We've got to get cracking if we're going to make it.
     SAMAD: Now sit back in your seats, go on. For Abba, please.
- [SG] Students discuss these questions in groups. Ask groups for their reactions. Do most groups agree or are there major differences between them?

Activity 21

Answers:
a F   b T   c T   d T   e F   f T   g F

Activity 22

- [P/SG] Students read the text of Track 61 and follow these instructions. Make a note of the words you think your students will find most difficult. See if your expectations correspond to what your students chose.

 Workbook Activities 6–9 *can be used at any stage from now on.*

Speaking: telling a story

Students organize pictures so as to make an effective story.

Activity 23

- [I] Students can discuss each picture and think about what is happening in each one. Then, individually, they attempt to put the pictures in order to tell a story. If they are having difficulty with the task, you can tell them that it is about someone suffering from loss of memory (amnesia). Remind them that they can make notes but they shouldn't write down the whole story.

  Possible answers: e, a, d, b, c, f

Activity 24

- [P] students tell each other their version of the story and then create a version that they both like.

  Possible answer:

  One day, Mary went shopping. While she was getting a can, a larger can fell off the top shelf and hit her on the head. For a moment she was unconscious, and when she came to she couldn't remember who she was.

  She walked out of the supermarket and straight into an army recruitment centre where she joined the army. Her husband and her children were left at home sad and unhappy.

  A few weeks after she joined the army, she fell off a climbing frame and hit her head. Suddenly she remembered her husband and her children. She went to her commanding officer and explained the situation. He allowed her to leave the army, and she got home to her family.

Activity 25

- Select individual pairs to tell their version of the story to the whole class.

Grammar: relative clauses

Students learn about different kinds of relative clause, including the use of different relative pronouns to introduce them.

Activity 26

- [P] Students begin this section by identifying the relative pronouns and the relative clauses which they introduce. Go over the example with the whole class, then pairs find the relative pronouns and clauses in the remaining sentences.

  Answers:

  a that we ate at the restaurant
  b where we went on vacation
  c that I drank from the kitchen sink
  d who lives next door
  e whose children were at the gym
  f when I was very tired and couldn't sleep

Activity 27

Answers:

a that = object
b where = object
c that = object
d who = subject
e whose (children) = subject
f when = object

Activity 28

Answers:

a The child who was at the party was asleep.
b The pie I made has a lot of calories.
c My mother grew up in a city where the prime minister was born.
d My aunt remembers the time when there used to be no computers.
e That is the child whose parents are very athletic.
f Did you see the place where I used to live?

- Students check their answers against **Mini-grammar 12A–B.**

Activity 29

- [SG] Students work in groups for this. Brainstorm some ideas for the first example, e.g.:

  "A city is a place where … anything can happen / people get mugged / there's a lot of excitement / there are too many people / there's too much traffic / there's a lot of things to do."

- [SG] Groups produce their own completions of these sentences. See which group comes up with the most interesting / unusual / amusing / thought-provoking completion.

- Remind students that we can use *which* and *that* for places and countries when the verb is transitive (*… which I'd like to visit*) and *where* when the verb is intransitive (*… where I'd like to live*). See answer *g* below.

  Possible answers:

  a … where there is a lot of excitement.
  b … where they charge the earth.
  c … who eats all the right things.
  d … where you meet exciting people.
  e … which you want to tell your friends about.
  f … where people chat on the Internet.
  g … which / that I'd like to visit. / where I'd like to go.
  h … when I like to go to the seashore.

Activity 30

- Go over this with students. Make sure they understand the difference between the two types of relative clause. Are there any clues in the punctuation of the two sentences which tell you what kind of clause you are reading? (Non-defining clauses tend to be marked by commas at the beginning and end of the clause.)

- Students check **12A–C in the Mini-grammar** for further guidance on the use of these clauses.

Activity 31

Answers:
a where (defining)
b who / that (defining)
c which (non-defining)
d who (non-defining)

 Workbook Activities 11–13 *can be used at any stage from now on.*

Pronunciation: what commas sound like

Students learn how to show pauses in speech (marked in writing by commas).

Activity 32

- Students listen to Track 62 and decide.
  Answer: a (because the speaker pauses before and after the relative clause)
- Students then think about the difference in meaning between *a* and *b*.
  Answer: In **a**, the speaker is talking about his only sister, who happens to live in Sydney. In **b**, the speaker has more than one sister and is talking about the one who lives in Sydney.

Activity 33

Answers:
Commas are needed in **b**, **c**, **f** and **g**, which contain non-defining relative clauses.
b The houses, where many people still live, are over 200 years old.
c His children, who sometimes played by the river, said they heard noises.
f Professor Macpherson, who is an investigator of strange phenomena, has never actually seen a ghost.
g The ghost in our house, which most of us have seen, only appears about twice a year.
The other sentences (**a**, **d**, **e**) contain defining relative clauses.

Activity 34

- Students practice saying these sentences, paying particular attention to the pauses before non-defining relative clauses. Then they listen again to Track 63 and compare their speech to that of the speakers on the track.

Activity 35

- Students first read this paragraph. All the sentences are simple statements, which makes the paragraph very bitty—it's not smooth. How do we make it read more smoothly? (By joining the sentences using relative clauses.)
- Students have to decide how to present this information using the appropriate relative clauses. They need to decide whether the clauses they use for this are defining or non-defining. The first two sentences are joined in example. What kind of clause is this?

- [P] Now students work in pairs to join the other sentences appropriately.
  Possible answers:
  My family, which is unusually large for a modern family, is very international. My brother who is an architect lives in Brazil. My sister who lives in Argentina is a singer. My parents, who live in Mexico, are French. My aunts and uncles, who move around a lot, have houses all over Europe. My grandparents, who are both in their nineties, live in France. I once saw a ghost in our house, which is in Paris.

Activity 36

- [P] Students can prepare this in class and complete it as a homework task. In class they should make notes about their family. Perhaps their family is not so international as that described in the paragraph above. Nevertheless, there must be something unusual or interesting about it. Suggest students focus on this.
- Other questions about the family students could make notes on include the following:
  —Where were the parents born? The grandparents?
  —What jobs do they do?
  —Has the family always lived in the same place?
  —What will the family be like in five / ten years' time?

 Workbook Activity 10 *can be used at any stage from now on.*

Functional language: agreeing and disagreeing

Students learn what language to use when expressing these functions.

Activity 37

- In this section, students listen to discussions of what books people like and dislike and specifically of what language they use to express agreement and disagreement. First, students listen to Track 64 and match books and summaries.
  Answers:
  Reaching the Top **f**
  Where the Flowers Grow **d**
  Watching Time Go By **b**
  Crying Over Spilt Milk **g**

Activity 38

Answers:
a ✓   b ✓
c ✗   d ✗
e ✓   f ✓
g ✗   h ✓
i ✓   j ✓
k ✓   l ✓
m ✗   n ✗
o ✗   p ✓

Activity 39

Answers:

a 1 (I agree up to a point with Rachel on this one.)
b 9 (Absolutely, Chris!)
c 2 (I couldn't agree more with Marsha.)
d 4 (I couldn't agree less with Garry.)
e 8 (I see what you're all saying, but ...)
f 6 (I'm with Marsha on this one.)
g 7 (I'm going to have to disagree with everyone here ...)
h 3 (Nonsense! I have to disagree with Garry here.)
i 5 (Well, I disagree with both Marsha and Chris.)

Activity 40

- Students listen to the track and complete the sentences with the phrases from Activity 39. Then they divide them into different kinds of agreement / disagreement.

Answers:

a I couldn't agree less with Garry. (SD)
b I see what you're all saying, but ... (MD)
c Nonsense! I have to disagree with Garry here. (SD)
d I'm with Marsha on this one. (SA)
e I couldn't agree more with Marsha. (SA)
f Well, I disagree with both Marsha and Chris. (MD)
g I agree up to a point with Rachel on this one. (MA)
h Absolutely, Chris! (SA)
i I'm going to have to disagree with everyone here ... (SD)

Activity 41

- Remembering the examples of different kinds of agreement and disagreement encountered in the previous activity, students decide how to categorize these expressions of agreement and disagreement.

Answers:

a MD	b SA	c MD	d MA
e SA	f MA	g SA	h MA
i SD	j MD	k SD	l SD
m SA	n SD	o SA	p SA
q MA	r MA	s SD	t MD
u SA	v MD		

- Students now look at these phrases and decide which ones can be used instead of those in the conversation on Track 64.

Activity 42

- Choose one of these topics and ask students to give you their opinions. Write a selection of these on the board, e.g.:

a 1 The money sportsmen get today is just ridiculous —far too much.
   2 They get a lot of money, but they have very short careers.
   3 Baseball players get paid so much money that the cost of going to a game is too high for most fans.

- Now ask the students to agree or disagree with one of these statements and add an opinion of their own, e.g.:
  S1: That's exactly what I think. And they spend their money on such stupid things—jewelry, big cars, tattoos!

- Ask the rest of the class which opinion S1 is agreeing with.

- [SG] Students continue with the role-play along the lines suggested in the Student's Book instructions.

Activity 43

- [SG] Allow sufficient time for students to prepare this role-play. They will need to make notes on their roles and perhaps practice it in groups before acting it out in front of the rest of the class.

 **Workbook Activities 14 & 15** *can be used at any stage from now on.*

Writing: book reports

Students decide on the important features of a book report and write one of their own.

Activity 44

- [P] Students read these reports and decide which book they would like to read. They should give reasons for their choice and be prepared to face disagreement from their partner.

- [P] Students think about what is missing from the reports. They can discuss a number of possible questions, which you can suggest to them, such as:
  —Did the reader like the book?
  —What did the reader like about the book?
  —What did the reader not like about the book?
  —Would he / she recommend the book? Why? / Why not?
  —What happens in the story?

Activity 45

- [P] Students go over these questions. Are they sufficient to enable them to write a book report? What other questions would they like to ask? Are there any questions which they wanted answers to in the previous activity that don't appear here?

- Now students decide on a book they have read and answer these questions about it.

Activity 46

- The answers to these questions should provide the basis for writing a book report similar in style to those presented in Activity 44.

 **Workbook Activities 16–18** *can be used at any stage from now on.*

Review: grammar and functional language

Students review the key language introduced in this unit.

Activity 47

Answers:

a Have you ever read the book I gave you?

b Have you seen the movie Michael Moore made about the American president?

c I just can't relate to people who don't like Turkish food.

d I read my favorite book, which was given to me by my sister-in-law, in just one day.

e In 1961, when I wasn't even born, things were so different.

f My aunt, who just had her 90th birthday, remembers a time when there were hardly any cars on the road.

g She often travels to Mexico, where she once lived, to see her friends.

h The manuscript, which can be seen at the British Museum from January 2nd until April 30th, is valued at about £350,000.

i When did you first meet Mr Graham, whose house is up for sale?

j When I was at school, writing compositions, which is easy for some people, was very difficult for me.

k Written by a first-time author, this book, which has already sold one million copies, is to be made into a movie.

Activity 48

• [I/P] These sentences all express opinions on a number of topics. Students work individually or in pairs. If working in pairs, they decide what their opinions are and complete the sentences accordingly, using relative clauses.

Possible answers:

a A good movie is one that makes you laugh as well as cry.

b A terrible restaurant is one where the staff don't care about the food.

c Good friends are people who help pick you up when you are down.

d A typical movie for young people is one which has lots of cuddly animals in it.

e A good place to take someone in this town is the King's Head, where they have live music in the evening.

f The best thing to read when you're on vacation is a book which you've read before.

Activity 49

Possible answers:

a You're so right.

b I don't think that's true.

c I agree with Jed. / I'm with Jed on this one.

d You must be joking!

e I take your point / I agree up to a point, ...

f I'm sorry, I can't accept that.

g You're not suggesting ...

h I disagree. / I have to disagree.

i I couldn't agree more.

Review: vocabulary

Students check the vocabulary used in this unit.

Activity 50

• [P] Go over the example with the class. Pairs compare their answers and ask questions of each other.

Pronunciation

Students check the pronunciation of some of the key words used in this unit.

Activity 51a

• Ask students to choose a word of two syllables or more from the list, e.g. *autobiography*. Ask students to say the word. How many syllables has it got? On which syllable does the stress fall? (On the fourth syllable: *autobi'ography*.)

• [P] Pairs write down other words of two syllables or more from the list and arrange them according to where the stress falls.

• Then students check their answers by listening to Track 65.

Answers:

Stress on the first syllable: *author, background, basic, blissfully, characters, editor, editing, fiction, former, letters, mainland, manuscript, massive, narrative, novel, outline, poetry, process, publisher, publishing, structure, travel, version, winning.*

Stress on the second syllable: *acclaimed, adapted, best-selling, deliver, description, original, prolific, rejection, uncool.*

Stress on the third syllable: *guaranteed.*

Stress on the fourth syllable: *autobiography.*

Activity 51b

• [P] Students find answers to these questions and check them by listening to Track 66.

Answers:

Words containing /f/ and /ɪ/: *fiction, figure, prolific.*

Words containing /f/ and /i/: *autobiography, blissfully.*

Word containing /f/ and /æ/: *fact.*

Words containing /f/ and /ɚ/: *former, first.*

Word containing /f/ and /eɪ/: *face.*

Word containing /f/ and /ʌ/: *fun.*

Activity 52

• [SG] Students follow these instructions to play the game. Do a demonstration with a group of students.

Workbook Activities 19–22 *can be used at any stage from now on.*

UNIT 13 Crime and punishment

Listening: crime doesn't pay

In this section, students listen to reports about crimes that went wrong.

Activity 1
- [P] Students look at these pictures and guess what went with wrong with these (attempted) crimes. For example, the man in the store with a gun and a paper bag over his head:

  T: What's wrong in picture *b*?

  S1: The man with the gun can't see very well.
- Ask students to make similar comments on the other pictures.

Activity 2
- Students listen to Track 67 to see if their guesses were correct.

  Answers: Story 1 d   Story 2 e   Story 3 a
  Story 4 c   Story 5 b

Activity 3
- Now students listen to Track 67 more carefully and get the information they need to complete the table.

  Answers:

  Story 1 a Weight of bags stolen meant robber couldn't run.
  b four money sacks containing pennies

  Story 2 a Driver of getaway car ran robber over after he had robbed a bank.
  b $500,000

  Story 3 a Burglar had his sentence increased by the judge after complaining a seven-year sentence would bring him bad luck.
  b TV and stereo

  Story 4 a Shoplifter was caught stealing books from a library.
  b law books

  Story 5 a Robber recognized during an armed robbery.
  b nothing

Activity 4
Answers:

a car made from strong, bullet-resistant, steel
b escape
c way out
d carefully chosen
e according to plan
f found guilty of
g condemned / given a punishment
h challenge a conviction
i put on trial
j stealing from shops
k tried
l during
m moved

Activity 5
- Ask students to listen to the news broadcast (Track 67) again. Note some of the words used to introduce the stories: *In* [town] … *Some news from* … *Today / Tonight* … *Finally*. Suggest that students use these words to introduce their stories.
- [P] Students choose their crime stories and write them up in the style of a news broadcast.
- [SG] Groups decide what order their stories should take. Often, the first story in a news programme is the most important, whereas the last story is often amusing or light-hearted. Groups can choose one person to read their news bulletin to the rest of the class and / or record their news bulletin.

▶ **Workbook Activities 1–3** *can be used at any stage from now on.*

Vocabulary: crime and criminals

Students read about crimes and learn words and phrases associated with criminal activities.

Activity 6
- Brainstorm the first couple of lines of this table with the class to give students an example of what's required:

  murder   murderer   to murder
  assassination   assassin   to assassinate
- [P] Students work in pairs to complete the rest of the table.

  Answers:

Crime	Criminal	Crime verb
a murder	murderer	to murder
b assassination	assassin	to assassinate
c computer hacking	hacker	to hack into a computer
d robbery	robber	to rob
e mugging	mugger	to mug
f burglary	burglar	to burgle
g theft	thief	to thieve
h pickpocketing	pickpocket	to pickpocket
i shoplifting	shoplifter	to shoplift
j arson	arsonist	to commit arson
k embezzlement	embezzler	to embezzle
l kidnap	kidnapper	to kidnap
m tax evasion	tax evader	to evade taxes

Activity 7
- [I/P] Go over the completed table with the class. See how many definitions of these crimes students can produce without looking at a dictionary. Correct them where they get things wrong and point out that where two words mean more or less the same (e.g. *murder* vs *assassinate*), the difference in meaning matters (e.g. *murder* = "to kill some on purpose even though it is against the law," *assassinate* = "to kill an important person such as a political figure").

- [P] Students work through the words, using dictionaries if they need to. They write definitions of the words. Go round the class offering help where appropriate.
- Students say the words. Their partner has to read out their definition.
- Listen to words and definitions with the whole class and give feedback where appropriate.

Activity 8

- Students use their dictionaries for this activity. A good dictionary will contain the information that students need here about how a word is used.
  Answers:
  a to   b of   c with   d to   e to   f for
  g of   h of   i for

Activity 9

- Here, students complete the texts with a verb (which might include a preposition, as in *a*, *confessing to*) or a preposition on its own (as in *d*, *for*).
  Answers:
  a confessing to
  b convicted of / arrested for
  c suspected of
  d for
  e charged
  f guilty of
  g sentenced to
  h wanted for
  i to
  j for

- [P/SG] Students check their answers with their partners. Then they decide what crimes these criminals committed.
  Answers:
  Jack the Ripper committed murder.
  Al Capone committed murder and tax evasion.
  Bonnie and Clyde robbed banks and stores.

Activity 10

- [P] Brainstorm these with the class. Are there criminals who, like Bonnie and Clyde, were admired by some people (e.g. Robin Hood)?

 **Workbook Activities 4 & 5** *can be used at any stage from now on.*

Speaking: Is crime ever justified? (discussion and role-play)

Students analyze and give their opinion on criminal cases.

Activity 11

- [P] Students first decide what crimes these people committed.
  Answers:
  a burglary
  b shoplifting
  c computer hacking

Activity 12

- [SG] When deciding what the punishment should be, students should consider what the reasons for these crimes were. Is there anything to be said in the defense of the accused? Students make notes as if they were the lawyers for the defence of the accused.
- Students should consider which of the three crimes is the most serious. Should the accused go to jail? If so, for how long?
- Students discuss these questions and present their findings to the rest of the class. Is there general agreement on what should be done to the three accused? Students should give clear reasons for the decisions.

Activity 13

- [SG] This role-play needs to be carefully prepared. Divide the class into groups of five, each with a defendant, a witness, a prosecuting attorney, a defense attorney and a judge. Groups decide which case they will take and who will role-play each part. Students study their part in the Activity Bank and make notes on it.
- Set up the classroom so that it resembles a courtroom with the judge, witness, defendant and attorneys in their proper place.
- Groups act out their "trial" for the rest of the class. Vote on which group delivers the most exciting / most authentic trial.

Functional language: making deductions

Students learn the language used in drawing conclusions from given facts.

Activity 14

- First students look at the picture. Ask some questions to start students thinking about what they're going to listen to, e.g. "What's the boy doing?" "Who is he watching?" "What's the man doing?" "Who is the woman?"
- Now students listen to Track 68 and fill the spaces in the Audioscript.
  Answers:
  a must be   b can't be   c could be
  d Maybe   e may have come   f definitely not
  g definitely

Activity 15

Answers:
a 12   b 11   c 8   d 3   e 6   f 2   g 14
h 4   i 1   j 9   k 7   l 5   m 13   n 10
- Students look back at the phrases used in Activity 14. Do the first example with the class (*a C*); then ask pairs to match each word or phrase with the correct heading.
  Answers:
  a C   b E   c A   d A   e B   f E   g C

Activity 16

- Work out the first sentence with the class:
  T: *I reckon she did it.* Is that present or past?
  S1: Past.
  T: Is the speaker certain or is it just a possibility?
  S2: It's just a possibility.
  T: So which box do we put this sentence in?
  S4: Box B.
- [P] Then students fit the remaining sentences in the correct box (*A–F* in Activity 15).
  Answers:
  a B   b A   c B   d B   e B

Activity 17

- [P] Students work in pairs to make deductions about the situations referred to here. They try their deductions on their partners who decide whether they agree or disagree with them. While they are doing this, go round the class offering help where appropriate.
- Listen to some of the deductions with the whole class. Why have the students come to their conclusions? Do the rest of the class agree with them?
  Possible answers:
  a It must be a car theft. / She might be stealing the car. / It must be her car. / I don't imagine she's stealing the car. / I reckon she has lost her keys.
  b They may be / must be planning a bank robbery. / They might just be looking at the bank for fun.
  c They are definitely going to steal from the store. / They must have stolen those computers from the store.
  d He must be about to commit a crime. / He's definitely going to commit a crime. / It's possible he's just having fun.
  e They must have set light to the building. / They are definitely arsonists. / They might have been watching the fire and now they're going home.

Workbook Activities 7 & 8 *can be used at any stage from now on.*

Pronunciation: sentence stress in deductions

Students learn how marked stress on a normally unstressed syllable can affect the meaning of a sentence.

Activity 18

- Students read these sentences. Ask them to read them aloud normally—that is, without any marked stress. Then ask them to listen to Track 69 and hear which words these speakers give special stress to. Students should mark these stresses on the sentences.
  Answers:
  a She 'might be a 'kidnapper.
  b They 'can't be 'burglars.
  c He 'could be an a'ssassin.
  d He 'may have come to de'liver the 'newspaper.
  e They 'must be 'going on va'cation.

- Without listening to the track again, students say these sentences with the same stress as the speakers. Then they listen to Track 69 again and see how close they were.

Activity 19

- This time, students try and work out where the stressed syllables are, before they listen to the track (Track 70).
  Answers:
  a She 'must be 'visiting her 'sister.
  b They 'might have 'stolen the 'flowers.
  c He 'might be a 'kidnapper.
  d There 'may be a 'pickpocket.

Workbook Activity 6 *can be used at any stage from now on.*

Activity 20

- [SG] Members of the group offer any information they have, e.g. what the painting is called, who painted it, where you can see it.
- Now students read about the painting in Activity Bank 26. What additional information can they find there?

Activity 21

- Students read about the theft of the Mona Lisa. Ask them to list any questions about the theft that they would like to have answered, e.g. who stole it? Why? What happened to it? How was the case solved? Did they catch the thief?

Activity 22

- [SG] Students discuss these theories in groups. Explain that one of these theories is correct. Each group should decide which theory is the most plausible and give reasons for their choice.

Activity 23

- [P] Ask students to think first of other crimes and mysteries that remain unsolved—the disappearance of a politician, the theft of a rare jewel, the collapse of a bridge, the appearance of a strange animal.
- Students should tell their story and give any explanation of the mystery they think is believable. What do other members of the class think of their story and their explanation.

Reading: When is a crime not a crime?

Students read a story which raises an interesting moral question about the nature of criminality and the limits of honesty.

Activity 24

- [SG] This is a warm-up activity to prepare students for what they are about to read. Students discuss these questions. There may be a wide range of opinions, from "I'd just keep it" to "I'd hand it over to the police." Don't make any judgements on these responses. Just ask students to keep them in mind when they read the story.

Activity 25

- Each student reads one of the two stories, and decides if their story is happy or sad. Try and make sure that half the class reads each of the stories.
  Answers:
  Finders keepers? is a sad story.
  Man 1 Bank 0 is a happy story (at least at the end).

Activity 26

- Each student answers the questions for the story that they read.
  Answers:
  Finders keepers?
  a Philadelphia 1981
  b Joey Coyle—28—unemployed
  c more than $1million
  d He found it in a box.
  e Yes.
  f He invested it foolishly and lost it all.
  g He was arrested, put in jail, then released; he died when they were making a movie of his story.

  Man 1 Bank 0
  a San Francisco 1995
  b Patrick Combs—28—writer
  c $95,093.35
  d He was sent a cheque.
  e No.
  f He gave it back.
  g He became a celebrity and had a successful career as a motivational speaker.

Activity 27

- [P] Students get information about their partners' story by asking questions *a–g*. They should both answer each question in turn, so that they can decide if for each question there are similarities or differences between the stories.
  Answers:
  Similarities:
  Both men are poor at the start at the story.
  Both men suddenly find themselves in possession of a lot of money they haven't earned.
  Differences:
  Joey is a manual worker.
  He quickly loses the money.
  He commits a criminal act by not returning the money.
  He doesn't benefit from his windfall.
  On the other hand, Patrick is (probably) well educated.
  He doesn't commit a criminal act.
  He returns the money to the bank anyway.
  He uses his fame to earn a good living.

Activity 28

Answers:
a tight   b cleared   c endorse   d stared
e mislaid   f paranoia   g giggled   h catapult
i roaring

Activity 29

- [P] Students study the sentence and decide if they can see an agent and an object in the sentence.
  Answers:
  a the charity
  b the money
- Students check the story that they have read to find other examples of passive sentences. They should only look for examples in which it is clear who the "doer" and who the "done to" are.
  Answers:
  Finders keepers?
  … about being discovered (the "doer" = the police, perhaps; the "done to" = Joey)
  and having "his" money taken away (the "doer" = the police or the rightful owner; the "done to" = Joey)
  Joey was arrested and thrown into jail (the "doer" = the police; the "done to" = Joey)
  he was released (the "doer" = the police; the "done to" = Joey)
  Joey's story was made into a Hollywood movie (the "doer" = a movie company; the "done to" = Joey's story)
  the movie was released (the "doer" = the movie company; the "done to" = the movie of Joey's story)
  Man 1 Bank 0
  the check had been cleared (the "doer" = the bank; the "done to" = the check)
  the money had been credited to his account (the "doer" = the bank; the "done to" = the money)

 Workbook Activities 9–11 *can be used at any stage from now on.*

Language in chunks

In this section, we look at aspects of language more closely. In particular, students learn to use idioms they have met in the reading text.

Activity 30

Answers:
a 9   b 7   c 2   d 5   e 1, 6 and 10   f 3   g 8   h 4

Activity 31

Answers:
a with her pulse quickening,
b beyond his wildest dreams
c nothing went right for him
d luck was about to change
e swore him / her / them to secrecy
f putting people in touch with
g make the most
h made a mess of
i to make matters worse,
j nothing to lose

- [P] Students choose four of these phrases and write sentences of their own to illustrate their meaning. For example, a sentence like *Her pulse quickened* doesn't tell you what the phrase means if you don't already know it. Whereas a sentence like *Her pulse quickened when she opened the envelope containing her exam results* is much easier to interpret.

Activity 32

- [SG] Groups discuss these questions. They give students an opportunity to judge the actions of the two men. Did either of them commit a crime? Did either of them do anything wrong?
- [SG] Questions *b* and *c* give students the chance to put themselves in the shoes of the two men. What would they have done in their place? Students say what they would have done and other students in the group express either belief or skepticism, e.g.:
  S1: If I'd been Joey, I'd have taken the money to the police immediately.
  S2: Oh yeah? I'll bet you'd have kept it. A million dollars is a lot of money.
  S3: But if you keep it, it's stealing, isn't it?
  S2: So what? It belonged to a bank. They've got plenty of money.
  S1: What would you have done if it had been $100?
- See if groups can agree on their responses. If not, take a straw poll of the class. Does the result show that most students are honest or dishonest?

Grammar: the passive voice

In this section, students are introduced to the uses and functions of the passive voice, with or without agents.

Activity 33

- Go over the material in **Mini-grammar 13B** with the class. Explain any difficulties. Then do the first sentence with the class. Students go on to match the remaining sentences with the best reasons.
  Possible answers:
  a 1 or 3
  b 1
  c 2 or 3
  d 4
  e 2 or 3
  f 2 or 3
  g 2 or 3
  h 4
  i 2 or 3
  Note: Sometimes more than one reason applies.

Activity 34

Answers:
a were taken
b is delivered
c was being moved
d is being fixed
e has been questioned
f had been broken into
g has been arrested
h have been delivered
i will / is going to be sentenced

Activity 35

- Tell students they are going to rewrite a report, making active verbs into the passive. Explain that the passive is used more in writing than in speaking and ask them why they think this is. Explain that using the passive makes something more impersonal, more "scientific," more formal, and that, especially in written reports, these are qualities that people expect to find.
- Do the first sentence with the class. What is the difference between *We followed the suspect* and *The suspect was followed*? What does the passive sentence leave out? (Answer: the agent, i.e. the person doing the action.)
- Now students change the remaining active sentences into passive sentences:
  Possible answers:
  The suspect was followed along Parker Street, which involved waiting as he paid the taxi driver. He entered the Wishbone Club and he was seen talking to two suspicious-looking young men, who were holding a baby. Someone came and the baby was taken away; the young men were left to talk by themselves. At 2 p.m., the two young men left the club and they were seen getting into a black car. The car was driven by a tall man with glasses. The black car was followed till it stopped outside the City Bank. Then we noticed that masks were being worn by the two men. The two men entered the bank and at this point the officers who were waiting in the bank were called and the alarm was sounded. We ran into the bank and the two men were arrested and handcuffs put on them. Then we put them in the car and they were taken to the police station. They appeared in court last week and were sentenced to six months in jail for attempted bank robbery.

Activity 36

Answers:
a were interviewed
b was found
c are kept
d is hoped
e will be installed
f will be published

Activity 37

- [I] Tell students they are going to solve a reading puzzle. Before they try and do so, they should read the five paragraphs of a story.
- [P] Students work together to try and find a sequence so that the story makes sense. While they are doing this, go round the class offering help where appropriate.
- Go through the story with the students and make sure they have the right sequence.
  Answers: c, e, a, d, b
- [P] Students discuss whether or not the policeman arrested the right person, and how / why he might know immediately who the guilty person was.

- Discuss the answer with the students.
  Answer: The lawyer and the engineer were both women. The voice had asked a man not to shoot. The priest is the only man.
- [P/SG] Students work to put together a news report which tells the same story. While they are doing this, go round the class offering help where appropriate.
- Listen to some of the news reports with the whole class. Give appropriate feedback.

 Workbook Activities 12 & 13 *can be used at any stage from now on.*

Writing: peer review

Students write a crime story and then work together to improve their pieces of writing.

Activity 38

- [I/SG] In this exercise, students read what other students say about working. (They're talking here about working in class.) Students should agree or disagree with these opinions individually then compare their responses to those of others in the group.
- Find out how many students prefer working on their own and how many prefer working with other people. You may find this information useful in your teaching.

Activity 39

- Ask students to skim-read this letter. Check basic facts—who wrote the letter? What kind of crime is described? Who was suspected? Who was convicted?
- The point here is that the gist of Juan Manuel's letter is clear, but it does contain a number of errors. Ask students to read the letter again and correct Juan Manuel's mistakes.
  Answers:
  want to tell
  happened / was committed
  was kidnapped
  People were
  took
  got mad
  couldn't have done
  suddenly
  had gone / went
  for him / the man
  trying to leave
  to jail
- Ask students to look at these mistakes. Ask them to list them under headings like grammar, vocabulary, spelling. Which mistakes are the most important as far as comprehension goes?

Activity 40

- [SG] Here students take on the role of teachers. In groups, they study the letter again and say what they think of the writing. In particular, they're asked to say how it could be improved.

- Students now read the piece of writing again and complete the form about it, including making some suggestions as to how to improve the writing. When they have completed the form individually, they can compare in pairs or groups to see if they agree on what could be improved in Juan Manuel's text.
  Possible answers:
  —The grammar mistakes could be corrected.
  —The spelling mistakes could be corrected.
  —The writer could include more details (e.g. the names of the people involved).
  —The writer could talk more about people's feelings to make the story more interesting.
  —The writer could have used more paragraphs.

Activity 41

- [P] Different pairs choose different topics (or you can assign topics to groups). Pairs make notes on what information they want to convey in their writing. Brainstorm some of the questions they should ask:
  —What was the crime?
  —Who did it?
  —Who was the victim of the crime?
  —Where / When did it take place?
  —Was the criminal caught?
  —What was his / her punishment?
- [I] Students write up their story in a paragraph. Set a time limit for doing this—you may like to set this as a homework task to give students more time to get their story right. A paragraph about the same length as Juan Manuel's letter should be long enough.
- [P] Students swap their stories with a partner and comment on each other's story, using the form from Activity 40.

 Workbook Activities 14–16 *can be used at any stage from now on.*

Review: grammar

Students review the key language introduced in this unit.

Activity 42
Answers:

a was sentenced	b had received
c had been stolen	d was alerted
e had been found	f was immediately claimed
g accompanied	h was discovered
i had been stolen	j (had been) vandalized
k was / had been abandoned	l had driven
m were found	n was ... identified
o was known	p was arrested
q was found	r pleaded
s sentenced	t is not expected

Activity 43

- [P] Ask students to read these notes quickly. What information does it give us about the crime? Ask students to say how the story could be divided into three parts. What would the title of the first part be?

Possible titles for the three parts of the story are:
1 The robbery
2 The arrest
3 The sentence
The task here is to expand the reporter's notes into a continuous narrative. Elicit the opening sentence from the class. The story might start like this:
On February 28th last year, two 19-year-olds, Roger Bartlett and Simone Rogers, broke into the home of 72-year-old Mrs Edna Brooks while she was sleeping.

- [I/P] Students write up the remaining notes in the same way. Students can either work on their own or in pairs for this. Ask students to read out their completed stories and ask the rest of the class to evaluate them.
  Possible answers:
  On February 28 last year, two 19-year-olds, Roger Bartlett and Simone Rogers, broke into the home of 72-year-old Mrs Edna Brooks while she was sleeping. They stole some money, her TV set and her DVD player.
  Bartlett and Rogers were caught because one of their fellow students, Tom Brooks, heard them boasting about the robbery in the college cafeteria where they are all students. Brooks is the grandson of Edna Brooks and he called the police who went round to Bartlett's house and found the stolen goods.
  At their trial, Bartlett and Rogers apologized for their crime. The judge ordered them to pay a fine and do community service.

Review: vocabulary

Students check the vocabulary used in this unit.

Activity 44

- [P] Students go over the words and expressions in the boxes and discuss their preferences with each other. Get feedback from pairs. Ask students to report on their partner's preferences.

Pronunciation

Students listen to words to hear how some letters are not alway sounded.

Activity 45

- Tell students to listen to Track 71 and find the words on the word list.
- Check that students have all heard the words.
  Answers: armored car, catapult, escape route, getaway, pickpocket
- Now play Track 71 again. This time they have to underline the letters that are not spoken, i.e. that are "silent."
  Answers: a<u>r</u>more<u>d</u> ca<u>r</u>, catapul<u>t</u>, escap<u>e</u> rout<u>e</u>, getaway, pi<u>ck</u>pocke<u>t</u>

- Now play track 72. This time they should notice that some of the letters that were "silent" in Track 71 are pronounced more clearly.
  Answer: a<u>r</u>mored ca<u>r</u>, catapult, escap<u>e</u> rout<u>e</u>, pickpocket

Activity 46

- Tell students to think of the sounds of words, not their meaning. Ask them to tell you an English word they like the sound of.
- Now have them look for two words from the Word List and two expressions from Word Plus which they like the sound of.
- Get students to tell you the words and phrases they have chosen.

Activity 47

- [P/SG] Elicit definitions of two or three words from the class, e.g.:
  beyond his wildest dreams = "much more than he expected"
  arson = "the crime of setting fire to a building"
  to stare = "to look at someone / something very intently"
- Then students write their definitions of two other words from the Word List or Word Plus and do the quiz with their partner as explained in the Student's Book.

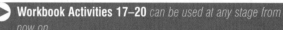 **Workbook Activities 17–20** *can be used at any stage from now on.*

UNIT 14 Stories from the heart

Reading: stories in poems

In this section, students read three poems that look back on the past with a variety of emotions.

Activity 1

- [SG] This exercise is designed to introduce students to the idea, which may be unfamiliar to some, of reading poetry. So this is an attempt to get students to give their views of poetry before they read any of the poems in this unit.
- Students discuss these questions. Get them to suggest other kinds of writing they could compare poetry to, e.g. fiction, newspapers, magazines, handbooks, (auto)biographies, pop song lyrics, interviews with stars. Ask groups to rate these kinds of writing and any others students come up with in comparison with poetry.

Activity 2

- Titles (of poems, of novels, etc.) are important: they try to make us want to read (the poem, novel, etc.). Students look at these titles *without looking at the poems* and jot down the first words that come into their head. Or you can ask them to call out words the titles suggest and write these on the board. Here are some examples of words these titles might make students think of:
  Midsummer, Tobago—hot, sun, beach, palm trees, rum
  Like a Beacon—sun, brightness, light
  Handbag—leather, bits and pieces, lipstick, notes, keys, diaries

Activity 3

- Now students have got some expectations of what they are going to hear from these poems. Play Track 73. Did students hear any of "their" words in the poems?
- Students can now uncover the poems and read them. Ask whether they prefer to read them silently on their own or have them read aloud to them.

Activity 4

- [SG] Students work in groups for this. They should read the poems closely and note down any similarities and differences they find in the ideas expressed in the poems.
  Possible answers:
  Similarities:
  looking back on the past (all)
  the Caribbean (*Midsummer, Tobago*; *Like a Beacon*)
  memories of the poet's mother (*Like a Beacon*; *Handbag*)

Differences:
tropical heat (*Midsummer, Tobago*)
cold city a long way from home (*Like a Beacon*)
war remembered; smells (*Handbag*)
The writers express feelings of nostalgia (*Midsummer, Tobago*; *Like a Beacon*) and compassion / sadness (*Handbag*).

Activity 5

- [P] Students work in pairs for this and take it in turns to ask and answer the questions listed about the three poems. They change pairs for each poem.
  Answers:
  Midsummer, Tobago
  1 wide 2 burnt
  3 the house appears to be sleeping in the summer heat—though it could also suggest that everyone in the house is sleeping through the heat of the day
  4 half-sleeping 5 go beyond, escape from
  6 sheltering
  Like a Beacon
  1 yearning / wanting 2 kind of banana
  3 reminder of home
  4 moving from side to side 5 light
  Handbag
  1 packed with letters 2 make-up for the lips
  3 make-up for the face
  4 not crisp any more, and a little damaged, especially at the corners
  5 smell 6 the essence of being a woman
  7 grief
- Each poem has a question that demands a fuller response from students. Go round the pairs and give any help students need.
- [P/SG] Finally, get students to share their answers with other pairs. Did they have the same answers to the questions about their poem? If not, do students want to change their answers now that they've heard other students' answers?

Activity 6

- Ask for volunteers for this. Let students tell the stories of the poems in their own words. Don't allow interruptions or corrections while students are talking.

▶ **Workbook Activities 1–4** *can be used at any stage from now on.*

Vocabulary: poetic effect

Students look at the way language is used in poetry.

Activity 7

- Explain that poetic language can sometimes differ from ordinary everyday language. Ask students to look at these lines from two of the poems and answer these questions about the way language is used in them.

- [P] First, get students to identify the things that are different about the way language is used. They should answer the first question in *a–d*:
  Answers:
  a None of these sentences have verbs.
  b Broad sun-stoned beaches.
    scorched yellow palms
    old leather handbag
  c sun-stoned
    summer-sleeping
  d past participle (*crowded*, *softened* and *worn*)
- [P] Now ask students to think about the two remaining questions in *a* and *c*. They can discuss these with their partners.
  Possible answers:
  a The lack of verbs makes the sentences read like quick thoughts, not fully worked out. It makes short sentences, emphasizes the nouns, creating strong pictures and images and means that the verbs have to be implied.
  c The joining together of two words makes us look more closely at what the words mean. These are not words we've ever come across before and we wouldn't find them in a dictionary. The ideas are packed tightly and we have to unpack them. Thus, *sun-stoned* tells us that the stones on the beach are being made very hot by the sun.

Activity 8
Answers:
a dog-eared
b foul-smelling
c brown-haired
d fair-skinned
e fun-loving
f good-looking
g sweet-smelling
h ready-made
i well-built
j soft-boiled
k hard-boiled
l mind-blowing

Activity 9
Answers:
a a rose, picked and given as a sign of love
b a plan hatched by a criminal
c the woman, finally driven crazy by the neighbors' noise
d a shot, fired in anger
e a letter, written in anger
f the actor's career, destroyed by jealousy
g a picture, painted in a fit of creativity

Activity 10
- [P] Brainstorm a few examples with the class. Then ask pairs to come up with adjective-noun

combinations of their own. These may be (should be) unusual and even weird, but students must be able to say what these new phrases mean and why they make sense, e.g.:
S1: *White hatred.*
S2: Why *white* hatred?
S1: Because when you're very angry with someone— you really hate them, right? Then your face goes all white and tense.

Activity 11
- [I/P] Students first write words they associate with the topic they've chosen. Then they use these words to create some phrases as suggested in *b*.
- They should use the phrases they've created in their poem, but don't expect them to do this straight off in class. To produce a worthwhile poem, students need to move the words around so that they express the ideas they have about home, friends, etc. First thoughts are fine, but further thoughts are better. Give time and space for this and be aware that many students may not wish to express their thoughts on these topics.

 Workbook Activities 5 & 6 *can be used at any stage from now on.*

Listening: storyteller
Students learn about a woman who works as a storyteller.

Activity 12
- Get the whole class involved in this. Accept a range of answers to these questions, e.g.:
  "She's from Africa / the West Indies / America."
  "She's a singer / politician / actor / storyteller."
- Now students listen quickly to Track 74 and see if their guesses proved correct.
  Answers: Jan Blake is from Britain (but she has a Jamaican background). She is a storyteller.

Activity 13
- Now students listen to Track 74 more carefully. This is a fairly difficult question because Jan answers it in a variety of ways. But the basic message is that telling stories and listening to them is about accepting the variety of human nature and exploring human imagination.

Activity 14
- Here students try to guess the answer to these questions. Let students glance through these questions but don't dwell on them. It doesn't really matter if the answers they give prove right or wrong —the point here is for students to focus on the important questions that Jan will be talking about in the next part of her interview.
- Now students listen to Track 75 and answer these questions.
  Answers:
  a She joined a traveling theater group.

b   to audition as a storyteller
c   bring a story, a game and a song from her own tradition
d   *Why Cat and Dog are no longer friends*
e   from her mother
f   She read the story again and again and again.
g   The audience liked it.

Activity 15
Answers:
a   the Spitalfields Theater
b   Crispin Robinson
c   Crispin
d   Crispin
e   Jan
f   Jan and Crispin
g   the audience
h   Jan
i   Jan, Crispin and the audience

▶ **Workbook Activities 7–9** *can be used at any stage from now on.*

Language in chunks
Students look at idiomatic expressions from the interview with Jan.

Activity 16
- [I] Ask students to read through the phrases *a–i*. Now they should go to the Audioscript for Tracks 74–76 and find how and when Jan uses them.
- [P] Working with a partner, the students discuss what each of the phrases means in the context in which Jan uses them.
- Go through the phrases with the students.
  Answers:
  a   something that's certain to be true because people have proved it to be the case—(talking about what stories are for)
  b   Do you understand? / Is what I am saying logical? (talking about how stories relate to human experience)
  c   I don't know / can't work out what it is (talking about something fundamental being found in all stories)
  d   to dig down (talking about listeners discovering hidden thoughts and images in themselves)
  e   exactly, so that I could repeat it exactly as it was written (talking about learning a story for her first audition)
  f   I've gone on / not thought about the past (talking about devoting her career to storytelling)
  g   described the events and the order they occurred in (talking of a story she had to explain to her accompanist)
  h   right at the limit of (talking about having to improvise a story they hadn't had time to prepare)
  i   not sure of what I'm doing / unsure of myself (talking about appearing unprepared on stage)

Activity 17
- Ask students to look at the phrases and think how they could say them in their language. Tell them they do not have to translate word for word (!), but should think of the equivalent kind of expression.
- If all the students share the same L1, you can listen to their translations and compare them. If they do not, have them translate the phrases in their language back into English. But this time they should translate word for word! The activity will demonstrate similarities and difference in the way we use language metaphorically.

Activity 18
- Tell students to read through the three paragraphs, *a–c*. They should look for things that people actually said and for things which people said but which are reported. Go round helping where appropriate.
  Answers:
  The three extracts only contain examples of direct speech, with the exception of the first line of paragraph c, *I asked the audience to join in and sing it*, which is an example of Jan reporting what she herself said to the audience.
- You could also ask students to add punctuation to these passages, e.g.:
  I said, "Oh oh! Where can you earn some decent money then?" and she said, "Oh, as a storyteller ..."

Activity 19
- Jan didn't exactly memorize her story, but she read it so many times that when she came to tell it to an audience, she didn't need any notes—it just all came out. Tell students that that's what they should be aiming for here.
- The process should be as follows:
  —Students choose a subject for their story. (Allow time for students to think about what their best subject might be before coming to a decision.)
  —They make notes on what they're going to say.
  —They write up their notes into a script they can deliver to an audience.
  —They tell their story to one or two partners.
  —They tell their story to the rest of the class.

Grammar: direct and indirect speech
Having been introduced to direct and indirect speech, students learn more about the relationship between these two forms.

Activity 20
- Students look quickly at the pictures and read what they say. Go over the example with the class. Ask them to pick out the speech-introducing phrases used in each of the three ways of reporting what Jane said (*She says ..., She said ..., ... Jane said*).
- Now students write three different ways of reporting what the other people in the pictures say.

Possible answers:

Jane
a She says she's going to read her latest poem.
b She said she was going to read her latest poem.
c "I'm going to read my latest poem," Jane said / said Jane.

Carlos
a He's asking if they'd like him to tell them a story.
b He asked if they'd like him to tell them a story.
c "Would you like me to tell you a story?" he asked / asked Carlos.

Renée
a She says she's heard their stories so many times before.
b She said she'd heard their stories so many times before.
c "I've heard their stories so many times before," Renée said / said Renée.

Danni
a She says she was going to paint a new picture, but she hasn't got any ideas.
b She said she was going to paint a new picture, but she hadn't got any ideas.
c "I was going to paint a new picture, but I haven't got any ideas," Danni said / said Danni.

Paul
a He says this picture is telling us a story.
b He said that picture was telling us a story.
c "This picture is telling us a story," he said / said Paul.

Activity 21

- Have students look at the two lists. Tell them that the phrases on the right can be reported by using the verbs on the left. Take them through the example and explain that if someone says "You *must* come with me ... ," they are usually insisting.
- [P] Students work through the activity.
- Go through the answers with the class.

Answers:

insist	m
accept	g
apologize	h
deny	e
refuse	f
compliment	l
suggest	a
forgive	n
complain	k
advise	b
order	d
boast	j
agree	o
explain	c
blame	i

- Now students convert the direct speech sentences into sentences where the speech is reported. They can use either the first person (see e.g. answer *b*) or the 3rd person (see e.g. answer *a*). They will use the introducing words in the left-hand column to start

the reported speech sentences. Do one or two examples with the class to make it clear what students have to do, e.g.

a *She suggested going / that they go / went to the gallery.*
h *He apologized for losing my pen.*

Possible answers:

a She suggested going / that they go / went to the gallery.
b He advised me to stay at home.
c She explained that I should just press the button and put in a CD, then press "play."
d He ordered her to come right then.
e She denied stealing / that she had stolen the painting.
f He refused to do my homework.
g He accepted her invitation to the movies.
h He apologized for losing my pen.
i She blamed George for breaking the window.
j He boasted of being / that he was the best artist in the world.
k She complained that that painting was much too expensive.
l He complimented her on her sculpture (, saying it was beautiful).
m He insisted that I went with him. He said I'd really enjoy it.
n She forgave him for spilling the paint (, saying it really didn't matter).
o She agreed that I was absolutely right and that it was a great poem.

- When students have converted all these direct speech sentences into reported speech sentences, they can refer to **14E in the Mini-grammar** and check their answers against the information given there.

Activity 22

- [P] Students look at the example. Do the same for another of the visitors to the exhibition, e.g. *h: The young man complained that it looked like a child had painted it.*
  Students report the speech of the other visitors in the same way.

Possible answers:

a The young woman insisted she hated going to art exhibition openings, because they were so boring.
b The other woman agreed that they were so tedious.
c The woman suggested to the man that they go and have a drink.
d The blond woman said that the artist had lived in Paris for five years.
e A young woman asked if the artist was trying a new technique when he did that.
f A man suggested to someone that they shouldn't bother coming because it was awful.
g Charlie's mother warned him not to touch the paintings.
h The young man complained that it looked like a child had painted it.

i The young woman told the artist that she loved / complimented the artist on the use of color in his work.

j The artist explained that he was experimenting with unconventional art.

- Get feedback from students. Have they all used the same introductory verbs? Are there times when more than one introductory verb can be used?

 Workbook Activities 10 & 11 *can be used at any stage from now on.*

Pronunciation: strong and weak forms (*was* and *were*)

Students listen to a number of sentences which contained stressed (strong) and unstressed (weak) forms of the verb *be*. They learn to pronounce both forms of the verb.

Activity 23

- Ask students to look at these sentences. They should try to say them aloud with whatever stress (strong / weak) they think the forms of *be* (*was*, *were*) should take.
- Now students listen to Track 77 and mark the stressed and unstressed forms of *was* / *were*.
- Students should listen to Track 77 again then try to imitate the stresses that the speakers use.

Activity 24

Possible answers:

a Fumiko said she was learning to paint.

b Brian said they were going to the Picasso exhibition.

c Maria asked if they were enjoying the museum tour.

d Wilton and Gaby said / complained that they were very tired.

- [P] The weak / unstressed forms of *was* / *were* are used in all these sentences. Students should read these sentences aloud to their partners using the correct pronunciation of *was* and *were*. Their partners repeat the sentence, changing the stress if they think it is incorrect.

Speaking and writing: reporting conversations and events

In this section, students look at the differences between reporting speech in spoken and written language.

Activity 25

- [P] Ask students to look over these pairs of sentences quickly. What signs are there of formal / informal language in the first pair of sentences? The use of *I'm like* ... to mean *I said* ... suggests informality in *a1*; whereas *He said that* ... in *a2* suggests a formal way of reporting something said.
- [P] Students go through the remaining pairs of sentences deciding which are formal, which informal. They should pick out words or expressions as evidence for their choice.

Answers:

a1 informal; a2 formal.

b1 informal; b2 formal

c1 formal; c2 informal

d1 formal; d2 informal

e1 informal; e2 formal

Activity 26

Answers:

a both   b both   c go

d be like   e both   f be like

Speaking: reading aloud

Students are introduced to reading aloud, a specialized form of speaking which involves particular forms of pausing, word and sentence stress and intonation.

Activity 27

- [P] Students can work in pairs, with each student choosing a different text. Students follow the instructions given in the Student's Book and read their texts to one another.

Functional language: expressing likes and dislikes

Students investigate different ways of expressing these functions.

Activity 28

- First, get students to look at the picture. Where are these people? What are they looking at? What do you think their opinion of the sculpture is?
- Now students listen to their conversation on Track 80 and fill the spaces with the words they hear.

Answers:

a at all

b isn't very good

c like

d couldn't stand it

e hate

f admire

g the worst

Activity 29

- Ask students to find one example of each type of comment. Then get them to draw up a table with columns or rows for each type and write these sentences in the correct row / column.

Answers:

a Positive comments

the best

adore

don't have anything against

don't mind

crazy about

really like

can't beat

b My opinions have changed

grown to like

gone off

taken a liking

warming to

c Negative comments
   can't stand
   loathe
   doesn't do much for me
   nothing worse than

- [SG] Students discuss questions *a–c*. Get feedback from the class on their opinions.
  Answers:
  a
  the best
  adore
  can't stand
  loathe
  crazy about
  really like
  nothing worse than
  can't beat
  b
  grown to like
  taken a liking
  warming to
  c
  adore—love
  loathe—detest, hate
  crazy about—really adore
  really like—interested in

- Do question *d* and see what other words students can add to the table under the three headings.
  Possible answers:
  a Positive comments
     I love it
     it's wonderful
     I've never seen anything like it
     it's truly amazing
  b My opinions have changed
     it grows on you
     I've changed my mind
     on second thoughts
     I have to say
  c Negative comments
     it's appalling
     I've never seen anything like it
     it's the worst thing I've seen since
     it's hideous
     I can't bear to look at it

Activity 30

- [P] Ask students to look at these works and give you their first impressions of them—basically *like / don't like*. Take one of the positive comments (hopefully there will be some!) and ask students how they would express their feelings to a friend (see the example in the Student's Book). Brainstorm some positive comments, possibly using some of the language introduced in Activity 29, e.g.:
  "I love this sculpture."
  "I've grown to like abstract sculpture."
  "I think this is a beautiful piece."
  Now ask students if they would express themselves differently if they were talking to the artist. If so, why?

- Do the same for any negative comments students may have. There may be a greater difference between how students would express negative comments to the artist and to a friend. Ask students to say why that might be and to think of ways of softening a negative comment.
- [P] Students then exchange opinions in pairs. Circulate and help the pairs as necessary.

Activity 31

- [SG] Groups discuss these two questions. Remind them of sayings like "Honesty is the best policy." Is this always so? When might it not be a good idea to be perfectly honest?
- Groups might like to consider further questions. Looking at it from another angle, for example, has a friend ever hurt you unintentionally by saying something negative about you? How did you react to this? Did you appreciate your friend's honesty or were you still unhappy about what he / she said?
- Get feedback from groups and find out what the range of opinions was.

Activity 32

- [SG] This could be a major activity, which you may want to spread over more than one lesson or you could treat it more superficially, depending on the time you have available and the needs and interests of the class.
- Divide the class into groups, with each group choosing one of these topics. Go round the groups and help them to decide on what questions to ask. What form should the questions take? For example, should the questionnaire use direct questions, e.g.:
  Do you think that modern art is a waste of time?
  Or should it use statements to agree or disagree with, e.g.:
  Modern art is a waste of time.
  Agree / Disagree / Don't know
  Or should it use a rating scale, e.g.:
  How much do you like modern art?   0 1 2 3 4 5
- Of course, different groups might choose different approaches. When groups have completed their questionnaires, they should circulate and mingle with students from other groups to exchange views and opinions.
- Group leaders describe the responses to their questionnaire and attempt to give some explanation of them.

Workbook Activity 12 *can be used at any stage from now on.*

Writing: movies and music
Students look at the relationship between music and emotion, especially as used in movies.

Activity 33
- [P] Play Track 81. Ask students to listen to the two music extracts and jot down the first adjectives that

come into their head. Pairs compare their words with those of other pairs. Is there a consensus?

- [P] Students then decide for what scenes from a movie these extracts would be a good soundtrack. For information, the music extracts are the third movement of Debussy's string quartet (Chilingirian Quartet, EMI records) and *Beanfields* by the Penguin Café orchestra (*When in Rome*, EEG records).

Activity 34

- [P] Students read the scenes from movie *A* and discuss suitable music for them. Ask them to describe the scene in a word. They should come up with words like *dramatic, mysterious, sinister, dark*. So what *kind* of music—not what particular piece of music—would fit this scene best?
- Pairs compare their ideas with other pairs then do the same for the scenes from movie *B*. Here the words they might choose to describe these scenes might include words like *fast, fearful, hunted*. How could the music chosen convey this sense of a chase?
- Now pairs think about these two movies. Ask them to guess what happens next in each movie. For example, in movie *A*, the figure in the doorway could pull out a gun and start shooting. Or he / she could walk up to a table and confront someone sitting there. Or (if you wanted to deflate expectations) he / she could walk slowly up to the bar, take off his / her hat, smile sweetly and ask, "Could I have a glass of water, please?"

Activity 35

Answers:
a outside
b circles of light
c person
d inside
e moves slowly
f view from above
g shining waves
h loud breathing
i falls forward suddenly

- The descriptions in the scripts are intended as notes to the director and the actors. They are like stage directions in a play.
- Such notes would not normally be acceptable if you were writing a novel rather than a play.
- To make this point, you could ask students to convert some of these notes into full sentences, e.g.:
The place is a small side street in a city. The time is ten years ago. The darkness is broken by pools of light from the street lights. A figure is walking towards us …

Activity 36

- [P/SG] Students choose one of these types of movie. Students form pairs (or groups) according to what type of film they have chosen. First, they decide on the answers to these questions, e.g.:
  a a castle in Transylvania
  b mid-19th century

c a carriage draws up to the castle and a man in a cloak gets out; the carriage leaves in a rush, horses neighing
d dark, sombre, flashes of lightning and crashes of thunder

Activity 37

- [P/SG] Now students take their answers to these questions and use them to write directions like those in the scripts in Activity 34.
- Get pairs / groups to read out their scripts and let the rest of the class give them a rating from 0 to 5.
- Ask other pairs / groups to say what music they would choose to accompany the scene they have just heard.

 Workbook Activities 13 & 14 *can be used at any stage from now on.*

Review: grammar and functional language

Students review the key language introduced in this unit.

Activity 38

- Ask students to read this story. Check comprehension by asking a few questions of the class, e.g.:
  "What did Graeme Wright have with him?"
  "What did the reporter tell him to do?"
  "How did Graeme Wright respond?"
  "Why did Graeme Wright put down the bucket?"
  "What was he going to do?"
  "How did the story end?"
- Now students rewrite the story using direct speech where the story uses indirect speech. Before they start, go over the example with the class and elicit a few more examples, e.g.:
Put that bucket down!
No, I won't!
Possible answers:
REPORTER: I really like your use of color, Tina.
REPORTER: Put that bucket down.
GRAEME: No, I won't.
REPORTER: Do as you're told.
GRAEME: I'm not afraid of anyone.
REPORTER: Put down that bucket or I'll call the police.
GRAEME: All right, I'll put it down. I wasn't going to damage the painting anyway.
TINA: People don't usually approach paintings carrying buckets of black paint.
GRAEME: I admit I was going to destroy one of your paintings. I wanted to get publicity for my own art show at the gallery down the street.
TINA: OK, I forgive you.
GRAEME: Would you like to see my show?
TINA: OK.

Activity 39

Answers:

a love / adore
b hate / loathe
c crazy about
d have grown to like / am warming to
e gone off
f doesn't do much for me
g nothing worse than
h taken a liking to

Activity 40

- [P] Start pairs off by brainstorming a number of professions, e.g. teacher, doctor, nurse, accountant, banker, architect, musician, movie director, engineer, gardener, soldier.
- [P] Tasks *a / b*: pairs write a short conversation (three or four exchanges at the most) between two of these professionals. They choose different topics and locations.
- When one pair has acted out their conversation (task *c*), ask the rest of the class to suggest how it could be rendered in indirect speech (task *d*). Pairs make notes.
- As a home task, you could then ask pairs to write up their conversation as reported speech. Ask students to decide which form is the more successful, the more dramatic, the clearer.

Review: vocabulary

Students check the vocabulary used in this unit.

Activity 41

- [I] Students make their own list of words then play the game as outlined in the instructions.

Pronunciation

Students look back at the key words introduced in this unit and list those they find difficult to pronounce. They compare their list with their partners.

Activity 42

- [I/P] Students draw up their own list and compare it with their partners.
- [P] Pairs make a joint list and divide the difficult words into sound or stress difficulties. Here are some likely examples of difficult words from the Word List:
  sound: *aerial anguish glittering odor plantain scorched softened sweet-smelling*
  stress: *brown-haired dog-eared harboring ready-made womanliness*

Activity 43

- [P] Get students to draw up a table to accommodate these nine diphthongs. In the first instance, ask students to put one word from the Word List under each sound *not* highlighted in yellow, e.g.:

/eɪ/ say	/ɔɪ/ joy	/oʊ/ boat
plant<u>ai</u>n	b<u>oi</u>led	mind-bl<u>ow</u>ing
/aʊ/ cow	/ɪr/ here	/ɛr/ bear
dr<u>ow</u>sing	ext<u>e</u>rior	<u>ae</u>rial

- Check with the class that these examples are correct. Then let students complete the table with as many other words from the lists as possible. Set a time limit for this and see which pair has written the most (correct) words under each sound.

Possible answers:

/eɪ/ say	/aɪ/ sigh	/ɔɪ/ joy	/oʊ/ boat	/aʊ/ cow
plant<u>ai</u>n made	fly by	b<u>oi</u>led	mind- bl<u>ow</u>ing odor outgr<u>ow</u>	dr<u>ow</u>sing f<u>ou</u>l outgr<u>ow</u> p<u>ow</u>der
/ɪr/ here	/ɛr/ bear	/yʊ/ pure	/u/ steward	
dog-<u>ea</u>red ext<u>e</u>rior	<u>ae</u>rial f<u>ai</u>r-haired	f<u>ue</u>l	j<u>ew</u>el	

Workbook Activities 15–19 *can be used at any stage from now on.*

Activity 44

- [I] This is a feedback exercise on what students have learned from the course, what they still have problems with and how they hope to improve. Go over this questionnaire with students, helping them to estimate their performance over the year accurately. You may find that students are inclined to be too pessimistic about what they have achieved. If so, remind them of what they have actually learned. It may be useful here to quickly run through *Just Right Upper Intermediate* with the class, reminding them of the topics and language covered (with the help of the Contents list on pages 3–5 of the Student's Book, for instance).

The results of this questionnaire should prove useful to you as a teacher. The questionnaire provides an assessment of how well students have done over the time they've been working on the course and an indication of the language areas they feel the need to improve.

Workbook answer key

UNIT 1

Activity 1
a	borrow	borrowing	borrower
b	donate	donation	donor
c	invest	investment	investor
d	lend	lending	lender
e	loan	loan	XXXX
f	gamble	gambling	gambler
g	spend	spending	spender
h	withdraw	withdrawal	XXXX
i	lose	loss	loser
j	win	winnings	winner
k	earn	earnings	earner
l	waste	waste	waster
m	save	savings	saver
n	deposit	deposit	depositor

Activity 2
a I asked if I could borrow some money from her until pay day.
b After winning a lot of money in the lottery, she decided to donate some to her favorite charity.
c He had a big family, so he needed to save some money for a rainy day.
d If you invest in this restaurant, you won't regret it.
e Why did you waste your money on that car? It's always breaking down.
f She went into the bank and deposited the check into her account.
g The Las Vegas casinos are full of gamblers. I saw one woman who won $100 on a slot machine and then put her winnings back into the same machine.
h She withdrew $200 from the ATM. She immediately spent it on a new pair of shoes.

Activity 3
a someone who doesn't like to spend money at all
b someone who spends money easily
c doing something well
d someone who takes a lot of chances and risks

Activity 5
a penny pincher
b on the right track
c daredevil
d spendthrift

Activity 6
a reckless
b can't be bothered to
c wardrobe
d extravagant
e amid the clutter
f raffle
g manageable
h statements
i keep track of
j tempted by

Activity 7
1 g
2 a
3 e
4 d
5 b
6 f
7 c
8 k
9 j
10 i
11 h

Activity 8
Yes / No	Open-ended	Subject	Tag
g, i, j	a, b, c, h, k	e	d, f

Activity 9
a fall
b rise
c fall
d rise
e fall
f rise
g fall
h rise
i fall
j fall

Activity 10
a 2
b 4
c 5
d 6
e 3
f 1

Activity 11
The answer is b.

Activity 12
a £20
b £2

Activity 13
a F
b T
c T
d T
e T
f T
g T
h T
i F

Activity 14
a shut up
b make matters worse
c get the message
d couldn't care less
e comes to the conclusion
f all eager
g a piece of cake
h weeping
i flabbergasted
j put me out of my misery

Activity 15
Open activity

Activity 16
Possible answer

In this essay I will discuss the advantages and disadvantages of being a spendthrift and a penny pincher and give my opinion about which it is better to be.

First of all, I'll discuss being someone who spends money easily—a spendthrift. Firstly, spending money is fun, and people who are generous tend to have more friends than people who are stingy. On the other hand, it is easy to get into debt and when this happens the life of a spendthrift can become miserable and out of control.

As for being someone who watches their money carefully—penny pincher—it's certainly good to be careful with money and to spend money wisely. Penny-pinchers are more likely to become very rich than spendthrifts, but at the same time, it is hard to enjoy your life if you are always counting your pennies.

In conclusion, I think it's good to be a penny pincher until you have enough money to live comfortably and then it's good to become a spendthrift and enjoy spending your money on yourself, your family and your friends.

Activities 17–19
Open activities

Activity 20
a penny pincher
b withdrawal
c spendthrift
d extravagant
e reckless
f stingy
g bankrupt

UNIT 2
Activity 1
a Maurice Gatsonides
b Walter Arnold
c 30 miles an hour
d 80%

Activity 2
a 9
b 2
c 1
d 7
e 4
f 8
g 12
h 5
i 3
j 11
k 10
l 6

Activity 3
a activated
b Sensors
c surface
d device
e phenomenon
f built-up
g toll
h uncontroversial
i joyriders
j invisible

Activity 4
a You couldn't go back slightly further, could you?
b Oh come on, it'll only take a minute.
c Could you do me a favour?
d Do you think you could take a picture of us?
e Would you mind taking a picture of me with the mountain in the background?
f Not too far!
g Please help us out. Just this once.
h Excuse me.

Activity 5
1 Excuse me.
2 Could you do me a favor?
3 Do you think you could take a picture of us?

4 Oh come on, it'll only take a minute.
5 Please help us out. Just this once.
6 Would you mind taking a picture of me with the mountain in the background?
7 Not too far!
8 You couldn't go back slightly further, could you?

Activity 6
a viewfinder
b zoom lens
c throwaway cameras
d photo booth
e photo opportunity
f darkroom
g photo finish
h picture frame
i digital camera

Activity 7
a alarm clock
b birthday present
c heart attack
d greenhouse effect
e human rights
f race relations
g washing machine
h contact lenses
i shopping bag
j windshield wipers
k steering wheel
l credit cards
m front door

Activity 8
a used to go
b lived / used to live
c was / used to be
d would start / used to start
e weren't / didn't use to be
f drove / would drive / used to drive
g drove / would drive / used to drive
h loved / used to love
i knew
j would take
k would go
l would / used to stop
m would spread / used to spread
n would have / used to have
o would run / used to run
p would worry / used to worry
q would set off / used to set off
r got stuck / would get stuck / used to get stuck
s seemed
t increased / would increase / used to increase
u would be
v saw / used to see
w would start / used to start
x would sound / used to sound
y had almost forgotten

Activity 9
a Did you use to play football when you were young?
b Did you remember to turn off the iron?
c I wouldn't listen to anything my mother said.
d I don't remember playing football when I was a kid.
e I used to enjoy listening to folk music.
f I forgot that I had taken a picture of my cat to school. / I forgot to take a picture of my cat to school.
g We didn't use to have much music in elementary school.
h We would go around to my friend's house in the evening.
i You didn't remind me to lock the back door.
j You mustn't forget to bring your homework tomorrow.

Activity 10
The correct answer is b.

Activity 11
a 2
b 2
c 1
d both
e both
f both
g 2
h both
i 2
j both
k both

Activity 12
a 9
b 4
c 5
d 8
e 3
f 6
g 7
h 2
i 1

Activity 13
a darkroom
b whole
c candlelight
d naked
e flame
f flame
g light bulb
h digital
i computer
j printed
k reproduction
l digital

Activity 14

a into Sydney harbor
b washing machine
c old pictures
d film cameras in latest survey
e applauds Jamaican reggae star
f statistics show sharp increase
g by man with photographic
memory
h hit by angry pop star
i to avert war
j by community leaders

Activity 15

Possible answers

a Lost cat found in washing machine
b Dog saves man from drowning
c Photographer invited to White
House
d Fashion photographer arrested for
car theft
e Crazy freeway driver caught at
120 mph
f Only 10 arrests at "most peaceful"
folk festival
g Romantic candlelight "here to
stay"

Activity 16

a 3
b 10
c 6
d 4
e 5
f 2
g 1
h 9
i 8
j 7

Activities 17–18

Open activities

Activity 19

a ✓
b ✗—We used to live in Seattle ...
c ✗—Could you give me a hand with
the washing up?
d ✓
e ✓
f It depends on what it is.
g ✗—Did you remember to turn off
the iron ...
h ✓
i ✓
j ✓

Activity 20

a newspaper
b mother tongue
c throwaway camera
d windshield wiper
e It's a fact of life.
f not a patch on the real thing
g more than a moment

UNIT 3

Activity 1

a stallion
b cow
c dog
d goat
e koala bear
f sheep
g snake
h kangaroo
i alien
j bat
k ostrich
l galah
m wolf
n wombat
o crocodile

Activity 2

The following creatures should be
checked:

a stallion
b cow
c dog
d goat
f sheep
g snake
h kangaroo
i alien
l galah
n wombat

Activity 3

a Yes. She stared and stared. Kathryn
says it was worth going 13,000
miles
to surprise her.
b Yes. He tried to be cool but he was
"lost for words".
c No. She describes him as a
'runaway husband' and later talks
about her divorce.
d Yes. He had grown a lot since he
used to be the same height as
Kathryn.
e No. There were a lot of stars.
f No. It just says they were armed
with
a camera.
g No. She makes a joke about taking
pictures of aliens, but it was
probably just a photograph of
cows.
h Yes. She says her stay at home
wasn't long enough.
i No. She flew via Bali and Kuala
Lumpur (and caught different
planes).

Activity 4

a 8, 14
b 5
c 3
d 16

e 10
f 12
g 11
h 17, 1
i 2
j 15
k 13
l 6, 4
m 7
n 9

Activity 5

bark
bleat
cluck
from the horse's mouth
hiss
howl
purr
roar
smell a rat
squeal

Activity 6

a Don't be so catty!
b ... the way he is so dogged.
c He was beavering away at painting
the room.
d ... there's no need to get so ratty.
e ... she's so mousy.
f ... was a real turkey.
g This whole situation is very fishy.
h ... it's a real pigsty.
i ... it's all dog-eared.
j ... it's always worth killing two
birds with one stone.
k Why did you let the cat out of the
bag?
l There's no need to use that
sheepish grin ...
m Stop fishing for compliments ...

Activity 7

a fast (adj), beautifully (adv)
b possible (adj), fantastic (adj)
c rough (adj), little (adj), well (adv)
d dangerous (adj), deadly (adj)
e tall (adv), proud (adj)
f fast (adv)
g lately (adv), hard (adj)
h wrong (adj)

Activity 8

a dangerously
b hard
c for a few months
d long and hard
e vertically
f always
g sadistically
h sometimes
i badly
j loudly
k purposefully

l very much
m tidily
n happily

Activity 9
a Danger: electrical cables overhead. [6]
b Do that again and I'll get really angry! [1]
c Don't ever borrow my laptop again without asking me. [8]
d Drive that fast again and I'll arrest you. Do you understand? [4]
e I wouldn't get on that if I was you. [2]
f I'm warning you not to come in here again. [3]
g If you don't finish getting ready immediately, I'm going to leave without you. [5]
h Watch out, there's a snake above your head! [7]

Activity 10
a orangutan—Borneo and Sumatra
b African elephant—parts of Africa
c black rhinoceros—Kenya, Namibia, South Africa, Zimbabwe

Activity 11
a
1 It collects information on animals and plants on the planet.
2 It keeps records of the numbers of animals and plants.
3 It tells us which animals and plants are in danger.
4 It gives the information to people / organizations who can protect the species.
b/c
critically endangered [1]
endangered [2]
vulnerable [3]

Activity 12
See Activity 1.

Activity 13
black rhinoceros; critically endangered; 2,550 ; hunted for its horn
African elephant endangered; 610,000; loss of habitat, ivory tusks
orangutan; vulnerable; 20–30,000; loss of habitat

Activity 14
a number, reduction, projected
b exploiting, exploited, decoration
c loss of habitat, desperate, support
d even, ban
e tree-dwelling

Activity 15
a as a result
b Moreover
c and furthermore
d Not only that, but
e However
f In contrast
g On the other hand
h In conclusion

Activity 16
Possible answers
a W
b T
c T
d W
e W
f T
g T
h W

Activities 17–19
Open activities

Activity 20
a sadistically
b dog-eared
c sociable
d a wolf in sheep's clothing
e They're fishing for compliments.
f I smell a rat.
g hold your horses

UNIT 4
Activity 1
The illustrated activities which are mentioned are ice-skating, tennis, swimming, aerobics, ballet and judo.

Activity 2
a 4
b 1
c 8
d 7
e 6
f 2
g 5
h 3

Activity 3
a 6
b 1
c 8
d 7
e 3
f 4
g 2
h 5

Activity 4
a consult
b take advantage of
c concludes
d courts
e accompanied by

f leisure
g facilities
h matches

Activity 5
a flower arranging
b mountain climbing
c stamp collector
d skydiver
e angler
f potholer
g beekeeper
h guitar playing
i water-skier
j quilting
k scuba diver
l skateboarder
m snowboarder
n bird watcher

Activity 6
a to
b on
c about
d about
e in
f with
g into
h out of
i for me
j me on

Activity 7
a The boys have been swimming.
b Mark has cleaned the window.
c It has snowed. / It has been snowing.
d He's been dancing.
e She's been cooking.
f They've been shopping.
g She's been painting.
h He's been digging.

Activity 8
a ever tried
b haven't
c haven't done
d ever been
e used
f noticed
g 'nt had
h been working
i have found
j lost

Activity 9
a 4
b 7
c 5
d 6
e 2
f 1
g 3

Activity 10
a F
b F
c T
d F
e T
f F
g F
h T
i T
j F

Activity 11
a daredevil
b Thermos
c synonymous with
d ultimate
e obsessed with
f freight
g stigma
h transatlantic

Activity 12
a Excuse me?
b Look
c Mmm
d what-do-you-call-it
e sorry to interrupt
f Could you repeat that?
g you know
h Do you know what I mean?
i Could you repeat that?

Activity 13
a 6
b 5
c 7
d 8
e 1
f 3
g 9
h 4
i 2

Activity 14
Open activities

Activity 15
a S
b D
c S
d D
e D
f D
g D
h D

Activities 16–17
Open activities

Activity 18
a ✗ – I've never had <u>much</u> trouble.
b ✗ – I am addicted <u>to</u> mountain-climbing.
c ✓
d ✓

e ✗ – I <u>heard</u> the singer ...
f ✓
g ✓
h ✓
i ✗—Trains<u>pott</u>ing is a boring hobby.
j ✗—You haven't been here before, <u>have</u> you?

Activity 19
a binoculars
b spelunker
c scuba diving
d Don't lose your grip.
e nonchalantly
f She gets a kick out of it.
g It doesn't do much for me.

UNIT 5
Activity 1
a It comes from a newspaper's website.
b The answers are a mixture of serious (Felicity Poole) and humorous (Danuta Ross) and everything in-between.
c The numbers that should be checked are 2, 3 and 5.

Activity 2
a Petra Weiss
b Hugh Foster
c Bud Karlowski
d Felicity Poole
e Miriam Stirling
f Sarah Green
g Bob Cartwright
h Carl Preston
i Katie Davis
j Phil Discarson
k Danuta Ross
l Caroline Hartley

Activity 3
a in better condition
b depends on
c as far back as
d pretending
e appropriate facial expressions
f get the message
g physical manifestations
h laughter lines
i villain
j free time
k burn calories
l tell jokes

Activity 4
a 2
b 3
c 1
d 7
e 8
f 4
g 5
h 6

Activity 5
Possible answers
a ... Martin would never have met his future wife.
b ... he wouldn't have met Patrick / probably wouldn't have taken up skydiving.
c If Martin hadn't met Caroline in Patrick's kitchen, ...
d If there had been space at a table inside the café...
e ... Patrick wouldn't have tripped over them / he might never have met Patrick.
f Patrick wouldn't have asked Martin to help him paint his house ...
g If Caroline hadn't talked to Martin about skydiving, she probably wouldn't have ended up marrying him.
h If Martin hadn't met Caroline, he might never have become a skydiving champion.
i If he hadn't enjoyed his first skydiving experience ...
j ... he wouldn't have met Caroline / become a skydiver.
k If he hadn't sat outside that day ...
l If Caroline and Martin hadn't enjoyed skydiving together ...

Activity 6
a angry
b annoyed
c bad-tempered
d calm down
e caught off balance
f cross
g fed up with
h furious
i grouchy
j grumpy
k temper
l irritable
m keep your cool
n mad
o moody
p sulky
q sick and tired of
r take it easy

Activity 7
a I am really cross with her.
b I went into a rage over John's behaviour.
c I was very angry at John's behaviour.
d She is in a bad mood because she lost her job.
e He lost his temper when he was told about the shark attack.
f She was absolutely furious at him for making a mess of her car.
g I am annoyed at / about the political situation.

h I'm fed up with working.
i I'm sick and tired of your bad behaviour.

Activity 9
The correct order is f, e, c, d, b, h, a, g.

Activity 10
a Habit formation is training people or animals to do something through repeated controlled practice tied to stimulus-response and rewards.
b They thought they were going to be fed.
c They learned to press a bar when a light went on.
d He was a young boy who had a pet rabbit.
e Because the scientists made a loud and frightening noise every time he was near his rabbit.
f He became frightened of them too— because of the experiment.
g They were not enthusiastic about on the idea.

Activity 11
a 'd come
b 'd had
c had bought
d wouldn't stop / hadn't stopped
e didn't move
f had saved
g wasn't
h had brought
i had arranged
j 'd asked

Activity 12
a 12
b 2
c 13
d 10
e 9
f 14
g 8
h 6
i 1
j 11
k 3
l 4
m 5
n 7

Activity 13
a Don't be so bad-tempered.
b I wish I'd been more careful.
c If only I'd got here earlier.
d Take it easy.

e Use your imagination
f He's absolutely out of control.
g She drives me absolutely crazy.
h Why should I tidy my room?
i I wish I was a little taller.

Activities 14–16
Open activities

Activity 17
a bad-tempered
b grumpy
c irritable
d really fed up
e calm down
f I feel trapped
g he gets on my nerves

UNIT 6
Activity 1
a see
b believe
c see
d believed; seen
e believe
f see
g see
h seeing
i believe
j believed

Activity 2
a 8
b 1
c 3
d 4
e 7
f 9
g 6
h 5
i 2

Activity 3
a T
b F
c T
d T
e F
f T

Activity 4
a Dr. Kenney
b the general public / people in industrialized countries
c John
d a few wealthy people
e millions of people
f Jenny
g governments
h private industry
i Dennis Tito

Activity 5
a futuristic
b the general public
c average person in the street
d the whole idea
e pretty basic
f improve greatly
g equivalent
h bring down
i in the first place
j stepping in

Activity 6
a 3
b 9
c 5
d 2
e 6
f 8
g 4
h 1
i 7

Activity 7
a Do you reckon it'll rain tomorrow?
b Do you suppose he'll win?
c What do you think will be the score?
d Did you see the game on Saturday?
e What do you reckon she'll do?
f Do you think they'll get there before we do?
g Who do you suppose will be there?
h Did you know they were going to be here?

Activity 9
a 5
b 6
c 3
d 4
e 2
f 1

Activity 10
a 6
b 2
c 4
d 5
e 1
f 3

Activity 11
a a conference and exhibition of technology
b a pop artist
c a Chinese artist
d someone who reads cards to tell your fortune
e a session when someone (who claims to have special talents) tells you what they "see" is going to happen in your future

f someone who takes advantage of the generosity of others by accepting material things and offering nothing in return

g a famous astrologer and predictor of the future

h the end of the world

i the temperature in San Francisco

Activity 12

a information technology

b electronic entertainment, electronic marketing—connected with entertainment and marketing online

c Tuesday–Sunday

d nontraditional, experimental

e someone who can see into the future

f spending time with you

g predictions

h west southwest (direction of the wind)

i miles per hour

j 73 degrees Fahrenheit (a measure of temperature used in the U.S.A.)

Activity 13

a 1
b 3
c 4
d 2

Activity 14

a will be gardening
b will have worked
c will you be doing
d 'll be enjoying
e will be taking
f won't be thinking
g 'll be arriving
h 'll be getting
i will be seeing
j Will he have finished
k will have left
l will have arrived

Activity 15

Title:	a	b
Notes:	d	c
Composition:	e	f

Activity 16

Possible answer

In this essay I would like to discuss space tourism and what it will be like. I think that the living conditions will be pretty basic. Space tourists will live on a spaceship and there will not be much room to move or to exercise. This will make it difficult for people to stay fit and healthy and there may be arguments among the people on

the spaceship, because they will have to live in a very restricted area.

The food on the spaceship will not be good. It will be dehydrated food, which can taste good, but which does not give the same sense of satisfaction as a real meal. There will be no entertainment on board the spaceship, so it will be important for space tourists to bring their own entertainment like DVDs and books, otherwise they will get very bored.

In spite of the conditions that I have mentioned above, I would love to be a space tourist. I think it would be very exciting to travel in space.

Activities 17–18

Open activities

Activity 19

a ✗ – I <u>reckon</u> we'll be living ...
b ✓
c ✗ – Do you <u>understand / see</u> what I mean?
d ✓
e ✗ – The winner of the lottery <u>is believed to</u> live in London.
f ✓
g ✗ – I'll have <u>finished</u> reading this book by Friday.
h ✗ – She'll <u>be lying</u> on a beach ...
i ✗ – ... an <u>IT</u> expert.
j ✓

Activity 20

a overpopulation
b robot
c clairvoyant
d astrology
e space tourism
f the general public
g in the first place

UNIT 7

Activity 1

a green
b red
c white
d red
e red
f blue
g blue
h red
i green
j blue

Activity 2

The man is wearing a bright lime-green T-shirt and faded blue jeans. He has
a beige baseball cap and bright white trainers.

The woman is wearing dark green trousers and a light blue T-shirt. She has a mustard-coloured jacket, bright red trainers and white socks.

Activity 4

a Each hat represents a different way of looking at a problem.

b to focus on the problem, not the individual, to look at a problem in many different ways, to allow a group of people to think effectively about a problem at the same time

Activity 5

white: facts and true information

red: intuition, feelings and emotions—how you feel about something

black: logic, judgment, caution, analysis —what can work and why, what won't work and why not

yellow: positive reason, suggestions and proposals—advantages of the suggestions

green: creativity, alternatives, combinations of ideas—more ideas are generated

blue: metacognition, thinking about thinking—tells the group what kind of thinking still needs to take place

Activity 6

a 7
b 3
c 1
d 5
e 6
f 4
g 8
h 2

Activity 7

a 5
b 3
c 7
d 8
e 1
f 4
g 2
h 6

Activity 8

a F
b T
c F
d F
e T
f T
g F

Activity 9

Activity 10

1

a Yes, I have.

b Yes, on my father's farm.

c I crashed into the gate and the car had to be repaired.

d I drove into a wall and now the radiator needs replacing.

2

a He used some very bad words.

b He said I needed my head examined. That was very unkind.

c If he had remembered what it was like to learn how to drive, he would have been more sympathetic.

d You can always get a new car.

e Are we going to have to walk home?

f Is that the end of the lesson?

Activity 11

a ac<u>ce</u>lerator

b <u>gear</u> stick

c <u>ra</u>diator

d rear-view <u>mirror</u>

e <u>stee</u>ring wheel

f <u>side</u> view mirror

g pe<u>des</u>trian

h <u>traffic</u> circle

i <u>engine</u>

j <u>neutral</u>

k <u>hand</u>brake

l <u>mirror</u>

Activity 13

a 7

b 4

c 5

d 6

e 1

f 3

g 2

Activity 14

a We had our house cleaned by the (cleaning) company in just three hours.

b I had the car resprayed at Gerry's garage.

c The bumper needs replacing.

d I had my bicycle stolen today.

e We had our house painted while we were on vacation.

f The roof needs fixing because there's a hole in it.

g My teeth need cleaning more thoroughly in the future, according to the dentist.

h The hard drive on my computer has a serious problem and needs replacing, according to the computer store.

i They had five pictures of the entire family taken by the photographer.

Activity 15

Conversation 1: c, p, a, q, g, e, l, r, j

Conversation 2: f, b, d, o, h, i, n, k, m

Activity 16

Sophie: 2

Patrick: 1

Activity 17

a1 – b5 – c3

a2 – b3 – c1

a3 – b2 – c6

a4 – b6 – c4

a5 – b4 – c5

a6 – b1 – c2

Activity 18

a1 E

a2 C

a3 B

a4 F

a5 A

a6 D

Activities 19–21

Open activities

Activity 22

a it needs fixing

b pedestrian

c metacognition

d I had my car washed

e lime-green T-shirt

f careful analysis

UNIT 8

Activity 1

Bernice Watson: Weight Watchers of Great Britain

Dr. Robert Atkins: the Atkins Diet

Dr. Barry Sears: the Zone Diet

Dr. Arthur Agatson: The South Beach Diet

Activity 2

a carbohydrates found in processed foods

b Bernice Weston

c Arthur Agatson

d Barry Sears

e people on the induction phase of the Atkins Diet

f fruits and vegetables which contain a lot of fiber

g members of Weight Watchers

h Robert Atkins

i monounsaturated fats found in olive and canola oils, meat and seafood

j *People* magazine

k Weight Watchers

l Robert Atkins

Activity 3

a 2

b 3

c 4

d 1

Activity 4

a 3

b 6

c 5

d 7

e 2

f 8

g 1

h 4

Activity 5

a 3, the Atkins Diet (low carb, no fruit)

b 4, the South Beach Diet (contains tomatoes, not allowed by the Atkins Diet)

c 1, Weight Watchers (it mentions "points" and includes pasta)

d 2, the Zone Diet (it mentions "blocks" and allows fruit)

Activity 6

a cucumber

b pancake

c pie

d beetroot

e pie

f mustard

g fruit cake

h candy

i hot potato

j two peas in a pod

Activity 7

a cup of tea

b the big cheese

c piece of cake

d the apple of my eye

e bread and butter

f cream of the crop

g breadwinner

h piece of the pie

i a bad egg

j full of beans

Activity 8
a T
b T
c F
d F
e T
f T
g T
h F
i T
j F
k T
l T

Activity 9
Good effects
a heart
b slow down
c brain, carbohydrates, good

Harmful effects
a sugar, fat
b milk, dark
c tooth decay
d fat, sugar, obesity

Activity 10
a 9
b 5
c 6
d 8
e 3
f 7
g 2
h 1
i 4

Activity 12
a 3
b 4
c 6
d 2
e 1
f 5

Activity 13
a 6
b 2
c 5
d 4
e 1
f 3

Activity 14
a X, a
b X, X
c X, X, X
d the, a, the, the
e the, X, the, the
f a, an / X, a / X
g the, the

Activity 15
1 c
2 a
3 e
4 d
5 a
6 a, b
7 c
8 a, b, e
9 f
10 e

Activity 16
a F
b T
c T
d F
e T
f F
g F
h T
i T
j F

Activity 17
Possible answer
This graph shows the reasons why Americans do not achieve the weight they wish to achieve on a diet.
It shows that most people fail because they don't exercise enough. Another main reason why they fail when they diet is because they feel that their metabolism is slowing down. Other reasons why they fail are that they splurge on their favorite foods too much, that they don't have enough self-discipline and that they snack too much.
Only 14% of people interviewed said that they fail when dieting because they only watch their calorie intake instead of watching their fat intake.

Activities 18–19
Open activities

Activity 20
a ✗—Put the skinless chicken into a skillet.
b ✓
c ✗—Who's the breadwinner in your family?
d ✗—This TV doesn't seem to be working.
e ✗—I have a complaint to make.
f ✓
g ✓
h ✗—Some doctors say animal fat is important to diet.
i ✗—The sun rises at 6.00 a.m. at this time of year.
j ✓

Activity 21
a cardiologist
b cool as a cucumber
c He brought home the bacon.
d chocolate
e emaciated
f I'd like to make a complaint.
g manager

UNIT 9
Activity 1
a pick, go with
b absolutely
c When all is said and done
d delicate
e first rate

Activity 3
1 e
2 b
3 a
4 h
5 d
6 g
7 c
8 i
9 f
10 e
11 b
12 a

Activity 4
a He has deep-set eyes under curly hair, a long straight nose, and a square chin.
b She has bright eyes, a turned-up nose, and a generous mouth.
c He has thinning hair, in fact he's nearly bald.
d She's absolutely gorgeous. She's slim and elegant with long thick wavy hair.
e He has thick wavy hair, protruding eyes, and a strong chin.
f She has straight hair, a weak chin, and small dark eyes.

Activity 5
Thin: absolutely puny [NG], emaciated [NG], kind of skinny [NT], rather slim [P], very underweight [NG]

Not thin: a little bit pudgy [NG], a little overweight [NG], a little plump [NT], extremely flabby [NG], extremely well-built [NT], fantastically muscular [P], incredibly obese [NG], absolutely voluptuous [P], rather stout [NG]

General description of looks and appearance: a bit of a mess [NG], absolutely gorgeous [P], extremely beautiful [P], fantastically hideous [NG], incredibly cute [P], incredibly handsome [P], incredibly ugly [NG], incredibly untidy [NG], rather attractive [P], rather elegant [P], rather plain [NG], rather scruffy [NG], rather ugly [NG]

Activity 6
a Nick Drake
b 1948–1974
c 3
d 1 Brad Pitt, 2 Coldplay,
  3 Beth Orton, 4 Norah Jones

Activity 7
a Tonya Swift
b Tonya Swift
c Jesse
d Sarah Beatrice
e Usha Jain
f Jesse
g Bentley
h Lucy Sparrow
i Sarah Beatrice
j Lucy Sparrow
k Lucy Sparrow
l Alejandra Valero

Activity 8
a background
b captivated
c entangled
d enchanted
e timeless
f charming
g melancholic
h haunting
i inspirational
j uplifting
k missions
l tender

Activity 9
a good
b absent
c high
d short
e fair
f auburn
g bad
h narrow
i fair
j cut

Activity 10
a an old black briefcase
b a huge black frightening storm cloud
c a haunting American folk song
d a tall, generous, elegant Colombian woman
e an unimpressive 19th-century operatic overture

f ancient Mexican cooking recipes
g expensive high-heeled Italian shoes
h large round blue-green eyes
i a beautiful talented small British radio actress

Activity 11
a How can I help you?
b Oh I'm sorry, Mr. Cartwright
c That's not very convenient
d if that's all right
e Oh, come on, Mr. Cartwright
f Mr. Cartwright
g Peter
h Peter
i I'd like a haircut, please
j What would you recommend?
k a bit off the top
l Just above the ears

Activity 12
Open activity

Activity 13
a 5
b 6
c 3
d 2
e 1
f 4
g 7

Activities 14–16
Open activities

Activity 17
a good-looking
b voluptuous
c well-dressed
d It's a kind of a mess.
e You'll damage your career prospects.
f She's absolutely gorgeous.
g What are you talking about?

UNIT 10
Activity 2
Possible answer
The effects of global warming are slowly becoming apparent. If we do not deal with the problem now, by the time the effects of global warming manifest themselves clearly, it will be too late.

Activity 3
a RL
b M
c RL
d SP
e RL
f SP
g RL
h SP

i M
j RL

Activity 4
a 6
b 3
c 4
d 5
e 8
f 9
g 1
h 2
i 7

Activity 5
a had been painting
b were watching
c had written
d arrived, found, had forgotten, had left, had been running
e had increased
f had told
g had been increasing / had increased
h have been living / have lived
i had been snowing for two hours, was settling
j have you known

Activity 6
a looked
b appeared
c was not taking
d took off
e slipped
f drove
g thought
h was being pursued
i made
j had attended / had been attending
k had taken
l took
m knew
n had been watching
o had been broken into
p could
q were
r hoped
s would be able
t got
u had told
v had
w had not answered / was not answering
x was

Activity 7
a blazing sun
b thunderous applause
c torrential rain
d storm of protest
e howling wind
f gales of laughter
g thunder and lightning
h downpour

i rainy season
j sunny disposition
k thunderstruck

Activity 8
a blazing sun
b rainy season
c sunny disposition
d howling wind
e torrential rain
f thunder and lightning
g downpour
h thunderstruck
i gales of laughter
j thunderous applause
k storm of protest

Activity 9
a Forecast 6
b Forecast 1
c Forecast 2
d Forecast 5
e Forecast 4
f Forecast 3

Activity 10
Forecast 1: c

Forecast 2: a

Forecast 3: b

Forecast 4: b

Forecast 5: a

Forecast 6: c

Activity 11
Forecast 1: silver lining, drop, breeze
Forecast 2: to last, return, a chance
Forecast 3: cloudy, chances are, hail, in the hills
Forecast 4: snowfall, blizzards, rural areas
Forecast 5: well, ease off
Forecast 6: flooding, rivers rise

Activity 13
a 9
b 8
c 10
d 6
e 1
f 7
g 5
h 4
i 3
j 2

Activity 14
a Could I say something here?
b if I just might make a point
c Wait a minute
d on top of that
e Incidentally, on the subject of
f looking at it from another angle
g if it wasn't enough to

Activity 15

	Weblog	Online journal
includes the date	✓	✓
the most recent entry comes at the top	✓	✓
the writer talks about her / his life	✗	✓
the writer talks about things connected to the world wide web	✓	✗
there are links to other websites	✓	✗

Activity 16
The top one is an online journal, while the lower one is a "blog".

Activity 17
a a child
b his mother (the writer of the journal)
c the writer of the journal (Liz Wright)
d an Internet bulletin board
e the House Rabbit Society

Activity 18
If you want to post your blog entry or online journal entry online, you can do this at a site like these: www.blogger.com, www.mydeardiary.com or www.opendiary.com

Activities 19–20
Open activities

Activity 21
a ✗ – ... she was talking
b ✓
c ✗ – ... that she had baked
d ✗ – ... strong sunshine, ... heavy thunderstorm
e ✓
f ✗ – To change the subject, ...
g ✓
h ✓
i ✓
j ✗ – Incidentally, ...

Activity 22
a torrential rain
b downpour
c heavy flooding
d incidentally
e freezing temperatures
f to change the subject
g hazardous driving conditions

UNIT 11
Activity 1
Friends: b, h, k
Art of the garden: f, i
Big Brother – Live Launch Show: a, d, e, j
American Idol: c, g, l

Activity 2
a Alison Graham
b Capability Brown
c the *Big Brother* programme makers
d Fantasia Barrino and Diana DeGarmo
e American Idol
f the character "Joey" from *Friends*
g *Big Brother*
h Phoebe in *Friends*
i the last episode of *Friends*
j Diarmuid Gavin
k the Duke of Blenheim
l Diarmuid Gavin
m Cameron Stuart
n Cameron Stuart

Activity 3
a bid their last farewells
b tying-up of loose ends
c there are no great fireworks
d talks us through
e dark horse
f fell out with
g pulls in big audiences
h brickbats
i fool the eye
j we'll just have to wait and see
k crowning achievement
l as dull as ditchwater

Activity 4
Positive connotations
legendary (A)
fame (N)
stardom (N)
renowned (A)
celebrated (A)
eminent (A)
eminence (N)
star (N)
legend (N)
renown (N)
have your name on everyone's lips (E)
Neutral
be in the spotlight (E)
come into the limelight (E)
come into the public eye (E)
famous (A)
be a VIP (E)
well-known (A)
be flavor of the month (E)
become a household name (E)
hit the headlines (E)
celebrity (N)

Negative connotations
notorious (A)
achieve notoriety (E)
notoriety (N)
infamous (A)
infamy (N)

Activity 5
across
1 eminent
2 flavor
3 celebrity
4 name
5 stardom
6 legend

down
1 eye
7 limelight
8 notorious
9 fame

Activity 6
a type 2
b type 1
c type 1
d type 2
e type 2
f type 2
g type 2
h type 2

Activity 7
a I hope she pays me back soon.
b People who are brought up ...
c ... I'm trying to work it out.
d ... should be pulled down ...
e ... will have to be put off ...
f Her acting career has suddenly taken off.
g Could you turn it down ...
h ... and speak up or ...

Activity 8
a type 4
b type 3
c type 3
d type 4
e type 3
f type 4
g type 1
h type 3
i type 2
j type 3
k type 4

Activity 9
a I don't know how you put up with it!
b The plane took off.
c Do you get on with her?
d I was sad when she turned me down.
e Will you please turn the radio off?

f Guess who I ran into today?
g They're going to pull it down today.
h I have to look after my sister.
i She's taking care of her grandfather this week.

Activity 10
The correct order is a, j, f, m, i, c, k, e, g, b, l, h, d.

Activity 11
a right
b don't you
c Does that mean
d haven't you
e did you
f would you say
g huh

Activity 13
a D / A
b D
c A
d A
e A
f D
g D
h D

Activity 14
a Brad
b Brad
c Both
d Both
e Diane
f Brad
g Brad
h Both

Activity 15
a 1
b 1
c 1
d 1
e 2
f 2
g 2
h 1

Activity 16
Marilyn Monroe
a June 1, 1926
b Los Angeles, California
c Norma Jean Mortenson
d 29, including *Niagara*, *The Seven-Year Itch*, *Gentlemen Prefer Blondes*
e August 5, 1962

Albert Einstein
a March 14, 1879
b Ulm, Germany
c theory of relativity

d German, later became a U.S. citizen
e April 18, 1955

Activities 17–20
Open activities

Activity 21
a notoriety
b infamous
c lose face
d get along with
e put up with
f don't you think
g a late developer

UNIT 12
Activity 1
a 9(F)
b 2(NF)
c 5(F)
d 11(F)
e 7(NF)
f 1(NF)
g 12(F)
h 4(NF)
i 3(NF)
j 6(NF)
k 8(NF)
l 10(F)

Activity 2
a play
b mention
c merits / merited
d report
e playing
f work
g mention
h merit
i works
j report

Activity 3
The correct summary is c.

Activity 4
a 1
b 1
c 3
d 1
e 2
f 2
g 1

Activity 5
a fork
b panty hose
c scratch
d to squat
e I'd gotten that far
f to groan
g blockage
h to poke out
i to stack up

j to slice
k to tune
l leaf

Activity 6
a Maximus
b Commodus and Maximus
c Marcus

Activity 7
a F
b T
c T
d F
e F
f T

Activity 8
a 1
b 10
c 2
d 7
e 3
f 4
g 6
h 9
i 8
j 5

Marcus' list: wisdom, justice, fortitude, temperance
Commodus' list: ambition, resourcefulness, courage, devotion

Activity 9
a 7
b 8
c 6
d 5
e 3
f 9
g 4
h 2
i 1

Activity 10
Two syllables: butcher, courage, justice, smother, temperance, wisdom
Three syllables: ambition, devotion, fortitude
Four syllables: resourcefulness

Activity 11
a 9
b 6
c 1
d 5
e 4
f 10
g 3
h 2
i 7
j 8

Activity 12
a9 Is that the girl that you used to sit next to at school?
d5 That's the rug that we bought for our living room.
e4 I want to show you the town that my sister moved to last year.
g3 It was the day that they came over to our house.
i7 Would you like a cushion that you can sit on?

Activity 13
Possible answers
a This is the woman (that) I told you about yesterday.
b Did you see that car that has a flat tire?
c He's the one whose book is about animals.
d My best friend Gemma, whose parents live in France, has decided to work in Paris.
e We were living in Chicago at the time when my novel was published.
f This is the house (that) we grew up in.
g Do you like this hat (that) I bought when I was downtown?
h I remember the day (when) we went to the beach and it rained all day.
i That's the author whose book is very popular at the moment.

Activity 14
a I do agree that Joaquin Phoenix was good.
b You're surely not suggesting Russell Crowe was right for that role?
c You must be joking!
d I take your point about actors sometimes not being right.
e I have to disagree with you on that one.
f I see what you mean about Joaquin Phoenix.
g I'm with Larry on that one.
h I couldn't agree less with both of you.

Activity 15
1 I have to disagree with you on that one.
2 I'm with Larry on that one.
3 I couldn't agree less with both of you.
4 I see what you mean about Joaquin Phoenix.
5 you're surely not suggesting Russell Crowe was right for that role?
6 I take your point about actors sometimes not being right.
7 I do agree that Joaquin Phoenix was good.
8 You must be joking!

Activity 16
The correct order is f, b, a, c, e, d.

Activity 17
Possible answer
As she walked down the street with the snow crunching beneath her feet, Janice thought about the Bancroft account. She had gone over the mystery again and again. What had happened to the missing $200,000? She had checked the books herself very carefully and had noticed that every month for the past two years $10,000 had disappeared. She had not spoken to anyone about it yet. She decided she was going to tell her boss about it the next day.
At the bus stop, two people were talking about the awful weather, but most people were silent as the 268 bus came to a halt and the passengers got off and the new passengers prepared to get on. But Janice never got on that bus …

Activities 18–20
Open activities

Activity 21
a ✓
b ✗—An autobiography …
c ✓
d ✗—I don't mind admitting …
e ✗—…, who lives in Australia.
f ✗—… the kind of person who loves adaptations …
g ✓
h ✗—… a great work of art.
i ✓
j ✗—… the girl whose mother is a dancer.

Activity 22
a literature
b autobiography
c the blurb
d fair enough
e rubbish
f temperance
g awe-inspiring

UNIT 13
Activity 1
Lines should connect the following items:
Jane's story—cellphone, bag, coffee cups, jeans, wooly hat
Angie's story—red coat, camera,

knife, gloves, "New York"
Michael's story—passport, credit cards, shorts, two beautiful girls, hotel key

Activity 2
a her uncle
b Jane
c Jane's uncle
d the man in the wooly hat
e the man in the wooly hat
f Angie and David
g David
h David
i Angie
j Michael
k The British man on the beach
l The British man on the beach
m The British man on the beach

Activity 3
a rang, for, working
b around, suspicious
c looked, like, bad
d wondered, right
e terrifying, happened, frightened
f knew, around, pressed, sharp
g looking, hanging
h joy
i eyes, far, foreign
j so, trouble, reason
k really, chat, conversation, smiles
l pretty, taken, again

Activity 4
a sentenced
b robbery
c guilty
d convicted
e embezzlement
f arrested
g shoplifting
h accused
i theft
j hackers
k arrested
l robbery
m hacked

Activity 5
1 d
2 c
3 b
4 a

Activity 6
a con*vict*
b *convict*
c *suspect*
d sus*pect*

a When it is a noun the first syllable is stressed, but when the word is a verb the second syllable carries the main word stress.

b for example: progress, record, produce, import, export

Activity 7
The correct order is c, f, h, j, k, d, i, a, g, e, b.

Activity 9
a a TV quiz show
b the host / quiz master of *Who wants to be a millionaire?*
c a contestant on *Who wants to be a millionaire?* who won a million pounds by cheating
d the man who helped Charles Ingram by coughing

Activity 10
a *Who wants to be a millionaire?*
b the big prize for *Who wants to be a millionaire?*
c an Anthony Eden
d the question about the Anthony Eden
e Charles Ingram
f Tecwen Whittock
g many in the audience
h Diana Ingram, Charles' wife
i a man sitting next to Tecwen Whittock
j Charles, Diana and Tecwen
k tapes from the show
l Charles and Diana Ingram
m Tecwen Whittock

Activity 11
a host
b contestant
c increases
d extract
e garment
f regular
g on purpose
h obvious
i court
j appropriate
k administering
l cheating

Activity 12
a Our car is being fixed at the moment.
b Jane Austen wrote this novel.
c A gang might have broken into our car.
d Do you think someone at the store stole the diamonds?
e The clothes can't have been taken by her, because she was with me.
f The assassin is going to be sentenced now.
g I'm sure that young man is being wrongly accused of murder.

h The diamonds must have been stolen between the hours of 8.00 and 10.00 p.m.

Activity 13
Possible answers
a Twenty grams of salt were put into a beaker and 20 ounces of water were added. The mixture was heated until the salt dissolved. The water was boiled till it evaporated. Salt was left in the beaker.
b Fifty-two people were asked what they thought about crime on TV. Fifty people said that they thought too much violence and crime was shown on TV. Two people said that they felt that the right amount of crime was shown on TV.
c The meeting was attended by 50 people yesterday. It was proposed that the time of the next meeting should be changed. This proposal was agreed on. The next meeting will be held at 6.00 p.m. instead of at 8.00 p.m.

Activities 14 and 16
The corrected version is:
My favorite crime movie of all time is *The Usual Suspects*, starring Kevin Spacey and Gabriel Byrne. The movie has a surprise ending, which I can't tell you. It is about a legendary gangster called Keyser Soze, whom the police have never arrested and everyone knows about, but who has never been seen. The movie begins when a boat is blown up and there are only two survivors, Verbal Kint (Kevin Spacey) and a Hungarian man. The Hungarian man is a terrorist and he is badly injured. When he is being interviewed by the police, Kint is forced to tell the whole story which began six weeks earlier. Kint tells the story of the powerful mastermind of the whole plot, named Keyser Soze. He tells us about a gang of five men who plan to do their last robbery and about how that robbery goes wrong. We also see the story of Dean Keaton (Gabriel Byrne), an ex-cop who becomes a criminal, but who is trying to start a life free of crime. The movie has a lot of action and suspense and by the end of the movie you are dying to know who Keyser Soze is. But then comes the big surprise which I can't tell you.

Activity 15
Possible answers
Name of writer:
Checked by:

	Yes	Not sure	No, not really
a			✗
b			✗
c	✗		

d I think the writing could be improved by:
- Dividing the text up into paragraphs to make the writing clearer
- Not repeating "the surprise ending, which I can't tell you"
- Proofreading carefully for mistakes

Activities 17–19
Open activities

Activity 20
a getaway car
b prosecuted
c during the robbery
d pickpocketing
e embezzlement
f to be charged with a crime
g he must have done it

UNIT 14
Activity 1
West Indian folk tales originally come from West Africa. They were changed in the West Indies by the addition of new animals.

Activity 2
The correct paragraph order is k, i, g, f, b, j, d, h, a, e, c.

Activity 3
a Because Dog has sworn to break the bones of the thief who stole his pears (and that was Finger Quashy).
b Because Dog's son had been playing with fire.
c Because Dog came into the room with a big stick.
d Because Rat told him that Finger Quashy had stolen some pears.
e Because she wanted Dog to think that she was innocent.
f Because Rat told him that she had.
g Because everyone knew Dog was a good cook and made nice meals.
h Because Dog blames them for the fire in his house—and for the fact that he doesn't have any clothes to wear any more.
i Because she was so fast.

j Because they were the best avocado pears for miles.

Activity 4
a on fire
b reduced to ashes
c pantry
d dignified
e leaped
f reprehensible
g distracting
h swearing
i blamed
j shot
k it's not a bit like you
l at his wits' end
m yelling his head off
n beside himself with fury

Activity 5
a days
b house
c retold
d sound
e memory
f sad
g nights
h told
i met
j longed for

Parents

Summer days.
White-painted house
gazing over the rolling cliff.

And the murmur of incoming tides.

The story told, retold, and heard so often.

The sound of his voice,
lion growly in the fading evening air.

This is a memory of vacations, a dog-eared
thought returned to whenever I am sad

and need to think of how it was in those
summer-lazy nights when we were young
and safe, and he told the tale

of how they met,
romantic still
in uneasy-living times.
Refugee hope.
And love, longed for by the young then, as now,
blossomed in the wartime dark.

Activity 6
a Summer days. Refugee hope.
b white-painted, dog-eared, summer-lazy, uneasy-living

c re-told, told, heard, returned, longed for

Activity 7
a 5
b 10
c 6
d 8
e 11
f 3
g 9
h 4
i 1
j 7
k 2

Activity 8
The Man in a Straw Hat by Vincent van Gogh is Exhibit 28.
The Man in a Felt Hat by Vincent van Gogh is Exhibit 27.

Activity 9
a F
b F
c T
d F
e T
f T
g F
h T
i F

Activity 10
a She says it was nice to see us yesterday.
b She said she had really enjoyed working with me in the recording studio.
c He said he had had a fantastic game of golf the week before.
d She said she hadn't been able to read the report I sent her.
e He asked whether we were going to go over for a barbecue that Saturday.
f He says he's just read the most fantastic poem.
g He says he hopes we'll both be able to come to the opening of his new exhibition next week.
h He said he had never felt better in his life.
i He says he was going to call me earlier, but something came up and he couldn't.
j He asked whether I would tell Mary that he would be late for the appointment.
k She says she really enjoyed meeting me.

Activity 11

a 6
b 9
c 1
d 2
e 8
f 4
g 5
h 3
i 7
j 10

Activity 12

a 5
b 14
c 2
d 9
e 10
f 12
g 13
h 7
i 4
j 1
k 3
l 11
m 6
n 8

Activity 13

Scene 1

a 4
b 1
c 7
d 5
e 2
f 8
g 3
h 6

Scene 2

i 1
j 4
k 2
l 3

Scene 3

m 4
n 2
o 3
p 1
q 5

Activity 15

a E
b N
c E
d U
e U
f E
g N
h N
i E
j U

Activities 16–17

Open activities

Activity 18

a ✓
b ✓
c ✗—He insisted that I arrived on time.
d ✗—They apologised for being late.
e ✓
f ✓
g ✗—I have really gone off VG's paintings.
h ✓
i ✓
j ✓

Activity 19

a aerial shot
b scorched
c drowsing
d heavy breathing
e a touch of home
f I can't put my finger on it.
g You've finally finished this book.